In Light of Another's Word

THE MIDDLE AGES SERIES

RUTH MAZO KARRAS, *SERIES EDITOR*
EDWARD PETERS, *FOUNDING EDITOR*

A complete list of books in the series is available from the publisher.

In Light of Another's Word

EUROPEAN ETHNOGRAPHY
IN THE MIDDLE AGES

Shirin A. Khanmohamadi

PENN
UNIVERSITY OF PENNSYLVANIA PRESS   *Philadelphia*

THIS BOOK IS MADE POSSIBLE BY A COLLABORATIVE GRANT
FROM THE ANDREW W. MELLON FOUNDATION.

© 2014 University of Pennsylvania Press

All rights reserved. Except for brief quotations used for purposes of review or scholarly citation, none of this book may be reproduced in any form by any means without written permission from the publisher.

Published by
University of Pennsylvania Press
Philadelphia, Pennsylvania 19104-4112
www.upenn.edu/pennpress

Printed in the United States of America
on acid-free paper

10 9 8 7 6 5 4 3 2 1

Library of Congress Cataloging-in-Publication Data

Khanmohamadi, Shirin A.
  In light of another's word : European ethnography in the Middle Ages / Shirin A. Khanmohamadi. — 1st ed.
    p. cm. — (The Middle Ages series)
  ISBN 978-0-8122-4562-2 (hardcover : alk. paper)
  1. Ethnology—Europe—History—To 1500.
2. East and West—History—To 1500. 3. Travel, Medieval—History—Sources. 4. Travelers' writings, European—History and criticism. 5. Authors, Medieval—Attitudes. 6. Civilization, Medieval.
I. Title. II. Series: Middle Ages series.
  GN308.3.E85K43 2014
  305.80094—dc23
                                    2013026522

*In memory of my father,
Mehdi Khanmohamadi
(1937–2010)*

CONTENTS

Introduction   1

1. Conquest, Conversion, Crusade, Salvation: The Discourse
   of Anthropology and Its Uses in the Medieval Period   11

2. Subjective Beginnings: Autoethnography
   and the Partial Gazes of Gerald of Wales   37

3. Writing Ethnography "In the Eyes of the Other":
   William of Rubruck's Mission to Mongolia   57

4. Casting a "Sideways Glance" at the Crusades: The Voice
   of the Other in Joinville's *Vie de Saint Louis*   88

5. Dis-Orienting the Self: The Uncanny
   Travels of John Mandeville   113

   Conclusion   145

   Notes   149
   Bibliography   181
   Index   195
   Acknowledgments   201

Introduction

Et cum circumdarent nos homines et respicerent nos tamquam monstra, maxime quia eramus nudis pedibus, et quererent si nos non indigeremus pedibus nostris, quia supponebant quod statim amitteremus eos, ille Hungarus reddidit eis rationem, narrans eis conditiones Ordinis nostri.

(People gathered round us, gazing at us as if we were freaks, especially in view of our bare feet, and asked whether we had no use for our feet, since they imagined that in no time we would lose them. And this the Hungarian explained to them, telling them the rules of our Order.) (*Itinerarium* 28.4)

William of Rubruck writes these words upon his return to Acre after a two-year mission to Mongolia from 1253 to 1255, as part of his report to King Louis IX of France on the state of Mongolian society and customs, one of the medieval period's most vivid ethnographic accounts. Here he is describing his immediate reception at the imperial court of the great khan, Mangu, where locals not only surround him and members of his Franciscan retinue, wondering at their display of bare feet in the subfreezing weather of Mongolian winter, but stare at them as if they were some kind of monsters, *tamquam monstra*. William is thus describing himself as he is seen in the gaze of the other he has come to describe, a feat striking, even disorienting, to modern and medieval audiences alike—the former who might not expect to find a mode of postmodern, self-reflexive ethnography in a medieval sampling of the genre, and the latter who might well turn to ethnographic reports with an interest in hearing of the world's exotic and monstrous races, not to learn that they are themselves seen as monstrous by diverse, little-known others. Surely William's moment of self-mirroring and even self-othering is exceptional and rare?

This book, on the contrary, tracks the persistent presence of such moments of startling and uncomfortable self-reflexivity and self-consciousness in some of Europe's earliest and most celebrated ethnographic descriptions—descriptions of observed manners and customs of cultural and religious outsiders. The ethnographic authors treated here, Gerald of Wales in his description of the twelfth-century Welsh, William of Rubruck among the Mongols, Jean de Joinville in his account of the various Muslim "Saracens" encountered on the Seventh Crusade, and the Mandeville author in his description of the world's diverse faiths from the Holy Land to the Far East, display an uncanny ability to see and write from the perspective of the others whom they mean to describe. They see and write, that is, "in light of another's word"[1]—relationally, dialogically, from more than one vantage point. Together their texts elaborate, I argue, a distinctive late medieval ethnographic poetics, one marked by a distinctive outlook on ethnographic encounter: a profound openness to alternative perspectives and voices; attention to the limits and hence dangers of taking a single-point European or Latin Christian perspective in engaging with cultural diversity; and frequent exposure of the discomfort experienced by Europeans in confronting and thinking through unfamiliar words and worldviews, in opening their own systems of thought to competing languages and having their beliefs thus "dialogized"—and relativized—through the encounter. Such openness and attraction to non–Latin Christian voices in a genre *about* outsiders certainly challenges the image of an insular and inherently xenophobic European Middle Ages. On the other hand, I do not wish to suggest that these medieval writers embraced alterity as early exponents of modern cosmopolitanism or multiculturalism,[2] or that these positions came naturally or easily to them. Rather they are each motivated, for different reasons tied to particular circumstances I will set forth in the individual chapters, to leave their narratives open to alternative perspectives and voices in spite of the considerable risks these posed to the stability of their overall personal and narrative perspectives, as well as to dominant Latin Christian beliefs and governing orthodoxies of their day.

The texts displaying such a striking poetics, moreover, derive not from the margins but rather the canonical centers of Europe's emerging genres of empirical ethnographies and literatures of observation. As scholars are increasingly appreciating, in the twelfth to fourteenth centuries, Europe's growing encounters with cultural difference through various cultural contact zones[3]—from zones of conquest along its own expanding borders to beyond, through missions, crusades, pilgrimages, and travels in the East—led to a growth in ethnographic curiosity about others and to the creative rebirth of empirical or observed ethnography, not seen in the West for some one thousand years.[4] Unlike the modern discipline of academic anthropology, ethnographic writing has a long premodern history and can be found wherever and whenever discrete cultural groups have moved across their borders to collide with customs and mores at variance with their own and had the means and motivation to record those differences. We cannot expect to identify these new medieval ethnographers through self-designation as "ethnographers" or designation of their works as "ethnographies"—instead they used terms like "descriptio" (description), "itinerarium" (journey), and "travels" to title their narratives. These terms suggest the extent to which ethnographic writing coupled with other genres of travel, including geography, topography, cosmography, pilgrimage, crusade, ambassadorial reports, and missionary reports, in the medieval period, as indeed, it would continue to do so until the modern era, when professional ethnography finally replaced the long-running unprofessional observations and "practical ethnographical 'science' of merchants, navigators, missionaries . . . [and] colonial administrators."[5] But we can identify medieval ethnographic writers by a common language they share with each other and with modern practitioners of ethnography in describing their discursive aims. For the practitioners of early European ethnography consistently write of an intent to describe and record the differing manners and customs (Latin: "ritus et mores"; Old French: "coustumes"; Middle English: "maneres and lawes") of the peoples they are observing.[6] The twelfth-century renaissance of classical learning notwithstanding, the rebirth of ethnography in the late medieval period took place without direct access to its most relevant classical literary and scientific models, such as Herodotus's *Histories* and Tacitus's *Germania*, underscoring the role of direct observation in the growth of the new genre. Along the expanding borders of twelfth-century Europe, Adam of Bremen wrote extensive descriptions of Scandinavian and Baltic peoples, and his continuator, Helmold, wrote an account of the pagan Slavic customs and religious rites.[7] Gerald of Wales, meanwhile, broke the mold of ethnography as an appendage to history to write arguably the first "ethnographic monograph" of the postclassical era, his *Description of Wales*.[8] While the twelfth century saw such sporadic ethnographic activity, events of the thirteenth brought about an impressive spurt of ethnographic accounts of the Mongols, who had staged a series of devastating eastern European campaigns before suddenly receding in 1242 on the death of Great Khan Ogodei. Elected pope in 1243, Innocent IV responded both by renewing calls for a crusade on Europe's eastern front and by organizing a series of missions to convert and collect information regarding the threatening empire to the east, which gradually came to be seen rather as a potential ally against the Muslims in the Middle East and as containing possible converts to Christianity. John of Plano Carpini's mission of 1245–48 to Mongolia stands as an important breakthrough in empirical ethnography for its details and for classifications of Mongol life according to categories that recall Herodotus's own.[9] But it was the Flemish William of Rubruck's mission of 1253–55, sponsored by Louis IX, that yielded the most outstanding medieval example of accuracy in observation, and the most immediate and realistic of accounts of the thirteenth-century missions to Mongolia, one still admired as a source on Asian religions of the era.[10] Also in the thirteenth century, Marco Polo's *Divisament dou monde* (Description of the World), surviving in 130 manuscripts, set a future standard for lay ethnography in its attraction of a wide audience to ethnographic writing. *Mandeville's Travels*, in the fourteenth century, indicated the full potential of that medieval and post-medieval audience for descriptions of worldly diversity, surviving in over 300 manuscripts and dominating the genre of travel and ethnographic writings well into the sixteenth century.[11] Of my sources, only Jean de Joinville's crusader account of life in Egypt and the Latin Kingdom, filled though it is with ethnographic content, is newly being treated as a seminal medieval "ethnographic" work. Its inclusion in this study serves as an important corrective to the frequent exclusion of the Crusades as a source of ethnographic production.[12]

The implications of the dialogic poetics of such seminal early European ethnographic writers as Gerald of Wales, William of Rubruck, and the Mandeville author are profound, and, as I show, rather different than the implications of multifocality as it has been elaborated in other, adjacent medieval representational disciplines such as chronicle writing and painting.[13] For the recourse to external perspectives on Europe in a genre about cultural difference evinces a new self-scrutiny and self-consciousness about European cultural identity as seen from an outside perspective, often enough a politically more powerful one: here, as elsewhere, dialogism emerges from the margins of power.[14] Dialogic engagement with alternative perspectives, moreover, implies the incorporation and integration of that alterity within one's own emerging self-definition, a thesis that has emerged in a number of recent "postcolonial medieval" studies of European encounters with difference.[15] The result, rather than the consolidation of European cultural identity through the encounter with difference, or a European self-confidence prefiguring that to come in the era of New World conquests,[16] is the loosening, relativizing, and redefining of European identity through such encounter. A genre about difference that ends up stressing the difference of the home culture; a genre about difference that, rather than consolidating the identity of its readers and writer, exposes that identity to new and destabilizing perspectives on it; a genre about difference that incorporates that difference as part of the home culture's self-definition: all of this rather turns what we know and think about ethnography, rooted as most of those assumptions are in its modern manifestations, on its head.

And all of this makes ethnography composed in light of another's word a difficult and dangerous proposition for medieval authors and their audiences. As the chapters that follow show, such a dialogic ethnography exposes ethnographer-writers as well as their audiences to the unfamiliar and heterodox voices, words, and gazes of medieval Europe's others, and, inextricably linked to these, to medieval Europeans' own considerable feelings of discomfort and disorientation before such worldly perspectives. In their display of such European disorientation, these ethnographies attest to a number of related features of late medieval European encounters that are central to the book's thesis. First, they stand as a record of premodern affect: namely, of the uneasy, disquieting feelings that often attended engagements with difference in spaces of dialogic encounter in the premodern period. Far from simply celebrating worldly diversity, these intercultural ethnographic accounts instead attest to the difficulty of true intercultural engagement with alterity and to the frequent discomfort of self-scrutiny and self-consciousness before the gazes of cultural and religious others. They show that the voices and gazes of the other— rather than a mere projection or fantasy of that self as Orientalist criticism would suggest—amounted to an irreducible force capable of significantly disorienting the medieval European self. And they attest, perhaps above all, to the productive force of such disorientation, which pushed ethnographers and their audiences well beyond the anchoring stability of Latin Christendom's received orthodoxies—those of crusade, mission, and classical anthropologies—into unscripted terrain, where there could and did emerge new modes of thinking about both self and other. Finally, such new modes of thinking and writing in light of another's word signal the strikingly still open nature of European identity itself in the twelfth through fourteenth centuries, an openness replete, as we will see, with both possibilities and hazards.

In tracing the reciprocal gazes of selves and others engaged in dialogic encounter, *In Light of Another's Word* also uncovers a history of the premodern ethnographic gaze and of the visual poetics of ethnography before empire. These, I show, diverge in several, decisive ways from modern ethnographic poetics. As Mary Louise Pratt and James Clifford have found in separate studies of ethnographic form, the conventions of twentieth-century "formal" ethnography developed in such a way as to deny the participation of the ethnographer in the field as observer, despite the fact that this participation has been a sine qua non of ethnographic authority in the modern era since the 1920s, just as it is intrinsic to claims to authenticity and authority in the major ethnographic works of the medieval period. In formal or "scientific" ethnography, "the subjectivity of the author is separated from the objective referent of the text."[17] The removal of the traces of the looking, recording ethnographer is effected to "conform to the norms of a scientific discourse whose authority resides in the absolute effacement of the speaking and experiencing subject," for according to scientific discourse, the "position of speech is that of an observer fixed on the edge of a space, looking in and/or down upon what is other."[18] This "objectivity" effect, as an array of critical anthropologists have argued, is afforded at the cost of the objectification of those being gazed at;[19] or as Jean-Paul Sartre noted more generally of the modern gaze in the 1950s, "objectification is the telos of the look."[20]

The poetics of the dialogic ethnographies of *In Light of Another's Word* are, by contrast, marked by rather different features. First, they exhibit a subjective approach to knowing the other, advancing a subjective view of social knowledge apprehension through the notion that accuracy is best achieved through multifocality, the accrual of ever more incomplete, "partial" (incomplete, subjective) perspectives on an object. This open-ended approach to representational truth is found in other foundational medieval representational disciplines, namely historiography and painting, which, as we will see, were close enough to the emerging field of ethnography to serve as an explicit model for some of its practitioners and implicit intellectual backdrop for all. What the medieval recourse to multiple perspectives in representational disciplines guaranteed was a more ambiguous, open-ended, and less coherent view of truth than any unifocal model allows, including and especially that of the modern ocular regime since the Renaissance rediscovery of linear perspective.[21] Rather than a gaze that aims for singular objectivity or totality in presenting knowledge about others, these writers repeatedly disclose the subjectivity and incompleteness of their gazes on others, implicitly or explicitly inviting the inclusion of other perspectives. Second, the ethnographies of this study are composed "deictically" (from *deiknonei*, to show), always referring back to the body of the speaker, and including information about the spatial and temporal relation of the speaker to his objects of description.[22] They are thus, third, fundamentally relational or dialogic, plotting the subject-author's relation to his objects, and, intersubjectively, theirs to him. Last, unlike modern ethnography, which emerged in the heyday of European empires when ethnographers cast inevitably complicit "imperial eyes" on native Asians and Africans and their customs, European ethnography before empire is characterized by more fluid, complex and unpredictable relations between Latin Christian subjects and their religious and cultural others,[23] and its gazes are likewise often more fluid and open-ended than the modern, fixed gaze of Orientalism and imperialism.[24] These differences of the medieval ethnographic gaze, when reinserted into the history of the Western gaze in relation to which they are rarely considered, complicate the conjoining of all Western techniques of visualization with the impulse to objectify, a critique forged by prominent cultural critics like Johannes Fabian and Edward Said.[25] Through intersubjective and dialogic gazing, the visual poetics of medieval ethnography offers an alternative story of the production of social knowledge in the West.

A range of studies of medieval vision and optics describe the differences of the premodern visual paradigm from modern, scientific ocular regimes in contexts outside ethnography and intercultural encounter. Suzannah Biernoff's study of optics, for instance, argues that in the medieval visual paradigm, truth could not be and was not distanced from the viewing body because of a number of features distinguishing medieval vision from the modern, including the lack of separation between viewer and objects and the synthesis of scientific and religious thought.[26] Similarly, ancient and medieval optics' extramission theory—whereby the subject's apprehension of an object depends on an emission of some sort of activating radiation from the subject on the object, and thus a relationship between subject and object—has interested intellectual historians like Martin Jay as evidence of intersubjective understanding and a participatory view of subject-object relation in the medieval period.[27] And in medieval literary criticism, scholars have argued for an intersubjectivity manifest in medieval courtly literature through the blurring of subject-object boundaries in amatory gazes.[28] In describing the operation of the premodern ethnographic gaze, I extend existing scholarship on the visual poetics of the gaze to a context addressed by neither critics of ethnographic form, who rarely focus on the premodern period, nor critics of medieval visual culture, who have not focused on ethnography or intercultural encounter. At the same time, I advance recent studies of premodern travel and encounter into the realm of poetics.

My first chapter, "Conquest, Conversion, Crusade, Salvation: The Discourse of Anthropology and Its Uses in the Medieval Period," surveys the sources of medieval ethnographic ideas regarding religious and ethnic difference found in the book. The chapter traces the discourse of medieval anthropology as it emerged to meet the challenges of human religious and cultural difference in five distinctive realms in the late medieval period: the conquest of the twelfth-century colonial fringe, the advancement of thirteenth-century missions to Asia, the theorization of non-Christian rights and responsibilities abroad, efforts to know the proximate Muslim enemy, and the theorization of the salvation of virtuous, primitive non-Christians. Each of these realms of anthropological activity was not only central to the overall development of anthropological thinking in the twelfth to fourteenth centuries but also serves as background to the particular chapters on medieval ethnography that follow.

I then turn to the dialogic ethnography of medieval Europe. Chapter 2, "Subjective Beginnings: Autoethnography and the Partial Gazes of Gerald of Wales," plots the doubled voice of Gerald's novel *Descriptio Kambraie*, a description of Welsh mores at once from a colonial, Anglo-Norman perspective underwritten by twelfth-century evolutionary anthropology and from the perspective of Wales's own mythic traditions of resistance and redemption. I show how the *Descriptio*'s rhetorical duality is typical of "autoethnography," ethnographic self-description that selectively appropriates colonialist representations in order to intervene in them. I argue that part of Gerald's intervention in colonial processes is the very act of writing the *Descriptio* itself, an act of "salvage anthropology" aimed at preserving a snapshot of contemporary Welsh manners and customs under increasing colonial infringement and Anglo-Norman acculturation. I close by considering the visual poetics of Gerald's gaze in the *Descriptio*, tracing the sources of his bifocality both in the representational disciplines of historiography and painting and in his own ethnic hybridity. The specificities of Gerald's ethnic hybridity apart, Gerald's insistence on the subjectivity, incompleteness, and partiality of medieval ethnographic description initiates a thread that runs through the whole of this study.

Chapter 3, "Writing Ethnography 'In the Eyes of the Other': William of Rubruck's Mission to Mongolia," is devoted to Friar William of Rubruck's record of Mongolian customs, the *Itinerarium*, written during his stay in that empire from 1253 to 1255. The chapter on the whole demonstrates how Christian universalism, which would become synonymous with a lack of receptivity to cultural difference in later eras, in fact features a great self-extension toward the other in late medieval practice. I first show how William eschews readily available European discourses of Mongol barbarism and demonization in favor of a representation of reasonable Mongol customs. I then show how the salvation aim structures William's representations, not only its profoundly detailed observations of Mongol life but also his depiction of his own religious and cultural difference from the viewpoint of his would-be converts. For contemporary preaching manuals predicated the preacher's success abroad on the disorienting and counterintuitive ability to externalize his own Christian viewpoints and to "see as other," as non-Christians see, a skill over which William shows mastery at the great interreligious debate at Caracorum. What is born of such ability to "see as other" is a dialogic ethnography composed as much in light of the other's gaze as one's own.

Chapter 4, "Casting a 'Sideways Glance' at the Crusades: The Voice of the Other in Joinville's *Vie de Saint Louis*," treats the fascinating events of the Seventh Crusade (1248–50) of Louis IX as later recorded in 1309 by his companion and seneschal, Jean de Joinville. Readers of this crusade account soon find that military endeavor slides into complex negotiations, which themselves turn on a veritable trove of shared vocabulary and cultural citations inherited from some two centuries of crusade contacts between Latin Christians abroad and local Muslims that testify to a working, dialogic, and syncretic Islamo-Christian culture on the ground. At the same time, Joinville shows the disorienting effects of partaking in the *Vie*'s many conversations with Muslims, of being pulled into inhabiting the perspective of the other: we watch as Muslim voices and views dialogize with Joinville's own, casting their own heretical "sideways glances" on official Christian perspectives to produce an alternative, heterodox image of the crusading endeavor.

Chapter 5, "Dis-Orienting the Self: The Uncanny *Travels of John Mandeville*," describes the way that at each turn the *Travels*' narrator performs the Christian self's uncanny and unsettling indistinguishability from its would-be pagan and Muslim "others." One might, with reason, say that such slippage is the logical end point of the cultural and religious interpenetration observed in previous chapters. But, as I argue, the crisis of the uncanny in the *Travels* ultimately finds its source in the fourteenth century's preoccupation with the question of non-Christian salvation and what, if anything, distinguished Christians from other religious communities. Of all the texts of the book, the *Travels* perhaps best reflects the poetics of writing "in light of another's word," displaying episodes that foreground external perspectives on Latin Christian practices, cite from the voice of the other, demonstrate the disorienting effects of other words and worlds on the European self abroad, and insist on the limits and contingencies of the European gaze—and of Latin Christian claims of universalism—upon and within a diverse world.

It is a critical commonplace that the European Middle Ages have frequently been constructed in relation to the modern era, whether as its backward and savage antithesis or, conversely, as a time of relative liberation from modernity's political and social discontents. Yet the ethnographic evidence of this study suggests something far more nuanced than either of these familiar poles allows. If the writers of *In Light of Another's Word* break with expectation in dialogically representing the other in his own words and language, so seemingly prefiguring the ideals of intersubjective ethnographic practice in the postcolonial period, their texts illustrate that they did so at great personal discomfort and risk in the face of the governing orthodoxies of their day. That we can hear the voices of medieval Europe's others in these narratives in spite of these orthodoxies allows us to take full measure of the forces of productive disorientation and destabilization at work on these early ethnographic writers through word- and world-altering encounter.

CHAPTER I

Conquest, Conversion, Crusade, Salvation

The Discourse of Anthropology and Its Uses in the Medieval Period

If ethnography, defined as discourse on observed manners and customs, has a very long history, anthropology, defined not as the academic discipline established in the twentieth century but as the set of ideas and theories attempting to account for cultural diversity or the unity of the "human," has an equally long history.[1] Anthropological thinking in the medieval period can be divided into two main discourses, each with its own distinctive assumptions and approaches to the other, the discourse of Christianity and the discourse of civility.[2] The medieval discourse of civility, derived from the Epicurean tradition of writers such as Lucretius and made available to medieval writers primarily through Cicero, posited a universal, linear model of cultural development according to which all cultures progressed through certain stages of development on a continuum from savagery to civility. This secular model was deployed in twelfth-century contexts of colonization or conquest along Europe's borders as a justification for the subjugation of native peoples. It was applied irrespective of the Christianity of its subject peoples, at once to the pagan Slavs on Europe's eastern border and the already-Christian Irish and Welsh on Europe's northwest border.[3] The discourse of Christianity, on the other hand, sought the conversion of the other, and so deployed a spatial model that distinguished "humanity," the realm of all possible converts according to universal Christian thought, from all that lay beyond it, the realm of the inhuman, semihuman, or monstrous. Medieval mappaemundi well demonstrate the spatial logic of the discourse of Christianity. Thirteenth-century European world maps such as the Psalter map picture the globe as an orb over which Christ presides, or in the case of the Ebstorf map, as an orb out of which Christ's very limbs—his head, hands, and feet—may be seen to project. The contemplator of such a map (and they were meant for religious contemplation) would have found Jerusalem at the center, the Garden of Eden circled at the eastern top, and a host of biblical stories drawn in as pictorial lessons before reaching the map's southern fringe. There medieval viewers would have confronted a series of monsters, figural representations of Pliny's legendary monstrous races: the Cynocephiles or dog heads, the cubit-sized Pygmies, the cannibal Anthropophages, the doubly sexed Androgynes. While for Pliny the monstrous races may have expressed the curious diversity and plenitude of natural history, for Christian thinkers as early as Augustine they presented very real doctrinal problems: were these races the descendants of Adam, and if not, how did they get there? Augustine devotes book 16, chapter 8, in the *City of God* to the question of "the origin of recorded monstrosities," where he writes: "There are accounts in pagan history of certain monstrous races of men.... What am I to say of the Cynocephali, whose dog's head and actual barking prove them to be animals rather than men? Now we are not bound to believe in the existence of all the types of men which are described. But no faithful Christian should doubt that anyone who is born anywhere a man—that is, a *rational and mortal being*—derives from that one first-created human being." He concludes his discussion, by his own admission, tentatively and open-endedly thus: "the accounts of some of these races may be completely worthless, but if such peoples exist, then either they are not human; or, if human, they are descended from Adam."[4] The monstrous races may well exist then and may be nonhuman; Augustine left medieval thinkers to grapple with the implications. We see in mappaemundi like the Psalter map one response to the problem: late medieval mapmakers drew in the monstrous races at the outer limits of the inhabited world where they stood, at once, for the limit of their own geographical knowledge and for the final frontier of the Christian message—for as all Christians knew, no pastoral outreach would be possible, required, or desirable toward nonhumans. The discourse of Christianity, then, depended above all on the distinction of the properly human, and hence possibly Christian, from the nonhuman. As such, the discouse of Christianity implicates a host of other discourses, including those of the monstrous races, the wild man, and the barbarian, devoted to the same definitional work.

Figure 1. The Psalter Map. British Library Additional ms 28681, f.9. Courtesy of the British Library.

In what follows I lay out some of the major sources for the discourses of civility and Christianity in the high medieval period. The former found particular application along the borders of Europe during its twelfth-century expansion, the latter, in the dreams of converting the Mongols during the thirteenth-century opening of Asia to Europe via the missions. Innocent IV's unique and remarkably influential contribution to medieval anthropology, his consideration of the conditional sovereignty rights of non-Christians living abroad, will be considered as an important signpost in the development of the medieval discourse of Christianity. I will then turn to the realm of the Crusades, and consider medieval European attitudes toward the proximate Muslim enemy by examining developments in Latin knowledge of and interest in Muslim religion and Arabic culture. Finally, I consider the medieval discourse of the virtuous pagan, forerunner of the Renaissance noble savage in its primitivist celebration of the uncultured piety and goodness of select non-Christians. This discourse, which dovetailed with the theological and philosophical discourses about the salvation of non-Christians, found a range of applications abroad in the late Middle Ages, from encounters with the Brahmins of India, such as in Mandeville's rendering, to the depictions of the natives of the Canaries in the fourteenth-century explorations and conquests of those Atlantic isles. Each of these realms of anthropological activity was not only central to the overall development of anthropological thinking in the twelfth to fourteenth centuries but also serves as background to the particular chapters on medieval ethnography that follow.

EVOLUTIONARY ANTHROPOLOGY IN THE TWELFTH CENTURY

Developmental, "progressivist," or evolutionary anthropology has its roots in the ancient classical tradition, in particular the Epicurean account of cultural development best exemplified by Lucretius. For the Epicureans, "the earliest condition of men resembled that of the beasts, and from this primitive and miserable condition they laboriously reached the existing state of civilization, not by external guidance as a consequence of some initial design, but simply by the exercise of human intelligence throughout a long period."[5] It is the notion of man's *independent* progress, as opposed to an externally induced kind, that would distinguish ancient progressivism, along with its medieval and modern descendants, from competing theories stressing the role of environmental, external factors in the formation of cultures such as ancient climaticism or modern diffusionism.

Many twelfth-century European writers were intimately familiar with the classical anthropological tradition, with lasting and profound impact on their perceptions and constructions of civilizational norms, achievement, and backwardness in the unfamiliar worlds they recorded around them. William of Malmesbury, who has been credited with being the first to rediscover the classical notion of barbarians and apply it to the Celts of his day, had an extensive knowledge of classical literature,[6] as did the Paris-schooled Gerald of Wales. Without pursuing the question of specific influence in particular texts, scholars of the Celtic fringe such as John Gillingham, R. R. Davies, and Robert Bartlett each acknowledge a general classical influence on the medieval ethnographers they treat. A consideration of the impact of Cicero on medieval ethnographic writers goes a long way toward closing this critical gap; for here is a classical author whose ideas about savagery "pervaded the medieval concept of barbarism."[7] We know, for instance, that Cicero, along with Seneca, another writer with progressivist leanings, is among the most cited of the prose writers in Gerald's numerous works,[8] and William of Malmesbury may have had as many as twenty-eight works by Cicero, his most esteemed classical author.[9] In reading such works as Cicero's *Pro Sestio*, Gerald and other medieval observers of "alien" cultural practices gained access to a mode of cultural analysis that converted these practices into signs of cultural primitivism and allowed them to plot cultures on an evolutionary scale that left no doubt as to the more advanced standing of Anglo-Norman culture.

Cicero was by no means the only source of classical ideas of culture available to writers like Gerald and William of Malmesbury: fragments of the picture of evolutionary cultural development were available via ethnographic descriptions in other classical sources, descriptions that implied developmental models of culture without, however, overtly stating these assumptions as a theory or generalization regarding human culture. We find such ethnographic descriptions in two of Gerald's known sources, Caesar's *Bellum Gallicum* and Sallust's *Bellum Iugurthinum*. Moments in these texts look much like those of Gerald and his contemporaries' descriptions of Celtic peoples. Caesar's *Bellum Gallicum*, for instance, notes the warlike aspect of the Germanic Suebi, their preference for milk and meat rather than corn, and sparsely populated lands (4.1–4); the Germans' lack of agriculture, and beast-filled forests; and the Gauls' capricious nature (4.5).[10] Sallust depicts the ancient Gaetulians and Libyans in a familiar language of savagery: a "rude and uncivilized folk [*asperi incultique*], who fed like beasts [*pecoribus*] on the flesh of wild animals and the fruit of the earth ... governed neither by institutions nor law, nor were they subject to anyone's rule. A restless, roving people, they had their abodes wherever night compelled a halt."[11]

Ethnographers like Caesar provided medieval writers with a glimpse of classical progressivist ideas, but it is through Cicero's rendering of Lucretius,[12] the earliest Roman exponent of progressivist anthropology and probably its most thorough exponent, that medieval thinkers were able to view a coherent picture of classical ideas of cultural progress, ideas that figure foundationally in the evolutionary anthropology of the nineteenth century and hence in the anthropological discipline at its origins. Lucretius's *De rerum natura*, book 5, along with Plato's *Laws*, book 3, is widely considered the locus classicus of the developmental anthropological tradition.[13] Roughly sketched, Lucretius's account of man's cultural development proceeds from the earliest phases in human history where man knew no agricultural tools and lived in the woods, forests, and caves, to the beginnings of human society where men made huts and tents, and "woman in mating with man gave herself to one only."[14] Next came language, the learning of various arts including fire and cooking, weaving, agriculture and the domestication of animals, and the earliest form of government, chiefdoms. Later kings founded cities, fortified them, and divided property between men. Next there came the reign of law, "for mankind, weary of violence, was grown weak from its feuds, so that it was the more ready of its own accord to subject itself to the restraint of laws."[15] Lucretius's account is not unmixed with moments of primitivist or antiprogressive nostalgia for times simpler and happier than the present, as when he regrets the invention of private property, or the ravaging advances in techniques of warfare. But his delight in the advancement of human arts and industries in such passages as below is clear: "Navigation and agriculture, fortification and laws, arms, roads, clothing, and all else of this kind, all the prizes of life and its deepest delights also, poetry and pictures and sculpture, these slowly, step by step, were taught by practice and the experience of man's mind as it progressed [*progredientis*]. Thus by degrees time draws forth everything before us and reason raises it to the realm of light. For things must be brought to light one after another and in due order in the arts, until they have reached their highest point."[16] This passage not only provides the first use of the word *progredientes*, from which "progress" derives, but also on the basis of its content and meaning, "[it] could be inserted aptly into literally dozens of works on the progress of mankind written in the eighteenth and well into the nineteenth century."[17]

We find much the same picture in Cicero, who was "intimately acquainted from the beginning of his literary career with Lucretius' outline of man's cultural history," but who, unlike Lucretius, was well known to twelfth-century medieval authors.[18] In the *De Officiis*, so frequently drawn from in Gerald's writings, Cicero praises the arts in a passage much like Lucretius's above:

> Why should I recount the multitude of arts, without which life would be a thing of no value? For how would the sick be healed, what pleasure would there be in health, how should we obtain either the necessaries or the refinements of life, if there were not so many arts to minister to us? In all these respects the civilized life [*exculta vita*] of men is far removed from the level of subsistence and comfort of the animals. And without the association of men, cities could neither have been built nor peopled, as a result of which laws and customs [*leges moresque*] were established, and then the equitable determination of rights [*iuris*], and a settled disciplined life [*certaque vivendi disciplina*]. When these were assured there followed a more humane spirit [*mansuetudo animorum*] and the sense of what is morally becoming, so that life is more secure, and that, by giving and receiving, by mutual exchange of goods and services [*mutuandisque facultatibus et commodandis*], we were able to satisfy all our needs.[19]

On the one hand, the arts are the key to the civilized life, provisioning man with necessities and refinements both; on the other, it is the social life of humans that has engendered their cities, the establishment of their laws, the growth of an exchange economy, a more stable, settled existence, and the growth of their civility and morality—the causes of the development of human civilization are multipronged and plentiful according to this optimistic passage. Cicero's use of *mansuetudo* for civility is echoed in medieval Latin sources.[20] In the *Pro Sestio*, also available to Gerald, Cicero lays out his clearest expression of the classical developmental model:

> For who does not know the condition of nature to have been once such that men, in the days before either natural or civil law had been drawn up, wandered dispersed and scattered about the fields [*fusi per*

agros ac dispersi vagarentur], and that each possessed no more than he could seize or keep by his own strength, through killing or wounding others? But those who first arose endowed with superior virtue and prudence, having recognized a kind of intelligence and teachableness in man, gathered these scattered individuals together in one place and converted them from wildness to justice and gentleness. Establishing first political societies for the common advantage, then the small associations of men which were afterwards named towns, then those groupings of domiciles which we call cities, they fortified all these with law, human and divine, as with walls. And between our present mode of life, refined through humanity, and that wretched one, the principal difference is the difference between law and force.[21]

When writing of the Welsh's dispersed manner of fighting ("If the Welsh would only . . . fight in ordered ranks instead of leaping about all over the place"),[22] plunder, and rule by force, as he did in the *Descriptio*, Gerald would have had access not merely to stock "barbarian" ethnographic descriptions such as Caesar's but to whole developmental models of culture in passages such as this one, which left a lasting imprint, as we shall see in the following chapter, on his seminal ethnographic work. For according to the evolutionary scale presented above, Gerald was free to conclude that the societies of Wales and Ireland had not progressed very far at all, still living as they did in unruly discord rather than "political societies for the common advantage" and in fields and forests rather than towns or fortified cities. And we can be certain of the influence on him of a like developmental model when he turns to the Irish in the following paragraph in the *Topography of Ireland*:

> Est autem gens haec gens silvestris, gens inhospita; gens ex bestiis solum et bestialiter vivens; gens a primo pastoralis vitae vivendi modo non recedens. Cum enim a silvis ad agros, ab agris ad villas, civiumque convictus, humani generis ordo processerit, gens haec, agriculturae labores aspernans, et civiles gazas parum affectans, civiumque jura multum detrectans, in silvis et pascuis vitam quam hactenus assueverat nec desuescere novit nec descire.[23]

> (They [the Irish] are a wild and inhospitable people. They live on beasts only, and live like beasts. They have not progressed at all from the primitive habits of pastoral living. While man usually progresses from the woods to fields, and from the fields to settlements and communities of citizens, this people despises work on the land, has little use for the money-making of towns, contemns the rights and privileges of citizenship, and desires neither to abandon, nor lose respect for, the life which it has been accustomed to lead in the woods and countryside.)

As we will see in the following chapter, Gerald's treatment of the Welsh will in fact be more ambivalent and equivocal than evolutionary influences allow, but his description of the Irish is another matter. Cicero's more subtle progression from pastoral to city life is laid utterly bare here, as Gerald performs the act of interpreting the classical developmental tradition for his reader, according to which city life is the highest expression of civility.

In importing the classical theory of human cultural development into his ethnographic depictions, Gerald has in effect moved beyond ethnography and cultural description into formulating medieval anthropology. Nor is he alone among twelfth-century ethnographers of the Celtic fringe in doing so. For although in the *Topography* we find an unusually complete medieval formulation of ancient progressivism, Gerald's contemporaries like William of Malmesbury, William of Newburgh, William of Poitiers, Ralph Glaber, and the author of the *Gesta Stephani* are so influenced by the same anthropological assumptions as to be unanimous in finding in Celtic lands a manifestation of what the ancients would have considered developmentally backward societies. Classical sources like Cicero shaped not only the twelfth-century ethnographer's categories of description—native habitat, the rule of law versus that of (seemingly, at least) force alone, agricultural versus hunting economies—but more importantly, his very modes of interpreting such descriptive categories as so many signposts on the road to civility. Thus William of Malmesbury, one of the earliest classically influenced ethnographers, is able to discover in the existence of town life and agricultural arts evidence of his own cultural superiority: "Ita pro peniuria, immo pro inscientia cultorum, ieiunum omnium bonorum solum agrestem et squalidam multitudinem Hibernensium extra urbes producit; Angli uero et Franci cultiori genere uitae urbes nundinarum commertio inhabitant" ([Whereas] the soil [of Ireland] lacks all advantages, and so poor, or rather unskillful, are its cultivators that it can produce only a ragged mob of rustic Irishmen outside the towns, the English and the French, with their more civilized way of life, live in towns, and carry on trade and commerce).[24]

Such continuity of classical and medieval ideas of progress would surprise some intellectual historians who have argued for the intrinsic incompatibility of models of historical progress with the Middle Ages, whose "history moved not according to natural development but a series of divine revelations and interventions."[25] But as historians of anthropology know, the notion of human progress was not intrinsically compatible with the thinking of later centuries when biblical assumptions regarding human degeneration since the Fall were still conventional, as they were even in the heyday of evolutionary anthropology in the nineteenth century. Most periods in history are fraught with antithetical, countering intellectual forces and, it would appear, the Middle Ages are no exception. Any doubt as to the possibility of a progressivist medieval anthropology is best resolved by the contemporary evidence from the twelfth century. That evidence indicates that a secular view of history had in fact been imported via classical sources into a medieval frame where it irrepressibly influenced the ethnographic writing of those who employed such sources. In fact, the developmental model of culture was very well suited to the arena into which it was imported, for as we have already glimpsed, it functioned in the twelfth century, as it would in the nineteenth century, to justify the secular aim of conquest and control of the native populations.

CONVERSION AND THE BOUNDARIES OF THE "HUMAN" IN THE THIRTEENTH CENTURY

If the twelfth-century expansion of Europe found developmental anthropology particularly suitable to its aims in nearby borderlands, the thirteenth century, an era of hope for the conversion of Asia to Christianity through missionary activity, was the age of elaborating the discourse of Christianity and defining the "human." In a range of discourses, both popular and elite, the thirteenth century evinces a heightened interest in establishing the contours of the human. New theorizations of what constituted the human emerged from scholastic thinkers like Albertus Magnus and Thomas Aquinas, as did new theorizations of the conditional rights of non-Christians abroad to cultural sovereignty through the papal decrees of Innocent IV.

While the thirteenth century might have witnessed the dream of converting Asia, in particular of bringing the Mongols within the Christian embrace, this by no means meant that the Mongols were universally regarded as particularly good candidates for conversion. On the contrary, the following description of the Mongols from Matthew Paris's *Chronica Majora* (c. 1240) is probably closer to the consensus view: "The men are inhuman and of the nature of beasts, rather to be called monsters than men, thirsting after and drinking blood, and tearing and devouring the flesh of dogs and human beings; they clothe themselves in the skins of bulls, and are armed with iron lances; they are short in stature and thickset . . . and of great strength; invincible in battle, indefatigable in labour; they drink the blood which flows from their flocks. . . . They have no human laws, know no mercy, are more cruel than lions or bears; they know no other country's language except that of their own, and of this all other nations are ignorant."[26] Matthew Paris's description, we will see, accords closely with the scholastic discourse of the barbarian. Missionaries to Mongolia such as Carpini and Rubruck were—indeed, needed to be—rather more generous in their attributions of Mongol humanity. How then was such "humanity" to be identified and distinguished according to the definitions of their day?

Given the place of Pliny's monstrous races at the outermost edges of the known world on medieval mappaemundi, medieval thinkers in search of demarcating the human from the barbarous or monstrous might well turn first to the definitions of Pliny the Elder, made available to them through Pliny's medieval encyclopedic abbreviators. The monstrous races of Pliny's *Natural History*, whom he terms *gentes monstri* and *homines* or *gentes silvestres*, appear in book 7 immediately after Pliny considers the innumerable *"ritus moresque"*—customs and manners—of all the world's gentes that he could not include in his cosmography. The relation between these monsters and the human becomes clear soon thereafter: the "monstrous" is that which stretches, twists, or turns inside out the norms of the human form, life cycle, and social habits of Pliny's antique day. The Pandorean Indians, for instance, live two hundred years, while childbearing among the Macrobii, who live only to forty years, is restricted to a single occurrence, and the Antemidorus never get sick. Many of the Plinian monsters display physical anomalies from the human, including giants, dwarf-like Pygmies, dog-headed Cynocephales, and doubly sexed Androgyni. Still others partake in aberrant diet (cannibal Scythians and Anthropophages) and dwellings (cave-dwelling Pygmies), are speechless (Cynocephales), practice religious idolatry (the sun-worshipping Gymnosophists) and unusual marriage customs (the Wife-givers), go naked (Bragmanni), or display skillful hunting (Troglodytes).[27]

From this list of monstrous attributes, one might glean what factors compose the "measure of man," to use John Block Friedman's phrase,[28] and distinguish the human from the monstrous: physical form; modes of diet; dwelling and habitat; sexual, marital, and childbearing practices; clothing; spiritual life; speech; and defense, Pliny suggests, are each constitutive of the "human." Pliny's ideas would have reached medieval readers through his ancient encyclopedic abbreviators, Solinus and Isidore of Seville, as well as the thirteenth-century encyclopedist Vincent of Beauvais. Solinus's *Collectanea Rerum Memorabilium* cites many of the most popular Plinian races, locating them in the farthest East or in Africa.[29] Solinus describes the manners and customs of a number of peoples, including the Arabians, the silk-trading Seres, Indians abstaining from meat, the Tabrobanes and their method of king selection.[30] He also offers a long ethnographic excursus on the Scythians, whom he describes in ways that will remind one of Matthew Paris's Tartars: living in caves, Scythians drink out of the skull cups of their enemies, love fighting, suck the blood out of the wounds they inflict, and, of course, delight in drinking one another's blood.[31] Isidore lists the Plinian races under his consideration of "Portents," where, he asserts, just as anomalous monstrous births take place among humans, so are there born whole monstrous races, including Cynocephali, Cyclopes, Blemmyas, Antipodes, Pygmies, and so forth.[32]

Isidore's and Solinus's treatment of the Plinian races may well have influenced the classifications of culture that John of Plano Carpini or William of Rubruck employed to describe the foreign Mongols before them, including their dwellings, food, clothing, laws, burial rites, marital rites, and religious beliefs—classifications that reinscribe much the same categories that serve as boundaries between the human and the nonhuman in Pliny, Solinus, and Isidore. But other cultural discourses were also available from which Carpini and Rubruck could derive those categories, including the widespread tradition of that internal other of medieval Europe, the wild man. This tradition was made available by way of the work of the great trio of thirteenth-century encyclopedists, Bartholomew Anglicus, Thomas of Cantimpré, and Vincent of Beauvais, as well as through older textual traditions such as the Alexander saga, the St. Jerome Bible, and the apocryphal *Letter of Prester John* (c. 1165).[33] In a composite sketch of the tradition, an "ethnography of the medieval wild man"[34] might look something like the following: the wild man is forest dwelling (thus a literal *silvester homo*) rather than a city dweller, giant or dwarflike Pygmy in size, hairy, hunting and gathering, eating the raw flesh of animals, without knowledge of agriculture or metallurgy, having great physical strength, warlike, given to sexual carnality, of meager intellect, lacking human speech, incapable of knowing God because irrational, and linked to the semidivine or the semisatanic. Such an ethnography indicates how readily one may treat the discourses of the medieval wild man and the monstrous races as coterminous, invoking as they do many of the same markers for "humanity"—habitat, diet, hunting, sexual practices, speech, religion—and each representing the projection of internal anxieties about the boundaries and norms of "human" behavior on an "other."

Thirteenth-century intellectual production indicates still further examinations by humans of the contours of the human. Specifically in the schools, Aristotelian scholars like Albertus Magnus, Thomas Aquinas, and numerous Aristotelian commentators were openly considering the same question of the boundaries of the human that popular discourses of "wild men" and "monsters" entertained in less conscious ways.[35] Indeed we even find leakage of vocabulary between scholastic and popular treatments of the topic: the Pygmy plays a pivotal role in Albertus Magnus's determination of what sets apart the human from the rest of the animal kingdom. In *De Animalibus*, a text whose main concern has rightly been identified as man himself, Albertus assigns the Pygmy and the ape intermediary positions between man and beast.[36] As manlike creatures, or *similitudines hominis*,[37] the ape and the Pygmy reached closest to the perfection of man in that they were capable of degrees of *disciplinabilitas*, "the control of mind over body that underlies every purposeful act,"[38] and thereby learning. They lacked, however, a final level of disciplinabilitas reserved for humans alone: the power of reason with which to transform these sensory data and memories into universal principles. Without *ratio* and the ability to grasp universals, the ape and the Pygmy were deprived of civility and its distinguishing elements, enumerated by Albertus as: the experience of shame and the ability to know vice from virtue, the use of language including a facility with rhetorical devices, political systems and laws, and non-forest dwellings.[39] In his inclusion of the forest habitat as a marker of incivility, Albertus Magnus participates in the popular ethnographic assumptions of his day. But Albertus Magnus distinguishes himself from other medieval thinkers in his anticipation of the evolutionary assumptions of modern anthropology through his offering of a measure by which the animal kingdom and man himself might be assigned a position on a hierarchical chain of being, and his posing of a theory of man's kinship with apes.[40]

But what of degrees of humanity within humans themselves? Albertus Magnus's treatments of the less than human in the *De Animalibus* closely echo his definitions of "the barbarian" elsewhere. In the *Ethics*, he writes: "Bestial men, however, are rare, since it is a rare man who has no spark of humanity. It does, however, occur, and usually from two causes: physical handicap and deprivation. For we call those who are not induced to be virtuous either by laws, by civility or by the regime of any kind of discipline 'barbarous.' Cicero, in the beginning of the *De Inventione*, calls them 'wild men leading the life of animals with the wild beasts'. . . . Or, in the same way, bestial men eat raw flesh and drink blood, and are delighted to drink and eat from human skulls."[41] Albertus Magnus's barbarians are men who lead the life of animals, who cannot be induced to civility and virtue by "the regime of any kind of discipline," discipline being linked, as we've seen, to reason. His final depiction of barbarians feeding on raw flesh, drinking blood, and eating out of human skulls resonates with Matthew Paris's description of Mongol life so closely as to make apparent to what degree each followed the barbarian script—already fully developed in Solinus's account of the Scythians[42]—and how much agreement there was among an array of thirteenth-century thinkers on the nature of humanity's other, the barbarian. When another great scholastic, Thomas Aquinas, depicted barbarians as "for the most part . . . robust in body and deficient in mind" and as "lacking in reason" in the *Commentary on the Politics*, he cannot be regarded as original. While Thomas offered some specificity for the causes of barbarian irrationality, his definition of the barbarian will be otherwise familiar:

> and so the men who are called barbarians absolutely are the ones who are lacking in reason, either because they happen to live in an exceedingly intemperate region of the sky, so that by the very disposition of the region they are found to be dull for the most part, or else because of some evil custom prevailing in certain lands from which it comes about that men are rendered irrational and almost brutal. *Now it is evident that it is from the power of reason that men are ruled by reasonable laws and that they are practiced in writing. Hence barbarism is appropriately manifested by this sign, that men either do not live under laws or live under irrational ones, and likewise that among certain peoples there is no training in writing.* (my italics)[43]

Humans are reasonable, lawful and robust in mind; barbarians are unreasonable, robust in body, lawless or ruled by irrational laws and evil customs, lacking the technology of writing.

Aquinas's attention to "evil custom" introduces a direct link between the attention to manners and customs—ritus moresque—and the judgment of inhumanity or semihumanity that is "barbarism." If the study of customs could lead to an assessment of the moral and intellectual worth of a people, the determination of unreasonable or corrupt customs among men could in turn lead to the justification for Christian intervention and even just warfare upon them. Aquinas hints as much when he asserts in a section of the *Summa Theologica* written between 1265 and 1271 that while non-Christians may not be compelled toward the faith, they may be compelled "ut fidem non impediant vel blasphemiis, vel malis persuasionibus, vel etiam apertis persecutionibus" (not to hinder the faith by blasphemies, evil suasions, or even open persecutions).[44] In this, Aquinas's thinking points to that of Innocent IV: for no thirteenth-century thinker developed the connection between social custom, sovereignty, and just warfare so clearly and so fully as Pope Innocent IV, whose work effectively influenced all thinking on the subject, including Aquinas's. Innocent's theory of limited non-Christian or pagan sovereignty provides a final component in our survey of the thirteenth-century anthropological discourse of Christianity, and arguably its most weighty component, as Innocent's thought was vastly influential in later centuries, when it was reinterpreted and adapted to fit approaches to pagans inconsistent with his own and with the medieval salvational aim.

THE CONDITIONAL RIGHTS OF NON-CHRISTIANS ABROAD: THE ANTHROPOLOGY OF INNOCENT IV AND ITS AFTERLIFE

Innocent IV was intimately involved in the thirteenth-century diplomatic, missionary, and information-gathering expeditions to the Mongolian empire, which together constitute the most significant anthropological activity of the Middle Ages. Immediately upon his election as pope in 1243, Innocent called for a crusade of Germans and Hungarians against the advancing Mongols, the subject of an emergency meeting of the Council of Lyon later that same year; at the same time he began organizing missions to convert and collect information about them.[45] Though it is Louis IX and not Innocent IV who sponsored William of Rubruck's mission, Innocent was responsible for nearly every other significant mission to Asia, including those of

Franciscans John of Plano Carpini, Benedict the Pole, and Lawrence of Portugal by way of the Near East, and Dominicans Ascelinus and Andrew of Longjumeau by way of Russia.[46] While his missionaries were learning anthropology "in the field," as it were, Innocent was developing at home a legal basis for papal relations with non-Christians. In his Commentary to Innocent III's decretal *Quod Super His*, concerning the vow to go on crusade to the Holy Land, Innocent IV addressed the fundamental question of the legality of invading infidel lands and offered two different answers. Where the land in question is the Holy Land, Innocent argues, invasion is justified for a number of alternative reasons, among them: the Holy Land is Christian by right and unjustly occupied by Saracens; Christ had consecrated this land and his followers were meant to live there; the Donation of Constantine made the pope the heir to the lands of the Roman emperors; and according to the Treaty of Jaffa signed (against heavy papal objections) in 1229 between the sultan of Egypt al-Kamil and the Holy Roman emperor Frederick II, Frederick held the title of king of Jerusalem. These arguments all fell under the already well-examined question of "just war."[47]

What is of more interest, and indeed occupied Innocent more, is the less well theorized question of just war upon lands held by non-Christians outside the Holy Land. Here Innocent's thinking is new and original. Building on the biblical model of Saul's election as king, Innocent argued that as rational creatures all men had the right to self-government and to private property and that papal interference with these rights was therefore illicit. Rational men also had the right not to be Christian: forcible conversion was unlawful, baptism required consent. But because the pope had a responsibility for the souls of all men, the papal domain did theoretically extend into non-Christian lands, that is, de jure if not de facto. The papal jurisdiction over all souls meant that the pope had a responsibility to send missionaries to non-Christian lands and to protect Christians abroad from persecution. It also meant, Innocent continued, that intervention in non-Christian lands was justified in cases where non-Christian practices violated natural law, as so-called sins *contra naturam*, and local leaders did nothing to punish or alter these practices.[48] While Innocent did not specifically define what he meant by a sin contra naturam, the two examples he did provide—sexual perversion and idolatry or polytheistic belief—represent practices Carpini, William of Rubruck, and others would record as part of Mongol "manners and customs" without regard to their sinfulness according to church norms. And despite the missionaries' descriptions of widespread practices of polygamy and idolatry among the Mongols, Innocent never addressed the implications of the presence of sins contra naturam within this immediate non-Christian theater.[49] The only response we are given to this test of Innocentian theory lies in the realm of practice: no papal crusade was ever called upon Mongol lands on the basis of the Mongols' polygamy, idolatry, or any other custom. Instead, the missionaries' records of these and other possibly "unnatural" Mongol cultural practices lay dormant, without provoking military applications throughout the Middle Ages, contributing instead to the storehouse of medieval European knowledge of non-Christian and Asian cultures.

Innocent's theory of papal relations with non-Christians would have a lasting influence on future canonists of the medieval and the early modern period, by whom it was applied in ways significantly divergent from Innocent's own context. Specifically, later canonists frequently interpreted Innocent's thinking to create justifications for wars being launched on non-Christian peoples. Two aspects of Innocent's theory were particularly significant for future thinkers: his inclusion of non-Christians within the pastoral jurisdiction of the pope on the premise of a common rationality and humanity, and his recognition of limited non-Christian sovereignty, within the albeit ill-defined confines of nature's law. Many fourteenth- and fifteenth-century canonists accepted Innocent's assertion of non-Christian humanity and rationality, only to justify intervention or conquest in pagan societies on the basis of Innocent's "sins contra naturam." In the fourteenth-century context of the Spanish Reconquista, for instance, the lawyer Oldratus de Ponte (d. 1335) argued that war upon Muslims was appropriate on the basis of their natural sins: as descendants of Ishmael and as a desert people, Arabs had a natural ferocity that led them to violate natural law constantly.[50] The fourteenth- and fifteenth-century Portuguese exploration and conquest of the Canary Islands—so named for the belief that they were inhabited by large dogs or monstrous peoples—provides a model case study for the application of Innocent's ideas in the context of colonization. There, Pope Clement VI applied Innocent IV's ideas rather directly to argue that, as a sin contra naturam, the natives' idolatry rescinded their sovereignty and justified war upon them. The Bolognese canonists Antonio de Rosellis and Antonio Minucci da Pratovecchio, who treated many of the legal questions concerning Portuguese claims to the Canaries, argued that the Canarians' refusal to receive missionaries constituted a sin contra naturam revoking their sovereignty.[51] Some canonists did apply Innocent's theory of sin against nature to argue in favor of Canarian sovereignty and against conquest. Felix Hemmerlin (d. 1457 or 1464) of Zurich, for instance, treated the Canarians' sharing of their women as an example of their natural innocence and virtue: "They did not have the possession of things in any individual sense but all things were common, as in the state of innocence. . . . Indeed, they lived according to natural law . . . and according to divine law."[52] But the question of war was the one to which Innocent's thought was most frequently attached: when in the seventeenth century, Hugo Grotius (d. 1645) turned to writing the *De Iure Belli ac Pacis*, the West's first international law text, he too cited Innocent's sins contra naturam as justification of war, demonstrating the four-hundred-year afterlife of Innocent's formulation.[53]

Canonists also justified the new European conquests and reconquests by writing against Innocent's notion of the humanity and rationality of non-Christian others, which, we recall, he had used to establish papal jurisdiction over non-Christian lands de jure, and arguing rather their semihuman or animal barbarity. Oldratus de Ponte published a *consilia* in which he termed Spanish Muslims wild animals requiring forcible Christian subjection; layering the bestial metaphors, he notes elsewhere that as descendants of Ishmael, the Arabs came from "a wild ass of a man" (Gen. 16:12).[54] In 1436, King Duarte of Portugal referred to the animal-like nature of Canarians to justify their conquest, citing as evidence a list that closely recalls medieval descriptions of the barbarian: their lack of writing, metal, or money; their lack of common religion, laws, and social intercourse; and their forest dwelling.[55] And in 1550, when Juan de Sepulveda famously promoted the conquest of American Indians against Bartolomeo de Las Casas's case for their peaceful conversion, he did so on the basis of their inhumanity, demonstrated by a number of alternative arguments. The natives are "natural slaves," he asserted, requiring enslavement and subjection, with the evidence to be found among other things in their sinful sexuality. They are rather monkeys than men, he continued, lacking disciplinabilitas. Their lack of humanity, he argued, is evidenced through a lack of culture, writing, laws, and histories, and through their barbarous customs, their cannibalism, and their lust.[56] In Sepulveda's portrait of the American Indian may be located the full arsenal of available medieval discourses of the semihuman or limited human that we have been surveying: the classical barbarian, the "animal" of the new natural sciences, Aristotle's natural slave, Aquinas's barbarous customs, and Innocent's sins contra naturam revoking sovereignty, suggesting significant overlap in medieval and Renaissance vocabularies of otherness, and its converse, humanity.

While this survey indicates much agreement about what made humans human in late medieval and early modern thinking, it also demonstrates that the same markers and categories of civility could be, and were being, deployed toward very different ends and arguments vis-à-vis the real peoples with whom Europeans were coming into contact. It began, we saw, with an approach to the Mongols that placed them beyond the confines of the human, as the quintessential barbarians on the basis of their violent nature, their aberrant diet and dress, lack of human laws, and so on. Similarly, in the late medieval and early modern period, canonists justified European conquests in the Canaries, Spain, and the Americas by arguing for the lack of "civility" among the peoples in these societies—evident in their animal-like ferocity, lack of disciplinabilitas, barbarous or contra naturam customs, diet, lack of religion or laws, and forest (or desert) habitats. For if the discourses of barbarism and the later projects of European colonization and expansion required and assumed pagan irrationality and inhumanity, the discourse of conversion and the project of universal salvation, supported by missionaries and their sponsors such as Innocent IV, generally required and assumed the opposite: pagan rationality, humanity, and even cultural sovereignty. Although Innocent IV developed a mechanism for the revocation of pagan sovereignty on the basis of sins contra naturam, he himself, significantly, never applied the formula. That remained for latter-day canonists writing in the wake of colonization or reconquest efforts, who recast Innocent's thinking away from the strategic humanism of the salvational aim and toward the rationalizations of new European empires.

Studies of these late medieval and early modern European expansions abroad reveal a decline in Europeans' interests in converting and saving the pagans with whom they were coming into increasing contact. This trend is already visible in the early colonial case study of the Canaries, where the arguments of humanists and missionaries in favor of the voluntary and peaceful conversion of natives gradually gave way to those of conquerors, colonists, and the canonists who overwhelmingly justified their actions.[57] With the New World expansions, the questions of spiritual mission and papal jurisdiction that so excited thirteenth-century minds became muted, and indeed the papacy's role gradually disappeared altogether from the secular adventures of kings, explorers, and conquistadors.[58] Hopes of conversion and salvation, epitomized in the thirteenth-century missions to Asia, begin to shift toward the aims of the modern civilizing mission, a shift again predicted in the Canarian experiment, where Prince Henry the Navigator (1394–1460) of Portugal petitioned Pope Eugenius for a mission not only to baptize but to civilize the natives with "civil laws and an organized form of government."[59] Already in the fourteenth century we see the medieval salvational paradigm, and its investments in the rational non-Christian or "virtuous pagan," giving way to a more secular and less inclusive paradigm promising civilization, and its remnant, the "savage," as the new sign of the other. As Columbus wrote Ferdinand and Isabella in the Letter to the Sovereigns, there were no monstrous men to be found in the Americas, only savages.[60]

THE PROXIMATE ENEMY: KNOWLEDGE ABOUT MUSLIMS IN THE LATER MIDDLE AGES

As with the medieval approach to pagans, the best attempts toward understanding Muslims ultimately derived from the missionary impulse. Early twelfth-century knowledge of Islam and its prophet were not promising: chroniclers like Guibert of Nogent, Walter of Compiègne, and others wrote of the life of Muhammad in ways that combined inaccuracy with insult, typical of the "life of Muhammad" genre. As Norman Daniel has shown, scores of medieval polemic writings on Islam turned to the life of Muhammad itself to delegitimize the validity of Islam.[61] In Alexandre du Pont's *Roman de Mahomet*, for instance, Muhammad is "the wisest and most learned of cardinals" in Rome, who is encouraged to do missionary work among Saracens in the East, and who agrees but only after being promised that upon his return he shall be appointed pope. When the cardinals fail to appoint him to the papacy, Muhammad takes revenge by preaching against Christian truth.[62]

But there was a significant shift in 1142 with the visit by the abbot of Cluny, Peter the Venerable, to Spain and his subsequent interest in converting Spanish Muslims. This interest led him to commission a collection of works about Islam, including the first translation of the

Qur'an by Robert of Ketton. Peter the Venerable used these works to compose his own *Book Against the Sect or Heresy of the Saracens*, aimed at converts.[63] In the 1220s and 1230s the mendicant orders directed their characteristic missionary outreach to Muslims in the Levant, which also marked a significant shift. The Dominican William of Tripoli learned Arabic, as was required by his order, lived in Acre, and eventually was able to compose the *De Statu Saracenorum* [On the state of the Saracens] in 1273, a text that argued for easy conversion of Muslims on the basis of the proximity between the Muslim and Christian faiths; it serves as an important source for *Mandeville's Travels*. For the first time, there began to emerge accounts of the various branches of Islam and explanations of its fundamental schism, such as that by the first native historian of the Latin Kingdom, William of Tyre. Postcrusade commingling between Franks and Muslims in the Levant led to a local appreciation of the reverence by Muslims for Christian figures like Jesus and Mary, a fact reflected in Frederick II's negotiated treaty during the Sixth Crusade for the return of Jerusalem to Christian rule in 1229, which specified that "no Saracen shall be forbidden freely to make the pilgrimage to Bethlehem."[64]

On the whole, however, proximity of belief between Christians and Muslims seems to have impeded rather than enhanced Christian understanding, leading "Christian theologians to measure Islam by Christian standards instead of viewing it ... as a different religion which had elements in common with their own."[65] As scholars have remarked, the polemical tilt to writings about Muslim religion impeded the pace of ethnographic knowledge about Muslims in the medieval period.[66] This meant that perhaps the most extensive medieval European description of the East before the mid-thirteenth century, the *Historia Orientalis*, probably by Jacques de Vitry, was filled will errors and shortcomings. These included information from crusader states that amounted to hearsay, a prejudiced account of Muhammad and the Muslim religion, and the measure and judgment of local Muslims (as well as oriental Christians and Jews) from a strictly Latin Christian perspective rather than on their own terms.[67] If knowledge about the tenets of Islam did improve with exposure, it did so only slowly: still in Joinville's early fourteenth-century crusading account, as we will see in Chapter 4, one finds Latin Christian surprise at shared revered figures in Islam and Judeo-Christianity.

If religious similarity did not readily lead to admiration or acceptance, increased interaction with Muslims in the multiconfessional spaces of the Levant, Spain, and Italy did work to increase knowledge and appreciation of Muslim secular culture. Translation movements in Toledo and Sicily delivered Aristotle and Plato clothed in Muslim commentaries to the Latin Christian world, making the scientific and philosophical renaissance of the twelfth and thirteenth centuries difficult to separate from Islamic culture. Newly translated Middle Eastern story collections, including the Spanish Jewish convert Petrus Alfonsi's *Arabian Nights*–like stories, told of an appealing Islamic world difficult to demonize.[68] While crusader contact is notorious for its dearth of intellectual results, it did lead to greater everyday knowledge about Muslims as well as to widespread "orientalization" of Latin culture in the Levant, as I explore in Chapter 4. While the dialogic dimensions of Joinville's chronicle are, as I will argue there, visible only in late crusading narratives, the similarities between Arab and European codes of knighthood and chivalry were appreciated from the very outset of the Crusades. The author of *Gesta Francorum*, a chronicle of the First Crusade, for example, writes thus of the Turks: "They have a saying that they are of common stock with the Franks, and that no men, except the Franks and themselves, are naturally born to be knights. This is true, and nobody can deny it, that if only they had stood firm for the faith of Christ and holy Christendom . . . you could not find stronger or braver or more skillful soldiers; and yet by God's grace they were beaten by our men."[69] And unlike religious proximity, these proximate codes of chivalry did in fact lead to mutual admiration between Arabs and Europeans. Perhaps no figure better exemplifies the international code of chivalry than that of Salahadin, Europe's "Saladin," about whose generosity, wisdom, and romantic prowess Europeans were telling stories in their vernaculars even as he threatened their Levantine coastline.[70] Stories, too, were told of Salahadin's being knighted, and perhaps most interestingly, of his deathbed baptism—Dante, who placed Saladin along with the pagan ancients in the relatively blameless space of Limbo within his *Inferno*, was not alone, then, in his concern for the salvation of this crusading rival. Indeed Dante's treatment of good Muslims as coterminous with pagan ancients is both telling and typical: the twelfth-century renaissance of the classics initiated not just an interest in the salvation of pre–*Lex Christi* pagans but, simultaneously, an interest in the salvation of post–*Lex Christi* virtuous or noble non-Christians, including contemporary Muslims.[71] From the twelfth century on, then, Muslims were increasingly assimilated to the virtuous pagan paradigm, as I discuss in the final section below.

DEBATING VIRTUOUS PAGANS: PRIMITIVISM AND THE PATH TO SALVATION

Opposed to the antiprimitivism of Lucretian-Ciceronian developmental anthropology, medieval anthropology also features a strain of cultural primitivism in its celebration of the simple, unacculturated, and natural goodness of some of God's people, the so-called virtuous pagans, precursors to the noble savages of the early modern period. The medieval descriptions of the Brahmins identified them as the exemplary virtuous pagans of Asia. This tradition dated as far back as the fourth century b.c. to historians of Alexander's wars with India, and later developed into the letters of Alexander and the Brahmin sage Dandimus, as well as the various Alexander romances that made their way into Mandeville's sources.[72] Distant and unknown lands, too, were associated with a natural goodness and bounty through the tradition of the Earthly Paradise or the Fortunate Isles. These were sometimes located in the East, other times placed in the West, as in the Celtic *Voyage of Brendan* and the *Purgatory of St. Patrick*. As the era of Atlantic exploration got under way in the fourteenth century, the Canaries came to be identified as the Fortunate Isles, and their newly found natives described according to the trope of the primitively noble pagan.[73] We know one such depiction was penned by Giovanni Boccaccio in Latin in a brief monograph called *De Canaria*, a translation from no longer extant Florentine merchant letters, likely in the vernacular, and dated December 17, 1341. The description of the Canarians in the *De Canaria* combined an account of their cultural primitivism, including their nudity, with an account of their good customs and nature, including their natural physical strength, intelligence, mutual trust, and lawfulness.[74] And when Columbus explored and conquered the island of Hispaniola, he described the land in the manner of an earthly paradise ("Spanola is a wonder, with its hills and mountains, fine plains, open country, and land rich and fertile for planting and sowing, to bring in profit of all sorts") and applied the trope of the virtuous pagan to its natives: "The people of all the islands I have discovered and taken, and those whom I have heard, both men and women, go about naked as when they were born, except some of the women cover one part of themselves with a single leaf of grass, or a cotton thing that they make for this purpose. They have no iron, nor steel, nor weapons, nor are they fit for them, because although they are well-made men of commanding stature, they appear extraordinarily timid."[75]

In the medieval period, concern with the virtuous pagans intersected closely with, and indeed was inextricably linked to, salvational questions going back all the way to the church fathers, a long elite theological and philosophical debate that only in the late medieval period found application to actual pagans in ethnographic encounters such as those in the Canaries or Hispaniola. While the interest in non-Christian salvation had concerned the church since its inception, the field of interest gradually expanded over the course of the Middle Ages, from, at first, concern only for the salvation of Old Testament patriarchs pre–Lex Christi, to concern for the salvation of pagan philosophers pre–Lex Christi in the twelfth century, to, finally, concern for the possibility of pagan, and Jewish and Muslim, salvation post–Lex Christi in the thirteenth century. The thirteenth-century expansion of the possibility of non-Christian salvation to living, virtuous non-Christians had profound consequences not just for approaches to non-Christian others but for the definition of the Christian community itself, which, by implication, no longer enjoyed exclusive access to salvation. These consequences were further heightened and sharpened in fourteenth-century philosophical, theological, and cultural thought, a turn I examine in detail in my discussion of *Mandeville's Travels* in Chapter 5. Here I wish briefly to sketch the earlier history of this concern with virtuous non-Christians, which began with the church fathers.

Many early church fathers, including Justin, Clement, and Origen, believed in the "concurrent value" of philosophy and Christianity, which held that through natural reason, man participated in the eternal reason of God and could thus attain truth. Clement and Origen influentially argued that Christ descended to hell to preach to those who had died before the Incarnation, thus making hell a place where future generations could learn about Christian teaching, and paving the way for universal salvation. In the late fourth and early fifth centuries, however, Augustine reversed the notion of Christ's preaching in hell, limiting the saved to those patriarchs awaiting the Savior alone and salvation to pre-Resurrection times alone, a position later adopted by the church.[76] In the sixth century, Gregory the

Great became famous for the saying, "nec fides habet meritum, cui humana ratio praebet experimentum" (faith for which human reason gives proof has no merit), so apparently denying the value of philosophy for salvation.[77]

Twelfth- and thirteenth-century thinkers evinced a renewed interest in the matter of the salvation of virtuous non-Christians, particularly of pagan philosophers themselves revived by the reflowering of classical interest known as the "renaissance of the twelfth century." Twelfth- and thirteenth-century thought on the question was split into two camps. The majority of thinkers, including Bernard of Clairvaux, Peter Lombard, Hugh of Saint Victor, and Alain of Lille, occupied the more conservative "sola fides" position, which held that faith alone, and not reason or philosophical understanding, was sufficient for salvation.[78] But an influential minority, best represented by Peter Abelard in the twelfth century and Thomas Aquinas in the thirteenth, occupied a far more liberal position on the question of salvation. Abelard argued, for instance, that reason was that which made man comparable to God's image, and should be used to investigate God, although post–Lex Christi, it was not enough.[79] Aquinas opened the way to non-Christian salvation much further, arguing that even after the Incarnation and Lex Christi, faith was available to men without the benefit of Christian teaching: the first principles of Christian faith were implanted in men by God, who made faith available to the virtuous through direct revelation. These latter prepared to receive his grace simply by—according to what would become the resounding formula of fourteenth-century thought on the issue—facere quod in se est (doing what was in them).[80] Virtuous pagans, according to Aquinas's formulation, need not do anything other than what was already in them in order for their virtue to be recognized by God and to be thus granted salvation. Conversion was unnecessary; virtue could reside naturally in God's people, without recourse or access to revealed law. Neither was this view treated as peripheral or heterodox: the main commentators of the fourteenth and fifteenth centuries—Duns Scotus, Durandus, Denis the Carthusian, Thomas of Strasbourg—all accepted the formulation without any alteration.[81] The implications of Aquinas's formulation—which amounts to a theorized acceptance of the other and a questioning of the distinctiveness of the Latin Christian self's relation to God—are profound for the fourteenth century's theorizations of what defined Christians against non-Christians, and are decisive, I show, in the striking approaches to non-Christians displayed in *Mandeville's Travels*.

As this brief survey suggests, the late medieval period was a robust one for the development of anthropological ideas that would continue well past the Middle Ages proper. While these ideas are meant to provide background to the ethnographic practice and writing of the chapters that follow, what will also emerge in those chapters is the gap between such theory and actual practice once a writer is faced with framing a particular ethnographic encounter. Thus Gerald of Wales aggressively applies classical developmental anthropology to the Welsh and Irish, but unexpectedly applies another, discordant discourse in a kind of resistant dialogue with developmental ideas. William of Rubruck goes out of his way not to apply ideas of inhumanity or incivility available to him in his day to the Mongols to whom he would preach. Joinville applies developmental anthropology to describe the incivility of nomadic Bedouins and Mongols, but when he comes to his main ethnographic focus, the Muslims of the Levant and the Holy Land, his desire for dialogue with them moves him toward new and unscripted terrain. Finally, Mandeville's text not only applies virtuous pagan theory to the Brahmins and others but exposes the crisis implicit in the challenge posed by non-Christian salvation to the exclusivity, distinctiveness, and integrity of the Christian community in the fourteenth century. Each of these writers, moreover, wrote ethnography in a particular way, and in the chapters that follow, the dialogic form of their medieval ethnographies will be as much the focus of discussion as is their content.

CHAPTER 2

Subjective Beginnings

Autoethnography and the Partial Gazes of Gerald of Wales

The earliest ethnography of Europe emerged from its borders, particularly as they underwent expansion in the twelfth century. Representative texts of such "border ethnography" include Adam of Bremen's account of Baltic peoples, and his continuator Helmold's description of Slavic customs, as well as a proliferation of texts about Britain's natives, the Irish, Welsh, and Scots, viewed by Anglo-Normans coming into contact with them along Britain's Celtic periphery. Gerald of Wales stands as the most important of these ethnographic border writers of the Celtic periphery, and among the most important ethnographers of the medieval period.

Gerald wrote his four Celtic works in the span of less than a decade, from the *Topographia Hibernica* (The topography of Ireland) and the *Expugnatio Hibernica* (The conquest of Ireland) in 1188 to the *Itinerarium Kambriae* (The journey through Wales) in 1191, to the *Descriptio Kambriae* (The description of Wales) in 1194. While Gerald called these his "minor works," and felt the need to defend his choice to expend "the flowers of my rhetoric" on "those rugged countries, Ireland, Wales and Britain,"[1] his Celtic works have in fact attracted more scholarly attention than any of his other writings. The *Journey through Wales* and the *Topography of Ireland*, in particular, have been the subject of numerous recent scholarly treatments, many of them interested in Gerald's construction of medieval Welsh and Irish identity and ethnicity at a time of pressing Anglo-Norman colonial incursion into the Celtic periphery.

But it is with the *Descriptio Kambriae* that Gerald managed the striking feat of reviving the classical genre of ethnography, a work devoted

37

centrally in theme to the description of the life and customs of a single people, for the medieval period. Gerald begins his *Description of Wales* much as he did his earlier Celtic treatise, the *Topographia Hibernica*, with a physical description of the contours of the land, a move traceable within British historiographical tradition as far back as Bede's *Historia Ecclesiastica Gentis Anglorum* and, of course, earlier still within Gerald's classical sources like Caesar's *Gallic War*. What comes next is far more innovative: in chapter 8 of book 1 of the *Descriptio*, Gerald turns his attention to the "natura, moribus, et cultu"—or nature, manners, and customs—of the Welsh people, and sustains that focus on Welsh manners and customs for the remainder of his treatise.[2] Writing without direct access to the major works of classical ethnography and anthropology such as Herodotus's *Histories*, Tacitus's *Germania* (also known as *On the Origin, Location, Customs and Peoples of the Germans*) (c. A.D. 98) or Lucretius's *De Rerum Natura*, Gerald nevertheless manages to reproduce in the *Descriptio* a form of writing not seen in the West for over a thousand years, the ethnographic monograph.[3]

We can tell Gerald thought that he was doing something new from his strain, also visible in the report of William of Rubruck, for adequate words to describe his task. In attempting to define his relation to his project and to the Welsh, Gerald works by way of metaphor. In the introduction to book 2 of the *Descriptio*, he likens himself to a historian, noting that he writes the *Descriptio* "more historico" (in the manner of a historian), a key methodological passage to which I will turn at the end of the chapter. And in the "First Preface" as well as again in the introduction to book 2, Gerald likens himself to a master *pictor* or painter, turning to the visual arts to capture the relation between himself and his object. In titling his work a "descriptio," Gerald is, of course, already invoking the visual arts. Indeed, the *Descriptio Kambriae* forms part of the rise in visual empiricism generally in the twelfth century. Evidence for such a "visual turn" has been found particularly in the cultural production of twelfth-century Anglo-Normans, including the Normans' use of visual evidence as "witness" to hereditary claims to land; the writing of social and natural histories supported by eyewitnessing claims; the proliferation of new genres of observation such as topographies of castles, towns, and cities, and descriptions of social customs of local inhabitants; a heightened use of character sketches, anecdotes, and trivial detail in history writing; and a rise in naturalist illustrations and illuminations of plants, animals, and birds.[4]

If Gerald himself was at the forefront of a general visual turn in twelfth-century cultural production,[5] there is no contemporary analogue for the extent and scope of his ethnographic achievement in the *Descriptio Kambriae*. His *Topographia Hibernica*, which prepared the way for the *Descriptio*, mixed history and myth with ethnographic description.[6] Other ethnographic endeavors of the twelfth century appeared as short excurses within long historical chronicles, as was the case with Otto of Freising's contemporary description of the Magyars in the *Gesta Frederici* and the ethnographic excurses on Celtic life and customs in works by William of Malmesbury, William of Newburgh, and the author of the *Gesta Stephani*. What, then, explains the way in which the *Descriptio Kambriae* emerged seemingly ex nihilo as a full-blown ethnographic monograph?

Historical examination and contextualization rarely support the emergence of novelty ex nihilo, and the case of Gerald's literary production is no exception. In this chapter, I turn to the context in which Gerald wrote in order to argue that the *Descriptio Kambriae* was an improvised, textual response to the perceived threat of cultural loss of traditional Welsh byways, a work designed to salvage a contemporary snapshot of "Kambriae nostrae," his "own Wales."[7] In writing the *Descriptio*, Gerald was enacting an early form of "salvage anthropology," the salvaging of native materials against the losses born of colonial incursion.[8] The *Descriptio* stands, as such, as an example of the improvised novelty of cultural production in "contact zones," spaces of dynamic, uneasy, and often asymmetrical colonial encounters that allow for new, dialogically derived cultural understandings and subjectivities.[9] Gerald's own hybrid identity is, of course, itself a product of the contact zone of the Celtic periphery, namely South Wales, which underwent steady Norman infringement throughout the twelfth century. The grandson of the Welsh princess Nest and the Norman Gerald of Windsor, Gerald is at once Norman and Welsh, a Cambro-Norman by-product of the Norman colonial project in Wales and especially its marcher borderlands in the South.

But Gerald's ethnography is as hybrid as his person, and as such is irreducible to a single language or function, even the striking one of salvage work. Instead, in its duality of languages, functions, and even audiences, I argue, the *Descriptio* may be viewed as an early form of "autoethnography" as theorized by Mary Louise Pratt: a native ethnographic self-description in dialogue with metropolitan representations of that self in ways that intervene in metropolitan modes of understanding. Autoethnographic texts are, importantly, not "autochthonous or 'authentic' forms of representation"; rather, they are hybrid documents featuring "a selective collaboration with and appropriation of idioms of the metropolis or conqueror . . . merged or infiltrated to varying degrees with indigenous idioms."[10] The *Descriptio*'s ambivalent mixture of two contradictory languages—the one Anglo-Norman, the other Welsh—each aware of and responding to the other, I argue, ultimately undermines the stability of metropolitan or colonial viewpoints. Finally, in addition to being "bilingual," the *Descriptio* is scrupulously bifocal: it is twice interrupted in order that its author may approach his object of study from an opposing gaze. In what follows, I examine the implications of this duality of discourses and gazes for Gerald's ethnography of the Welsh, and for medieval ethnographic poetics generally.

AUTOETHNOGRAPHY AND DOUBLED DISCOURSE IN THE *DESCRIPTIO KAMBRIAE*

In keeping with the connections between ethnography and the description of cultural practices marked as alien from those of the writer and audience, Gerald opens his description of the Welsh thus:[11] "Kambriae nostrae descriptionem, gentisque naturam, aliis alienam nationibus et valde diversam, hoc opusculo declarare" (I now propose, in this short treatise, to write a Description of Wales, my own country, and to describe the Welsh people, who are so very different from other nations) ("First Preface," 211). Already Gerald's signature ambivalence becomes visible: the grandson of Nest in one breath authorizes his decision to write a *descriptio* of the Welsh on the basis of its being "nostra" and declares the Welsh utterly different from other peoples, "aliis alienam nationibus et valde diversam." The components of Welsh—and, nearly always simultaneously, Irish[12]— "alienness" that follow are largely shaped by the developmental anthropology of his day, according to which difference was measured by the yardstick of distance from Anglo-Norman norms (see Chapter 1). But as I show below, the *Descriptio Kambriae*'s participation in the distinctly colonial idiom of developmental anthropology is disrupted and offset by its selective appropriation of powerfully resonant native Welsh themes, so doubling its languages and functions.

Anglo-Norman discourses on Welsh incivility or savagery are prominently voiced in Gerald's ethnography of the Welsh, whether he is considering their "good points" in book 1 or their "less good points" in book 2. Gerald wastes little time in getting to a depiction of Welsh incivility in the *Descriptio*: to his initial announcement of subject matter, the *mores* of the Welsh, is appended "Et primo de audacia ejusdem, agilitate, et animositate" (Their boldness, agility and courage). Welsh boldness and agility easily shade into excessiveness and ferocity in what follows: the Welsh are, Gerald declares, a "gens armis dedita tota" (an entire people trained in war) (1.8); they are "Vindicis enim animi sunt, et irae cruentae" (vindictive by nature, bloodthirsty and violent) (1.17). Gerald here follows the barbarian script: an inexplicable ferocity is a fixed feature of Celtic difference and of "barbarians" wherever twelfth-century German and French writers—among them Otto of Freising, Adam of Bremen, Gunther of Pairis, Helmold, the anonymous author of the *Gesta Stephani*, William of Newburgh, William of Malmesbury, Gervase of Tilbery, and Gerald of Wales—came into contact with them.[13]

Economic life takes a central place in delineating civil societies from savage ones according to classical developmental anthropology. Gerald clearly has in mind this model, made available to him from Lucretius via Cicero, when he writes of Welsh industry thus: "Totus propemodum populus armentis pascitur et avenis, lacte, caseo, et butyro. Carne plenius, pane parcius vesci solent. Non mercimoniis, non navigiis, non mechanicis artibus, nec ullo prorsus nisi martio labore vexantur" (In this way the whole population lives almost entirely on oats and the produce of their herds, milk, cheese and butter. They eat plenty of meat, little bread. They pay no attention to commerce, shipping or industry, and their only preoccupation is military training) (1.8). The eating of milk and meat rather than bread is shorthand for the presence of pastoral economies according to the developmental account of civility, where it occupies a middle space between complete savagery and urban civility, here marked by Gerald through the technologies of "commerce, shipping, or industry." Gerald sketches the logic and stages of developmental anthropology most clearly in his depiction of the Irish in the *Topography of Ireland* (see Chapter 1), in which he groups civility, markets, town life, and the rights of citizenship, opposing these terms to barbarism or primitivism, country or woodlands living, and pastoral lifeways.

The developmental model linked habitat with civility, and the habitat of the Welsh and other Celtic peoples constitutes another category of their incivility according to Anglo-Norman writers. Celtic lands are frequently said to have open pastures and forests[14] and these natural environments are, moreover, linked to the humans living in them, rendering them "uncivil," as in the following treatment of Welsh habitat in the *Descriptio*: "Non urbe, non vico, non castris cohabitant; sed quasi solitarii silvis inhaerant. In quarum eisdem margine non palatia magna, non sumptuosas et superfluas lapidum caementique structuras in altum erigere, verum tecta viminea, usibus annuis sufficientia, modico tam labore quam sumptu connectere mos est" (They do not live in towns, villages or castles, but lead a solitary existence, deep in the woods. It is not their habit to build great palaces, or vast and towering structures of stone and cement. Instead they content themselves with wattled huts on the edges of the forest, put up with little labour or expense, but strong enough to last a year or so)" (1.17). According to this description, the twelfth-century Welsh are an antisocial, solitary people content to live in the woods, a seminomadic existence implied in the description of their huts as *usibus annuis sufficientia* (strong enough to last a year or so). That the passage describes the Welsh almost solely on the basis of what they do *not* do—"non urbe, non vico, non castris . . . non palatial magna, non sumptuosas"—suggests the extent to which Gerald is enacting an implicit comparison with contemporary Anglo-Norman life, which as we know from abundant contemporary evidence was indeed town oriented, and built around stone palaces and castles, those symbols of Norman conquest throughout England and Wales. Gerald's description of Welsh forest dwelling is far from value free: as we know both from Ciceronian developmental anthropology and from stock medieval encyclopedic sources such as those of Pliny and Solinus, a people content to live in the woods win themselves the label of *silvester* (pl: *silvestres*, literally savages), from the Latin for forest, *silva*.

Welsh political life constitutes a final, major category of ethnographic interest to Gerald and other writers of Celtic custom. Anglo-Norman writers were here, too, most struck by the differences from the political organization of their own realm. Gerald is not alone in noticing the lack of centralized authority or single kingship in Celtic lands, though he is unusual for recommending against it as he does at the end of book 2. Observers found in Wales and Ireland, particularly the upland and western regions out of reach of the Anglo-Norman orbit, political organization more kin based than lord based.[15] The overriding significance of kinship structures in Welsh life is not lost on Gerald, as we see at the end of the *Descriptio* when he notes the fractious effects of the "antiquus in hac gente mos" or ancient Welsh custom of "brothers dividing between them the property which they have" (2.4), that is, of Welsh partible inheritance. Similarly, he describes Welsh kinship: "Genus itaque super omnia diligent; et damna sanguinis atque dedecus acriter ulciscuntur. Vindicis enim animi sunt, et irae cruentae; nec solum novas et recentes injurias, verum etiam veteres et antiques velut instantes vindicare parati" (As they have this intense interest in their family descent, they avenge with great ferocity any wrong or insult done to their relations. They are vindictive by nature, bloodthirsty and violent. Not only are they ready to avenge new and recent injuries, but old ones too, as if they had only just received them) (1.17). Here Gerald refers to the practice of blood feud, in effect throughout the twelfth century in Wales and phased out gradually a century later when Wales began to assume the centralized organization of a feudal state.[16] To Anglo-Normans, whose king had achieved a near-exclusive claim on war making and "had taken homicide out of the realm of private compensation and feud and subjected it to the processes of royal justice,"[17] the blood feud, though subject to intricate laws, signaled utter disorder and violence.

The *Descriptio Kambriae*, then, arguably functions as a work of colonial ethnography. Through his widespread application of developmental anthropology in the text, Gerald may have provided the Anglo-Normans with a cultural profile of their conquered subjects that buttressed their preexisting assumptions about their cultural superiority in relation to them. That Gerald had a primarily Anglo-Norman audience in mind for the *Descriptio Kambriae* is suggested by its Latin-language composition, as well as his dedication of it to an English ecclesiast, Stephen Langton, archbishop of Canterbury.[18] Gerald, moreover, notoriously ends his ethnography of the Welsh by offering military advice to the Normans on "How the Welsh can be conquered" and "How Wales should be governed once it has been conquered." These combined textual features appear to place the dual-affiliated, Cambro-Norman Gerald in the uneasy position of playing "native informant" to the colonizer. Other features of the text, however, overtly challenge the Anglo-Norman viewpoint and champion Welsh ones. That Gerald's military advice to the conquering Normans is immediately countered by advice to the Welsh on resisting the Normans—suggesting that at times, Gerald had a native Welsh audience in mind as well—is altogether typical of his ambivalence and duality of perspective. These alternative perspectives sit uncomfortably together in Gerald's treatise on the Welsh, just as they reside uneasily in his own hybrid body, forcing him to occupy what Jeffrey Cohen has aptly called a "difficult middle" between two seemingly opposing states.[19]

Uneasy though it may be, the hybridity of the *Descriptio Kambriae* is pervasive, extending from its deployment of contradictory language to its unfixed functions and even audience. To begin with its doubled discourse, Gerald's lengthy Anglo-Norman viewpoint on native Welsh life and customs is countered in the *Descriptio* with a radically different voice emerging out of the Welsh's own mythic narratives of resistance and redemption. Having dismissively waved away the "remarkable" and "completely wrong" prophecies of Merlin (2.7), Gerald reconjures their essential content soon thereafter in the words of another prophet, an old Briton living in Pencader,[20] with whose prophetic voice he ends the *Descriptio*. The old man of Pencader, not unlike Gerald, is of mixed affiliation, having sided with Henry II against his own people in the expedition of 1163 against South Wales. But when asked by King Henry "what he thought of the royal army, whether it could withstand the rebel troops and what the outcome of the war would be,"

> respondit, "Gravari quidem, plurimaque ex parte destrui et debilitari vestris, rex, aliorumque viribus, nunc ut olim et pluries, meritorum exigentia, gens ista valebit. Ad plenum autem, proper hominis iram, nisi et ira Dei concurrerit, non delebitur. Nec alia, ut arbitror, gens quam haec Kambrica, aliave lingua, in die districti examinis coram Judice supremo, quicquid de ampliori contingat, pro hac terrarum angulo respondebit."

> ("My Lord, King," he replied, "this nation may now be harassed, weakened and decimated by your soldiery, as it has so often been by others in former times; but it will never be totally destroyed by the wrath of man, unless at the same time it is punished by the wrath of God. Whatever else may come to pass, I do not think that on the Day of Direst Judgment any race other than the Welsh, or any other language, will give answer to the Supreme Judge of all for this small corner of the earth.") (2.10)

The old man of Pencader answers in the language of Welsh political redemption, announcing the return of the not-to be-repressed colonial remnant of the British Isles, its mythic, native Welsh. While the resistance sounded by this Welsh voice finds striking context as a final note for the *Descriptio Kambriae*, it is otherwise in no way unusual or atypical as Welsh expression: throughout the twelfth century, such prophecies figured prominently in contemporary Welsh narratives as the means for Welsh deliverance from foreign domination, forming the "cardinal axiom" of Welsh historical mythology that Britain would one day be reunified and returned to the rule of the Welsh.[21] Gerald has, then, concluded his ethnographic treatise by speaking in a characteristically native Welsh idiom.

But Gerald's advocacy of the Welsh is, I believe, discoverable at an even deeper textual level of the *Descriptio*. Just as his choice to close his text with a paradigmatically Welsh voice disrupts the colonial ethnographic perspective of the *Descriptio*'s previous pages, so Gerald's very composition of the *Descriptio* itself may be seen as an intervention in the colonialist agenda with respect to the Welsh: an improvised, textual response to the perceived need for cultural salvage against colonial incursion into local Welsh culture. For such widespread incursion and acculturation in the direction of the self-styled more "advanced" Anglo-Normans was precisely what Wales was undergoing within Gerald's lifetime. In the span of the late eleventh through fourteenth centuries, Welsh, Irish, and Scottish societies underwent changes much like southern and midland England had undergone from the ninth through twelfth centuries, an "Anglicization" of the British Isles or "penetration of English peoples, institutions, norms, and culture (broadly defined) into the outer, non-English parts of the British Isles."[22] In Wales and Ireland, Anglicization proceeded through the establishment of English settlements, which aggressively asserted their own societal and cultural norms along with the English language in southern Wales and southern and eastern Ireland.[23] The impact of Anglo-Norman colonization expressed itself increasingly all over twelfth-century Wales, but especially in the south, through the changing of place names, the exploitation of native forest and fishery resources, the spread of arable cultivation, and the development of markets and gradually even of small towns.[24] By 1300, the British Isles constituted a world increasingly subsumed under a single economic orbit and a single currency, constituting, in R. R. Davies's estimation, a "world in which Anglo-French cultural, architectural and ecclesiastical norms increasingly dominated, and even threatened, indigenous and local traditions."[25] Scholars of medieval Scotland have recently begun to unearth and examine the region's cultural losses with respect to Gaelic law, language, and the very memory of the Gaelic past.[26] Likewise, first in marcher Welsh and then native Wales over the course of the twelfth century, Anglo-Norman literary culture penetrated indigenous literary traditions, transforming them such that in Wales too it would be possible to discover "the themes, topoi, and literary sentiments common throughout the court circles of the Anglo-Norman world," in Welsh scriptoria, the insular scribal tradition became edged out by Anglo-Norman script, and native Welsh church buildings began to reflect Romanesque patterns.[27]

A close reading of the *Descriptio Kambriae* suggests that these processes of social and cultural accommodation, well under way in the period in which Gerald wrote, may have motivated his composition of the novel treatise. For just as in the nineteenth-century European incursion into Asia, Africa, and the Americas gave rise to the widespread appeal to anthropological "salvage"—the call to preserve traditional cultures from the ravages of modernity and acculturation—so too in the medieval era's greatest period of expansion, we find that same call in the work of the twelfth century's most accomplished ethnographer of the Far West. In the "First Preface" of the *Descriptio*, Gerald speaks of "my own native land"[28] with the romantic sentimentality proper to salvage work: "Nos, ob patriae favorem et posteritatis, finium nostrorum abdita quidem evolvere, et inclite gesta, necdum tamen in *memoriam* luculento labore digesta, *tenebris exuere*, humilemque stilo materiam efferre, nec inutile quidem nec illaudabile reputavimus" (my italics) (I have been inspired to think that it may be a useful and praiseworthy service to those who come after me if I can set down in full some of the secrets of my own native land. By writing about such humdrum matters I can *rescue from oblivion* those deeds so nobly done which have not yet been fully recorded). And in the "Second Preface," similarly, "et posteritati consulens, inclita nostri temporis acta *sub silentio perire* [perish] *non permisi*" (my italics) (For the benefit of those who will come after, I have also rescued from oblivion some of the remarkable events of our own times). Given that Gerald—whose attitude generally displays the realism and lack of nostalgia characteristic of Cambro-Norman society—nowhere else characterizes the processes of accommodation that were proceeding all around him as forms of loss, instead setting about to fix and record soberly such native Welsh customs as still existed for posterity, these small expressions of the importance of memory and of acting against the ruins of silence ring out with disproportionate power.

In writing the *Descriptio* as a work of salvage, Gerald, I believe, displays what Mary Louise Pratt calls a canny "autoethnographic" consciousness: "a particular kind of cultural self-consciousness . . . of one's life-ways or customs *as they have been singled out by the metropolis*, be it for objectification in knowledge, for suppression or for extermination" (original italics), that is, processes of colonization and conquest. Autoethnography, Pratt shows, "selectively appropriates some tools of objectification . . . to counter objectification ('We are not as you/they see us')."[29] In splicing and recombining colonial developmental discourse with the redemptive voices of Welsh mythology, Gerald manages to exceed and disrupt colonial discourse and outlook. Gerald also frequently manages, of course, to confound his audiences. Autoethnography's rhetorical heterogeneity makes it legible in different ways to differing audiences, thus by nature liable to semiotic slippage or indeterminacy. But it is most confounding to those who approach its representative texts, or for that matter cultures themselves, "as discrete, coherently structured, monolingual edifices."[30] Instead of expecting the *Descriptio* to express a single or "pure" position, we need to recall that autoethnographic texts are distinctly impure and inauthentic forms of self-representation. Autoethnographic texts are, moreover, frequently penned by mixed-race authors who are ambivalently positioned as cultural intermediaries in a colonial administration, figures who could as readily turn "native informant."[31] Gerald, for instance, acted as a royal clerk for ten years, in which time he served as colonial surveyor of Ireland for Henry II, and acted as cultural liaison between the king and the various princes of Wales, many of them Gerald's blood relations.

That autoethnographies are often confounding is not to be regarded as a regretful by-product of their rhetorical complexity, but rather as one of their central and defining features: in mixing colonial and native perspectives, they confound and disrupt metropolitan modes of understanding. Where, after all, can dutiful mimicry of Anglo-Norman perspective be said to end and native resistance to begin in a text like the *Descriptio Kambriae*? What does Gerald's freewheeling, if uneasy, mixture of Welsh and Anglo-Norman discourse do to an evolutionary scale of culture—and thus the metropolitan mode of anthropology—that requires them to be kept distinct and opposed, as cultures of "barbarousness" on the one hand, and "civility" on the other? And what additional threat to metropolitan discourse is posed if, instead of being distinct from or opposed to native idiom, it is in fact actually joined in a complex, mutually defining, dialogue with it? For such can be shown of the metropolitan and native discourses cited by Gerald in the *Descriptio*. Anglo-Normans were far from neutral about the quintessentially Welsh voices of redemption and resistance that Gerald places in the mouth of the old man from Pencader at the end of his treatise on the twelfth-century Welsh. Voices of Welsh resistance, instead, appear to have rattled Anglo-Norman rulers of Gerald's day. Local Welsh uprisings appear to have enjoyed a special symbolic capital for all of England, that wielded by the resistance of the native population of the land over which the newcoming Anglo-Normans sought to assert dominium.[32] Indeed, some scholars have argued that it was the threat of real Welsh uprising in the marches and native Wales such as those of 1136–38 that made Geoffrey of Monmouth's positive depiction of native Britons in the *History of the Kings of Britain* politically inflammatory until the end of the twelfth century. Only then, when the body of Arthur had been "discovered" at Glastonbury Abbey and so the hopes of his "return" contained, was British (Welsh) history ready for expropriation and appropriation by the kings of England and general consumption and enjoyment by its public.[33] Culturally, the most ostensible sign of such consumption was of course the new vogue in Arthurian romance material. In politics, the appropriation of Welsh symbols to buttress the English Crown seems to have begun immediately thereafter, with Richard the Lion-hearted's reputed possession of Caliburn, Arthur's sword,[34] and was deemed useful into the late thirteenth century, when Edward I seized and displayed what was allegedly Arthur's crown during his final conquest of Wales.[35] In light of the mantle of Welsh resistance, Norman appropriations of Welsh political symbols apparently aimed to diffuse native foundational claims to the land even as they expropriated such native symbols for their own competing claims to British sovereignty. Anglo-Norman rulers, then, were not only aware of but in intimate dialogue with Welsh claims of sovereignty over England, suppressing, countering, and expropriating them as they deemed necessary. In viewing Gerald's expression of ambivalence in the *Descriptio* and elsewhere an idiosyncratic condition, or a mark of his monstrosity, critics have considerably simplified the evidence. Both within the body of Gerald and well beyond it, the Anglo-Norman discourse of civility underwriting Welsh colonization, on the one hand, and the Welsh discourse of native resistance and redemption, on the other, occupied two sides of a single coin, joined together as are colonizer and colonized in a reciprocal dialogue of force and resistance, appropriation and mutual redefinition.[36] Colonization in the contact zone of the Celtic periphery imbricated the cultures of the Anglo-Normans and the Welsh in such a way that each thought and acted in light of the other's word and world.

Anglo-Normans, then, were as ambivalent about the Welsh as Gerald himself is ostensibly ambivalent about Anglo-Normans. This rather straightforward point is worthy of some pause. For while it can be readily shown, it is nevertheless rarely noted that the duality and ambivalence that we have come to associate so closely with Gerald of Wales is discoverable in the Anglo-Norman world at large—that, in fact, colonial derision for Welsh cultural byways was combined in twelfth-century Anglo-Normans with a telltale colonial desire for the same.[37] We have already noted the best evidence of Anglo-Norman desire for Welsh things—the fantastic vogue in Arthurian story and romance, the keen desire for native Welsh symbols to buttress the English Crown. This desire is contemporaneous with the steady Anglo-Norman infringement on Welsh lands, underwritten by the derisive colonial outlook of evolutionary anthropology. Why, then, do we so rarely meet "the two Wales"— the one of colonial derision (Wales under steady colonial infringement in the twelfth century), the other, of colonial desire (the celebrated Wales of Caerleon on Usk, the plenary court of the legendary King Arthur)—on one critical page? Perhaps the reason they are usually kept apart is that the notion of colonial desire still bears a strong "heretical" force: the acknowledgment of the power of the periphery to leave its imprint on the culture of metropolitan centers of power, as well as the more commonly plotted reverse cultural flow.[38] This notion, heretical as it may be, nevertheless lies at the heart of the thesis of *In Light of Another's Word*, whose every chapter demonstrates the redefinition of European horizons and subjectivity and the emergence of a more self-conscious "Europe" through its dialogic engagement with ethnographic others within and beyond its borders.

In citing metropolitan discourse in order to upend it, autoethnography is very close indeed to voicing the "sly civility" of colonial mimicry, a civility with which Gerald has already been eloquently charged.[39] His composition of a full-blown ethnography of the Welsh people even as their traditional cultural lifeways were under substantial pressure of acculturation is further evidence of his canny awareness of the colonial processes occurring around him and their derogation of local, native culture. Gerald's attempt to paint a "still life" of Welsh customs and mores in the *Descriptio Kambriae* may have been an attempt to still, for a time, the ongoing acculturation of such native customs to dominant Anglo-Norman cultural, political, and economic norms.

STILL LIVES OF THE WELSH

Gerald's *Descriptio* freezes the Welsh in a given frame of activity, as if to drive off the flux and change of Welsh life of the period, taking place especially but not exclusively in the south. His earlier cited depiction of the Welsh economy in book 1.8 is typical: "Totus propemodum populus armentis pascitur et avenis, lacte, caseo, et butyro. Carne plenius, pane parcius vesci solent. Non mercimoniis, non navigiis, non mechanicis artibus, nec ullo prorsus nisi martio labore vexantur" (In this way the whole population lives almost entirely on oats and the produce of their herds, milk, cheese and butter. They eat plenty of meat, little bread. They pay no attention to commerce, shipping or industry, and their only preoccupation is military training) (1.8). Gerald deploys this same technique in his depiction of the Irish in the third book of the *Topographia Hibernica*, the ethnographic section of the *Topography*. In section 93, devoted to "the nature, customs and characteristics of the people," for instance, Gerald writes:

> Ceterum, licet ad plenum naturae dotibus excolantur, barbarus tamen tam barbarum quam vestium, necnon et mentium cultus, eos nimirum reddit incultos. Laneis enim tenuiter utuntur . . . nudi et inermes ad bella procedunt . . . lapides quoque pugillares . . . prae alia gente promptius et expeditius ad manum habent. . . . Est autem gens haec gens silvestris, gens inhospita; gens ex bestiis solum et bestialiter vivens; gens a primo pastoralis vitae vivendi modo non recedens.

> (Although they are fully endowed with natural gifts, their external characteristics of beard and dress, and internal cultivation of the mind, are so barbarous that they cannot be said to have any culture. They use very little wool in their dress. . . . They go naked and unarmed into battle. . . . They are quicker and more expert than any other people in throwing. . . . They are a wild and inhospitable people. They live on beasts only, and live like beasts. They have not progressed at all from the primitive habits of pastoral living.)[40]

At a glance, such depictions seem to be marked by modern ethnographic poetics rather than the dialogic mode of ethnography in light of another's word. Despite the first-hand observation implicit in the *Descriptio* genre that Gerald innovates, and despite his multiple references to himself as a *pictor* of his subject matter, the reader can discover in this picture no trace of Gerald's moving eyes or "I" on the scene of description, deictic modes of description that would imply Gerald's presence in the frame of description and his hand in its construction. Further, the use of the ethnographic present (as in "the X are matrilineal") and the removal of Gerald's own subjective eye from these ethnographic descriptions creates a temporal disjunction, what Johannes Fabian has called the "denial of coevalness,"[41] between the times of the ethnographer and that of his subjects. This disjunction makes a still life of Irish and Welsh life and custom that belies the historical processes of change at work in these cultures in the twelfth century. For instance, Gerald's critiques of Irish clerical life in the *Topography* and elsewhere—its overly monkish and insufficiently pastoral nature, the nonpayment of tithes, clerical marriage, and so on—proceed without the least acknowledgement of the vigorous reform efforts in the Irish church of the twelfth century, much as in western Europe generally.[42] And while Gerald is explicit about the aim of Anglo-Norman conquest of the Welsh in the *Descriptio*, he makes no effort to expose its penetrating impact on the very social structures, habits, and customs he is at pains to describe and preserve for us. In this, Gerald gives expression to the conservative side of ethnographic salvage work, whose valorization of traditional lifeways over modernizing ones has been critiqued as politically regressive.[43]

The use of the "ethnographic present" inevitably leads to charges of inaccuracy and reductivism, and Gerald's case is no exception: Gerald has been critiqued for his charge that all Welsh chose to live in temporary dwellings near forests,[44] and for his depiction of Welsh housing as consisting solely of fragile huts.[45] At times, Gerald's own details undermine his overgeneralizations: when Gerald recommends against the importing of cloth, salt, and corn from England, he betrays the participation of Wales in larger market circuits (2.8), and in book 1.17 of the *Descriptio*, when Gerald depicts farmers ploughing and reaping, he indicates the use of agricultural techniques in Wales at the time, as was indeed the case.[46] The latter detail, moreover, attests to the denaturing effect of Gerald's silence regarding the social effects of marcher and Norman colonization on native social structures: most lowland arable areas in Wales subject to "ploughing and reaping" were held by wealthy marcher families,[47] leaving native Welsh to engage in pastoralist modes of subsistence out of necessity rather than innate preference, as ethnography written from an imperial standpoint would have it.

But Gerald's ethnography departs from those of modern ethnographers precisely here: his cannot be reduced to ethnography written "from an imperial standpoint," for it is an ethnography assiduously committed to being composed from more than one standpoint, with a decidedly unmodern—or, we might say, a premodern and postmodern—lack of concern for whether or not these resolve into a single, unified picture. Indeed, if we follow his metadiscursive commentary in the *Descriptio*, we find that it is the prospect of offering a single, unified picture of his subject matter—at the risk of both oversimplification and false representation— that most troubles Gerald.

GERALD'S PARTIAL GAZES

Readers of the *Descriptio* discover halfway through that Gerald's book itself has been divided into two halves: the "good points" and the "less good points" of the Welsh people. He addresses the reader in explanation:

> Quoniam, in priore libro, gentis Britannicae naturam, mores, et modos satis evidenter explicuimus; eaque praecipue quae virtuti consona, et in unum collecta ad laudem ejus et honorem vere poterant explanari; de cetero competens ordo deposcit, ut in sequenti operis partitione, more historico, ad ea quoque quae virtutis et laudis lineam egredi videntur calamum vertamus.

> (In Book I, I set out clearly the character, way of life and customs of the British people. There I collected together and explained in detail all the good points which redound to their credit and glory. In Book II, I must, as a serious historian [*more historico*], arrange my material in proper order and put before you things which seem less praiseworthy and transgress the path of virtue.) (Preface to book 2)

Gerald here likens himself to one who writes *more historico*, in the manner of a historian, who in his eagerness to arrange his material "in proper order" must approach and reveal his subject matter from more than one perspective. Continuing to find analogies for his novel task as ethnographer, Gerald next likens himself to "the painter who professes to imitate nature by his artistry" who would "lose . . . his reputation if he concentrates too much on those aspects which please him and through very shame leaves out anything which he finds unseemly," for, he adds, "evil is never far removed from good, and vice is only with difficulty distinguished from virtue."[48]

In his search for the proper analogy to describe his own novel task, Gerald has turned to two nearby medieval representational disciplines, historiography and painting, both of which not only strove toward mimesis but did so through the practice of multifocality in perspective. As Gabrielle Spiegel has shown, medieval historiography treated history as a mirror or (in another painterly analogy) "image" of truth, a perceptual field to be represented rather analyzed, and chose as the primary vehicle toward achieving representational truth the use of multifocality or multiple perspectives—the citation of many primary sources, each with its own perspective or gaze on what occurred—as opposed to a single, unified perspective on the past.[49] "Impartiality" in chronicle writing, then, was nothing short of the accrual of multiple, unresolved, and competing perspectives on a single event: "the pluralism of perspectives that the chronicler included in his narrative, therefore, served not the goal of neutrality, *but a higher partiality*, one capable of generating an illusion of objectivity or 'truth,' a 'truth' negotiated by the chronicler among the competing views that his chronicle set forth"[50] (my italics). Spiegel calls this juxtaposition of opposing views in medieval chronicle writing "a kind of primitive historiographic *sic-et-non*."[51] In the scholastic reasoning put to theological and philosophical questions, the practice of sic et non, literally "yes and no," allowed for, indeed encouraged, the coexistence of countervailing, opposing truths, in the eliciting and setting forth of complex truths. Reality, then, according to a number of medieval representational disciplines, was neither simple nor simple to apprehend. Gerald's assertion that "evil is never far removed from good, and vice is only with difficulty distinguished from virtue" fills out this same worldview, in which contraries sit in close proximity and defy easy categorization or distinction.

Medieval painting serves as a second major realm invoked by Gerald in which multifocality was often deployed. As Miriam Bunim has shown, in early medieval art, "very often different parts of the same object are presented from different points of view."[52] In *The Renaissance Rediscovery of Linear Perspective*, Samuel Edgerton similarly describes the premodern, prelinear perspective of a fourteenth-century anonymous painting of the *Civitas Florentiae* (city of Florence) from a fresco in the Loggia del Bigallo as a painting "representing what it felt like to walk about, experience structures, almost tactilely, from many different sides, rather than from a single, overall vantage.... [J]utting building corners, balconies, and rooftops are thrust out and huddled toward the viewer from both sides of the picture. If we do not get a keen thumb's eye notion of the layout of Florence, we do get a feeling for the sculptural impact of an encompassing medieval city."[53]

If reality is complex, medieval thinkers seem to have reasoned, it was best to approach it from more than one angle. This characteristically premodern openness to external viewpoints, seen in disciplines outside the nascent ethnographic one to which this book is devoted, provides the intellectual background and context out of which ethnography "in light of another's word" was cultivated and emerged. The medieval ethnographic dialogic mode, after all, can no more be said to have emerged ex nihilo than did the groundbreaking *Descriptio Kambriae*. While Gerald is more explicit than the other ethnographers of this study in revealing his debt to historiography and painting, he was not alone among them in having access to medieval representational disciplines adjacent to the new ethnography and to the assumptions about truth that subtended them. And what the medieval recourse to multiple perspectives in representational disciplines ensured was a more ambiguous, open-ended, and less coherent view of truth than any unifocal model allows. This multifocal complexity is what Gerald's division of his ethnography into two books achieves, for the portraits he offers in the two books cannot be resolved into a single unified picture and instead offer divergent, even contradictory perspectives and judgments on the same Welsh traits. In book 1, chapter 8, for instance, Gerald touts the unmatched boldness of the Welsh in the defense of their country, only to counter this would-be positive image in book 2 through critique of their warlike ability to live on plunder without regard for the ties of peace or friendship (2.2) and a tendency for cowardice in battle (2.3). Similarly, Gerald trumpets the frugality (1.9) and the generosity and hospitality (1.10) of the Welsh in book 1, only to seemingly reverse course in book 2, where he discusses their lust for land and possessions (2.4). Some of these apparent contradictions are resolved as two sides of a single complex coin: bold patriotism may be the other side of ruthless war and plunder; generosity to guests requires one's own land and possessions. As Gerald has warned his readers, "evil is never far removed from good, and vice is only with difficulty distinguished from virtue." But other depictions, such as Welsh boldness in war, on one hand, and cowardice in war, on the other, simply do not add up to a single resolvable perspective on the Welsh. Each generalization rather exposes the incompleteness of the other.

For ethnographers like Gerald as for medieval practitioners of historiography and painting, gazes are always partial—biased and incomplete pictures that must be offset by more incomplete pictures, an ever-open field of proliferation to differing vantage points. At the same time, Gerald's general commitment to multifocality in the *Descriptio* has a rather more personal stake than it does for other writers: at the *Descriptio*'s end, he locates the ultimate source of its dual discourses and perspectives in his own ethnic duality. In announcing his turn to the Welsh perspective, a *second* announcement of a turn to an alternate perspective, at the stunning end of the *Descriptio*, he provides the following explanation: "Sed quoniam pro Anglis hactenus diligenter admodum et exquisite disseruimus, sicut autem ex utraque gente originem duximus, sic aeque pro utraque disputandum ratio dictat, ad Kambros denuo, in calce libelli, stilum vertamus, eosque de arte rebellandi breviter sed tamen efficaciter instruamus" (I have set out the case for the English with considerable care and in some detail. I myself am descended from both peoples, and it seems only fair that I should now put the opposite point of view. I therefore turn to the Welsh in this final chapter of my book, and I propose to give them some brief, but I hope effective, instruction in the art of resistance) (2.10). For Gerald, reason dictates (*ratio dictat*) that just as (*sicut*) he is himself two-sided, so (*sic aeque*) he should now endeavor to present his readers with the other, and opposite, perspective on a multifaceted subject, the representation of the Welsh under the Normans. Gerald's ratio for turning to the opposite perspective here, then, is fully personal, flowing from his complex and difficult ethnic hybridity. Inextricably intertwining ethnographic perspective with ethnicity and subjectivity, he declares his ethnographer's perspective, again, to be anything but impartial, but rather precisely "partial," that is, biased and incomplete, situated, and contingent on the accidents of personal history and desire. He thereby expresses a relational view of truth, in which one's subject position, where one is standing, is part of that truth, a deictic and perspectival approach to ethnographic objectivity. At the beginning of European ethnography, in a guise that in no way anticipates its direction in the modern era, unifocal ethnographic "objectivity" is roundly rejected as unreasonable. It may be Gerald's specific and individual case as an ethnic hybrid along a colonial frontier that forces him to self-consciously theorize and delimit the difference of his own gaze, namely, its necessary bifurcation and duality. In the chapters that follow, we explore many more instances of the disorienting inclusion of heterogenous perspectives in writings about others before the formation of European empire and the single-point, imperial gaze of its ethnography, decisions that flow not from the accidents of personal history but are no less motivated. In turning to these other cases, we do not leave behind Gerald's situated and personal gazes, his insistence on the necessary subjectivity and incompleteness of the premodern gaze on its ethnographic objects.

CHAPTER 3

Writing Ethnography "In the Eyes of the Other"

William of Rubruck's Mission to Mongolia

The thirteenth century witnessed a remarkable opening of the Asian landscape and peoples to Europe. The great thirteenth-century missions, many of them instigated by Pope Innocent IV in part as a defensive strategy of knowing the Mongol other on Europe's eastern border, produced an impressive set of ethnographic treatments of Asia's Mongolian peoples, including those of John of Plano Carpini, Benedict the Pole, and Andrew of Longjumeau, and perhaps most gripping of all, William of Rubruck's own. William's mission, and the thirteenth-century missions generally, may now be viewed as part of medieval Europe's great dream of converting Asia, and its mythical eastern Christian king, Prester John, or else allying with it against the common enemy of the Muslims of the Middle East. The missions of John of Plano Carpini and William of Rubruck influenced later medieval missions to Asia by John of Montecorvino, Jordanus Catalini, Odoric of Pordenone, and John of Marignolli. This collective late medieval ethnographic interest in Asia would find no parallel until the coming of the Jesuits in Asia in the sixteenth and seventeenth centuries.

    If Gerald of Wales stands as the twelfth century's most accomplished ethnographer, Wiliam of Rubruck may well represent the thirteenth century's. The fineness of William of Rubruck's *Itinerarium* or *Journey*, a report of his mission to Mongolia in 1253–55, notwithstanding, its contemporary reception was mixed at best. The *Journey* enjoyed scant contemporary attention and was unknown even to encyclopedists like Vincent of Beauvais, who recorded the earlier

57

Mongolian mission of John of Plano Carpini; Vincent of Beauvais personally knew King Louis IX, at whose request William made the journey "ut omnia scriberem . . . quaecumque viderem inter Tartaros" (to put in writing . . . everything I saw among the Tartars) (preface).[1] Were it not for the great admiration of Roger Bacon, who copied much of the *Journey* in his *Opus Maius* (c. 1264), William's fascinating account of his two-year mission from the Latin Kingdom of Jerusalem through the twin imperial courts of Baatu (1242–55) and the great khan, Mangu (1251–59),[2] would probably not have come down to us. Its low circulation is suggested, further, by its mere five extant manuscripts, four located in England.[3] Though published partially by Richard Hakluyt in 1600 and completely by Samuel Purchas in 1625, the *Journey* continued its path of relative obscurity, overlooked by historians of its own Franciscan order and other orders, even after the discovery and publication of all its manuscripts by the Société de Géographie of Paris in 1839. At the same time, the *Journey*'s reputation for distinction grew among travel collectors and publishers: Purchas called William's account a "Jewell of Antiquitie," while Sir Henry Yule, the great editor of Marco Polo, wrote of William's book: "the generation immediately preceding his [Marco Polo's] own has bequeathed to us . . . the narrative of one great journey which, in its rich detail, its vivid pictures, its acuteness of observation and strong good sense, seems to me to form a Book of Travels . . . which has never had justice done to it, for it has few superiors in the whole Library of Travel."[4]

Like Yule in the early twentieth century, William's modern commentators have been struck by the vividness of detail and acuteness of observation that inform William's descriptions of Mongolian life, qualities that allow the *Journey* to stand today as a major ethnographic source for medieval Mongolian practices.[5] Whether for this reason or on account of the relative reliability of its narrator,[6] studies have tended to treat the *Journey* as a document of hard science rather than a complex narrative object—endowed, as Mary Campbell has put it, with "a plot and a character"[7]—and a complex cultural object reflecting a particular mode of medieval ethnographic thinking and poetics. In what follows, I argue that William's ethnographic choices in the *Itinerarium* are shaped by the exigencies of medieval "missionary ethnography": a peculiar, ambivalent, and strategic acknowledgment of non-Christian humanity and difference deployed in order to incorporate the non-Christian other into the fold of Christian promise. A number of the most distinctive qualities of this ethnographic work—namely, Rubruck's intersubjectivity, or interlocking subjectivity, with various encountered non-Christian others, his acute openness to Mongol cultural difference, and his unwitting religious syncretism—can be shown to result, however paradoxically, from his great self-extension toward the other in the service of universal Christendom. William's peculiarly visual and painterly language renders the *Journey* especially suitable to a related study: the aesthetics of the premodern ethnographic gaze. William's text is filled with his gazes upon Mongols, and theirs upon him. William's missionary gaze—a gaze, as we will see, that requires him to see himself through the eyes of his non-Christian audience, however difficult and uncomfortable a sight this may be—captures something quite apart from a safely distanced and objectified Mongol other. It records a disorienting, dynamic, and dialogic contest between viewing selves and viewed others, in a mode of representation that unsettles the boundary between cultural subjects and objects, knowers and known within the *Journey*'s pages. The *Journey*'s destabilization and interpenetration of various cultural and religious boundaries further attests to the rather open and fluid nature of premodern Europe's boundaries with its cultural and religious others that characterizes writing ethnography before empire and before the rise of Orientalist representation.[8]

WRITING MISSIONARY ETHNOGRAPHY

"On the third day after we left Soldaia, we encountered the Tartars; and when I came among them I really felt as if I were entering some other world [*aliud seculum*]. Their life and character I shall describe to you as best I can."[9] William of Rubruck narrates his first encounter with the Tartars, as Europeans called the Mongols, in the language of absolute difference, an entry into an "aliud seculum," or other world. The idea of Mongol alterity had already developed into something of a literary motif by the mid-thirteenth century. Matthew Paris's *Chronica Majora* (c. 1240), for instance, links thirteenth-century Mongols with the frightening barbarity of the so-called enclosed nations—popularly believed to be shut in at the "gates of Alexander" in the Caucasus Mountains and to be released upon the coming of the Antichrist.[10] Such association was hardly unique: medieval writers as diverse as Quinlichinus of Spoleto, Rudulph of Ems, Peter Comestor, Roger Bacon, Ricold of Monte Croce, Albertus Magnus, Vincent of

Beauvais, and Marco Polo also made the connection.[11] Matthew Paris then proceeds to depict Mongols in the discourse of semihuman barbarism: "The men are inhuman and of the nature of beasts, rather to be called monsters than men, thirsting after and drinking blood, and tearing and devouring the flesh of dogs and human beings; they clothe themselves in the skins of bulls, and are armed with iron lances; they are short in stature and thickset . . . and of great strength; invincible in battle, indefatigable in labour; they drink the blood which flows from their flocks. . . . They have no human laws, know no mercy, are more cruel than lions or bears; they know no other country's language except that of their own, and of this all other nations are ignorant."[12] In making this depiction, Matthew Paris draws from a stock of high medieval ethnographic ideas on the nature of nonhuman or semihuman barbarism and monstrosity and their distinction from the category of "the human," a boundary with which thirteenth-century scholastic as well as popular sources indicate a veritable preoccupation (see Chapter 1). As John Block Friedman has shown, medieval man's differentiation from the monstrous races, and hence his proper "measure," was established through the boundary-setting categories described in Chapter 1, physical stature, diet, housing, domestic practices, speech, and so on.[13] The widespread medieval discourse of the wild man and scholastic discourses of the barbarian draw on much the same boundary-setting categories. As Richard Bernheimer and Roger Bartra have shown, an "ethnography of the medieval wild man" correlates closely with Matthew Paris's depiction of semihuman Mongols: forest dweller, hunter and gatherer, eater of raw flesh, ignorant of agriculture or metallurgy, strong, carnal, hairy, warlike, unintelligent, unable to speak, and irrational, and thus incapable of knowing God (see Chapter 1).[14] Likewise, Cicero's definition of the barbarian, so influential on future scholastic thinkers like Albertus Magnus and Thomas Aquinas, likened the barbarian to *sylvestres homines*, so revealing the basic continuity of ideas between the categories of "wild men," "monsters," and the "barbarian" and that which differentiated these from the "human."[15]

If William of Rubruck was in all likelihood aware of these popular and scholastic ethnographic currents,[16] it becomes evident upon reading the *Journey* that his own treatment of the Mongols springs from quite different sources and motivations. William's initial language of absolute, unutterable difference gives way to the very opposite aim and promise: "quorum vitam et morem vobis describo prout possum" (Their life and character I shall describe for you as best I can). Mongolia may be *quoddam alium seculum*, but William, sent by Louis IX to describe what he sees there, is intent on setting down just what kind of other world it is. What follows is a thorough examination of the life and customs of the Mongols, prompting Roger Bacon to call William's report the *"De Moribus Tartarorum"* in his *Opus Maius*.[17] Deploying mostly the same categories being invoked in medieval Europe to differentiate humans from nonhumans—categories that in later centuries would emerge as staples of modern ethnography's "manners and customs" discourse[18]—William devotes consecutive chapters to the dwellings, diet, clothing, hunting, laws, marriage and burial rites, religion, women's work, and other social customs of the inhabitants of the Mongol Empire.[19]

But William does not deploy the categories as tests for Mongol humanity. When Mongolian social structure and customs fall within modes of living and practice deemed inhuman or subhuman according to the ethnographic classifications of his day, including the Plinian discourse of the monstrous, the medieval wild man tradition, or the widespread notions of the barbarous of which he would have likely had some awareness, William rarely uses the opportunity to condemn the observed practices. Instead, he applies the classifications emptied of their moral implications for Mongolian society. For instance, William describes a clearly nomadic culture in his depictions of Mongolian habitats; if Mongols do not live in caves, rivers, or forests, nevertheless, William is aware, "nowhere have they any 'lasting city'" (2.1). But in William's hands, the nomadic nature of Mongol life does not negate its order; instead, he closely details the internal logic and structure of movable courts such as that of Baatu's: "Baatu's . . . dwellings had the appearance of a large city stretching far out lengthways and with inhabitants scattered around in every direction for a distance of three or four leagues. And just as every one of the people of Israel knew on what side of the Tabernacle to pitch their tent, so these people know on what side of the residence [*curia*] to station themselves when they are unloading the dwellings. For this reason the court is called in their language *orda*, meaning 'the middle,' since it is always situated in the midst of his men" (19.4). William discovers in Baatu's court not the prescribed aimlessness and unreason of nomadic society, but precisely the opposite: an internally consistent method of dwelling, an order worthy of the Israelites, betrayed even in the (he presumes, equally logical) native language. Similarly, Mongol hunting and gathering, "by which they obtain a large proportion of their food," becomes less a sign of barbarity than a well-honed skill worthy of description: "When they intend to hunt wild animals, they gather in great numbers and surround the area where they know wild beasts are to be found, gradually converging until the animals are enclosed in the middle in a kind of circle; then they shoot them with their arrows" (5.3). When William speaks of the assortment of small animals that constitute the Mongol diet, including mice, dormice, marmots, and conies, he does not malign the flesh-and-milk diet, but praises Mongol skill in acquiring such prey: "They have many other little creatures besides which are good to eat and which they are quite able to tell apart" (5.1). We learn of the thick animal skins Mongols wear in the wintertime not as part of a portrait of wild men, but because William and his cohort sport the same clothing before making their long journey to Mangu's court: "The following day we were each brought a rough sheepskin coat, trousers of the same material, boots—or buskins made in their style with leggings—of felt, and fur hoods after their fashion [*secundum morem eorum*]" (20.6).

Of the crucial question of speech and writing systems in analyses of human culture and civilizations William is surely aware: he takes pains to describe the numerous non-European writing systems—Chinese, Tibetan, Tangut, Arabic, and Uigur—at work in the Mongol Empire (29.50) and repeatedly stresses the importance of good interpreters or good knowledge of the native language for successful conversion throughout the *Journey*. Indeed he closes the *Journey* by urging the "need of a good interpreter—several good interpreters, in fact." Far from berating the Mongol tongue as incomprehensible or impure—the hallmark of barbarian discourse—William expresses open admiration for those who speak it, and sets about to learn the language himself when the tutorial is made available to him, as it is by Lady Cota, the young Christian wife of Mangu. Mongol polygamy is related without moral censure: "they observe the first and second degrees of consanguinity, but none of affinity, for they can have two sisters at the same time or in succession." And even the "turpis consuetudo" (shameful practice) of a son marrying all his father's wives (except his own mother) upon the father's death is explained according to Mongol belief structure, and thereby rendered internally logical: "in the case of a widow they think that after death she will always revert to her first husband" (7.4).

Throughout the *Journey*, Mongol beliefs, however alien to European ones or misguided in William's view, are related with the greatest care and attention. These range from the idiosyncratic belief among Mongols that the drinking of *comos*, a milk beverage, is inconsistent with the tenets of Christianity (a view, William regrets, that deters many a would-be Christian in the territories) to the more dramatic prohibition, on pain of death, against touching the threshold of court residences, which William's colleague inadvertently violates. In the relatively few cases where he does express judgment of what he describes, he is not prevented from proceeding in the same degree of specificity, as when William justifies visiting the idol temples of the Iugurs, members of an apparently monotheistic Buddhist sect, "ut viderem stultitias eorum" (in order to see their stupid practices) but follows up this declaration with a multi-chapter-long discourse on Iugur rites, including their worshipping positions, temple architecture, idols, priests' dress, community life, silent reading practices, alphabet, and burial rites (24–25). In this and other instances, the cause of objective information gathering—putting down everything he sees in writing, as best he can—overwhelms William's personal feelings with regard to what he is recording.

William, then, goes out of his way to affirm Mongol humanity, eschewing in all but rare instances the varied discourses of dehumanization available to him in favor of an affirmation of Mongolian humanity and reason. The logic of William's representational choices and his ability to transcend received stereotypes become intelligible when viewed in light of the exigencies and assumptions of the conversion aim, which assumes first, pagan rationality, and second, that through an appeal to reason rational pagans could be turned toward Christianity. The assumption of non-Christian rationality is beautifully attested by William's maneuverings at the great interconfessional debate at Caracorum between Buddhists, Muslims, Nestorians, and Latin Christians— in R. W. Southern's estimation "the first world debate in modern history between representatives of East and West"[20]—to which I will turn in some detail later. At the same time, William's relative tolerance of practices falling outside Latin Christian norms and usage in the *Journey* ought not to be naively attributed to his, or the salvational aim's, celebration of difference as such. Rather, as William's most enthusiastic reader and preserver Roger Bacon recommended in the *Opus Maius*, the detailed knowledge of the other is precisely required for the aim of conversion: "He who is ignorant of the places in the world, lacks a knowledge not only of his destination, but of the course to pursue. Therefore whether one sets forth to convert unbelievers or on other matters of the Church, he should know the rites and conditions of all nations [*ritus et conditiones omnium nationum*] . . . for very many have been foiled in the important interests of Christianity because they were ignorant of the distinctions in regions. . . . [T]hey have also met with countless dangers, because they did not know when they entered the regions of believers, or of schismatics, Saracens, Tartars, tyrants, of men of peace, barbarians [*barbarorum*], or of men of reasonable minds."[21] The modern history of anthropology tells of the leading role played by missionaries in the formation of the anthropological discipline in the mid-nineteenth century, when missionaries' descriptive tracts of Asia, Africa, and the Americas served as essential data for theorizing by armchair anthropologists. Here, in Bacon's thirteenth-century tract, the roots of the long collaboration between the study of the other, as anthropology is often defined, and missionary work is laid bare: one must, simply put, know the other in to convert him. This explains William's relative intolerance of the malpractice of Christianity in the Mongol territory by Nestorian Christians, whom he frequently charges with "corruptions"[22] institutional and personal. The Nestorian priests in Cathay, for instance, he deems drunkards, usurers, polygamists, and simoniacs, with the result that "when any of them rear the sons of aristocratic Mo'als, even though they instruct them in the Gospels and the Faith, nevertheless by their immorality and their greed they rather alienate them from the Christian religion" (26.14). The fact that here, among Nestorian priests, William is wholly intolerant of polygamy, whereas earlier he had described Tartar polygamy without recourse to moral censure, highlights the strategic nature of the missionary's disposition toward cultural and religious difference: William's detailed and objective descriptions of Mongol practices are presented in the service of knowing the other in order to convert and save him; descriptions of corrupt practices among Christians can serve no such objective.

William's report buttresses the view that while the medieval discourses of barbarism and the later projects of European colonization assumed and required pagan irrationality and inhumanity, the discourse of conversion and the project of universal salvation, supported by thirteenth-century missionaries and their sponsors like Innocent IV, required much the opposite. Early colonial history reveals that the heyday of the missionary approach to the other was not long lived: studies of late medieval and early modern European expansion abroad narrate a decline in Europeans' interests in converting and saving the pagans with whom they were coming into increasing contact. This trend is visible in the fourteenth-century experiment in colonizing the Canary Islands, described in Chapter 1, in which the arguments of humanists and missionaries in favor of peaceful conversion of natives gradually gave way to the brutal measures of conquerors, colonists, and canonists.[23] Already in the fourteenth century, then, the medieval salvational paradigm, and its investments in the rational non-Christian, were giving way to a more secular and less inclusive paradigm promising civilization, and its remnant, the "savage," as the new sign of the other.

This is in essence the argument advanced by anthropologist Johannes Fabian in his book *Time and the Other: How Anthropology Makes Its Object* (1983). There he argues that whereas the premodern salvational scheme acts in ways essentially inclusive and incorporative of its others, that is, pagans, whom it seeks to incorporate into the fold and save by conversion, modernity's projects of civilization and progress by contrast require the exclusion and temporal distancing of their other, the savage, whom they must by definition leave behind: whereas "the pagan was always *already* marked for salvation, the savage is *not yet* ready for civilization."[24] For Fabian, the project of conversion represents a unique and essentially premodern moment in the history of approaches to the other. The ample dehumanizing medieval discourses of barbarism, monstrosity, and wild men that we have glimpsed show that medieval approaches to the other can hardly be cast as always inclusive, and such generalization certainly risks reductivity. As I argued in Chapter 1, moreover, the long legacy of medieval ethnographic ideas for early modern and later thinking about Europe's others makes the line between medieval and modern ethnographic systems blurrier than is usually assumed. Nevertheless, as I show in the remainder of the chapter, William's ethnographic practice and poetics in the *Journey* bear out Fabian's intuition about the likely differences of a premodern ethnographic poetics, and more particularly, of the difference of the premodern ethnographic gaze on the other.

DEICTIC POETICS

Ambivalently, the conversion aim locates the other in a state of difference from the self even as it enfolds him within a salvational scheme accorded all humanity. Incorporation, inclusion, embrace are metaphors that suggest spatial relations between the selves and others of conversion, and I will consider now the way in which the conversion aim affects the spatial and visual representation of encounter in premodern ethnographic writing. William's preoccupation with visual matters throughout his ethnographic tract lends his text unusually well to an examination of premodern visual culture.[25] An attention to visual descriptions and to scenes of looking between selves and others in the *Journey* reveals an ethnography characterized by the subjective markers of *deixis*, distinguishing it sharply from the much-critiqued objectifying "ethnographic gaze" of travelers and natural and social scientists who write in the service of colonial domination in later centuries.

"Our experience of things here in the earth we owe to vision.... [H]earing causes us to believe because we believe our teachers, but we cannot try out what we learn except through vision."[26] So Roger Bacon characterized the visual sense, and upon reading the *Journey*, he no doubt appreciated William of Rubruck's practice of much the same philosophy therein. For William considers as certain only what he has witnessed himself and frequently calls into question the veracity of received sources of authority such as Isidore and Solinus. In the course of his investigations, William dispenses with the myths of Prester John ("nobody knew anything about him" [17.2]), of Jews at Alexander's Gate ("there are other barriers that shut out Jews, about which, however, I did not succeed in discovering anything for certain" [37.20]), and of human monsters ("I enquired about the monsters or human freaks [*de monstris sive de monstruosis hominibus*] who are described by Isidore and Solinus, but was told that such things have never been sighted, which makes us very much doubt whether [the story] is true" [29.46]). He, moreover, updates Isidore's geography: the Caspian Sea, he notes, "at no point" makes contact with the ocean—"what Isidore says, to the effect that it is a gulf extending inland from the Ocean, is incorrect" (18.4).

William, furthermore, marks many of his observations of culture and nature with statements indicating his eyewitnessing of them. Of Mongol musical instruments, for instance, he notes, "I did not see [*non vidi*] our sort of lute or guitar there, but I did see many other instruments which are not used in our part of the world" (2.9); and of Chinese medicine: "their physicians are well versed in the efficacy of herbs and can diagnose very shrewdly from the pulse. But they do not employ urine samples, not knowing anything about urine: this I saw [*vidi*] [for myself], since there are a number of them at Caracorum" (26.9). Elsewhere he details that staple of "manners and customs" discourse, funereal rites, with the same visual markers: "I have not ascertained that they bury treasure with the dead.... [F]or the rich they build pyramids, namely little pointed houses; and in some places I saw [*vidi*] large towers of baked tiles, and in others houses of stone, although stone is not to be found there. I saw [*vidi*] a man recently dead for whom they had hung up between high poles sixteen horses' hides, four towards each quarter of the earth, and they had laid down *comos* for him to drink and meat for him to eat—and for all that they were claiming that he had been baptized. I saw [*vidi*] other graves to the east" (8.4). William of Rubruck's explicit alignment of the visual sense with the gathering of cultural and natural information suggests the coincidence of visual empiricism and social science from their beginnings. Scholars of the Renaissance such as William Ivins have noted the confluence of the rise of the sciences of botany and anatomy in the sixteenth century and certain technologies of vision in the pictorial arts, such as the woodcut, printings from etchings, and Albertian pictorial perspective.[27] Even before the so-called rationalization of space of the early modern period, we see the intimate link being forged between looking and the act of cultural description and categorization in medieval ethnographic texts such as William's. Roger Bacon similarly accorded vision privileged rank among the senses in the acquisition and testing of human knowledge, calling it "the flower of the whole philosophy," through which "and not without it, can the other sciences be known." Indeed, further indicating the contemporary interest in the boundaries of the human, Bacon asserts that the visual sense alone distinguishes "human wisdom" from the knowledge of beasts: "If, moreover, we should adduce taste and touch and smell, we assume a knowledge belonging to beasts."[28] Taste, touch and smell, senses common to man and beast, do not yield information of significant quality or quantity; and as we've seen earlier, "hearing causes us to believe" but "we cannot try out what we learn except though vision." Only vision, it seems, produces empirical knowledge and "human wisdom." Thus Bacon tantalizingly connects the endeavor of knowledge acquisition via vision to the very definition of man, doubling the link between vision and anthropology: not only is cultural science established by visual description and examination, but it is the act of looking that in turn constitutes man as such, and as the proper object of his own anthropological inquiry.

The many failures of language described and enacted within William's *Journey*, neatly juxtaposed with the keenness of William's observational gaze among the Mongols, lend support to Bacon's view of the relative poverty of nonvisual senses. This is a text that paradoxically announces the inefficacy and inadequacy of language at every turn. In scene after scene, William either explicitly faults language and its transmission or, more disturbingly, implicitly announces its failure by allowing an uneasy silence to fall upon the scene of his narration. At each of William's appearances at court, readers observe a familiar ritual: William's interrogation regarding the contents of Louis IX's letter to Sartach, the son of Baatu—on account of his reputed Christianity—and William's reiteration of these contents in nearly identical language, to seemingly little avail. If such oral examination calls into question the purpose of the written missive in the first place, so too does its frequent misinterpretation along the way.[29] William's consistent attempts to confine the contents of the letter and mission to the preaching of the faith, to carve a space neither diplomatic nor military for himself and his cohorts in Mongol lands, routinely fall on deaf ears and are finally met with damning silence at the court of Mangu. There, having been asked to leave the territories, William requests permission to return to Mongolia on future missions: "At this he [Mangu] fell silent [*tunc ipse tacuit*] and sat for a long while as if in thought. The interpreter told me not to say any more; but I was waiting anxiously for his response. At last he said, "You have a long journey ahead'" (34.7). William's speech problem is partly attached to the marginal voice accorded the missionary in Mongolia, as he knows: "From that moment there was never any time or place in which I could have expounded the Catholic faith to him. For a man may say in his presence only as much as he [the Chan] chooses, unless he is an ambassador; whereas an ambassador may say anything he wishes, and is always asked whether there are further things he would like to say" (34.4); hence William's final self-defeating recommendation to Louis is that preachers no longer be sent to the Mongols.

When William is in a position to preach the Christian message, it nevertheless rarely meets its addressee. In the course of two years among the Mongols, "we baptized there a total of six souls," he writes near the end of his narrative. Such frustration is already prefigured at its beginning, at Scatacai's camp, where he is first asked about Louis's letter and the purpose of his mission: "And he asked what we would say to Sartach. 'Words of the Christian faith,' I replied. 'What are they?' he enquired, since he was eager to hear them. So I expounded to him the creed [*symbolum*] of the Faith as best I could through my interpreter, who was neither intelligent nor articulate. And when he had heard it, he nodded in silence [*Quo audito ipse tacuit et movit caput*]" (10.5). William's interpreter, Homo Dei, or Abd'ullah,[30] all too frequently fumbles the message of God: in an impromptu debate with Buddhists met with on the way to Mangu's court, William finds that his interpreter, "tired and incapable of finding the right words, made me stop talking" (25.8); among Nestorians in Mangu's territory, Homo Dei again "proved inadequate," and William concludes that "to speak in doctrinal terms through an interpreter like this was a great risk—in fact, an impossibility, as he was ignorant of them" (27.4); at Mangu's court, William finds his interpreter "in no time ... grew tipsy" (28.15). William learns to rely on his own, albeit limited powers of speech, attempting to learn the Mongol language from Lady Cota, Mangu's Christian wife, though he admits of missed opportunities to instruct her in the faith due to this same language gap—"Ego autem sedebam ibi mutus non valens aliquid dicere" (I would sit there in silence, being in no position to say a word) (29. 42). William concludes his otherwise triumphal rhetorical performance at the great debate at Caracorum, where he represents himself as having cowed the Buddhists or *tuins* and the Saracens into seeming acquiescence to Christian viewpoints, on a note that casts doubt on all earlier accomplishments: "There was present an old priest of the Iugur sect, which holds that there is one God but nevertheless makes idols; and they [the Nestorians] had a long discussion with him, relating everything down to the coming of Christ in judgment, and also using analogies to explain the Trinity to him and to the Saracens. Everybody listened without challenging a single word. But for all that no one said, 'I believe, and wish to become a Christian'. When it was all over, the Nestorians and the Saracens alike sang in loud voices, while the *tuins* remained silent; and after that everyone drank heavily" (33.22–23). It would seem that hearing falls short even of Bacon's limiting assessment of its powers in the *Opus*, causing no one "to believe" in contexts of conversion such as this, where it matters most. The debate at Caracorum calls into question hearing's efficacy for conserving and reproducing the knowledge of authorities in multilingual, multifaith contexts and rather foregrounds the cultural specificity of the production of knowledge and ideas about faith. When William does attempt to bridge these cultural gaps during the debate, he is most successful when he thinks visually, rather than with language, a point to which I will turn shortly.

William's problem with language in the *Journey* extends, in the final analysis, beyond specific moments of translation, the problem of unfamiliar tongues, or differences of authorial communities. Sometimes, he is simply at a loss for words, in any language. Early on, he makes what seems an innocuous comment in declaring of his encounters with Tartars: "We were all right as long as we were in the wilds, but I cannot put into words [*non possum exprimere verbis*] the tribulations I suffered whenever we came to their encampments" (13.4). These sorts of statements, of not being able exprimere verbis, accumulate in the course of his narrative, bearing with them an additional element: the requirement of illustration as supplement to otherwise inadequate discourse. In a section describing women's dwellings, he writes, "Matrone sibi faciunt pulcherimas bigas, quas nescirem vobis describere nisi per picturam, immo omnia depinxissem vobis si scivissem pingere" (the married women make themselves very fine wagons, which I could describe to you only by drawing—and indeed I should have drawn everything for you had I known how to draw) (2.4). Further suggesting the analogy between painterly arts and his own ethnographic work—much as did Gerald of Wales before him—William's search for the right descriptive words often yields visual metaphors, as when he writes: "Quando ergo vidi curiam Baatu expavi, quia videbantur proprie domus eius quasi quedam magna civitas protensa in longum et populis undique circumfusa usque ad tres vel quatuor leucas" (On sighting Baatu's camp, I was struck with awe. His own dwellings had the appearance of a large city stretching far out lengthways and with inhabitants scattered around in every direction for a distance of three or four leagues) (19.4). When he encounters "Scatacai's wagons loaded with dwellings," he uses the following description to resolve the apparent contradiction of a movable city, in a clear rejection of the received dichotomy between nomadism and city dwelling: "videbatur michi quod obviaret michi civitas magna" (I felt as if a great city were on the move towards me) (10.1). In these moments and many others in William's text, pictures work where language fails.[31] Readers of the *Journey* are supplied with many such communicative and supplemental pictorial scenes, some of them like self-enclosed vignettes, as when William's colleague, "me ignorante, cucurrit ad Bulgai maiorem scribam, innuens ei per signa quod moreretur si iret viam illam" (without my knowledge . . . ran

Writing Ethnography "In the Eyes of the Other"   71

to Bulgai, the chief secretary, and conveyed to him by means of signs that he would die were he to make that [final return] journey) (36.14). Finally, at Mangu's court, it is the appeal of pictures that accomplishes William's work, conveying the word of God:

> Ingressus autem oratorium habens bibliam et breviarium in pectore, primo inclinavi me ad altare et postea ipsi Chan. . . . Ipse autem Chan fecit sibi afferre libros nostros bibliam et breviarium, et quesivit de ymaginibus diligenter quid significarent. Nestorini responderunt ei pro velle suo, quia interpres noster non erat nobiscum ingressus. Etiam quando prima vice fueram ante eum habebam bibliam in pectore, quam fecit sibi afferri et multum respexit eam.
>
> (I went into the oratory holding the bible and breviary to my breast, and I bowed first to the altar and then to the Chan. . . . The Chan had them bring our books—the bible and the breviary—and enquired keenly what the pictures meant. The Nestorians gave him whatever answer they chose, as our interpreter had not accompanied us inside. When I had appeared before him on the first occasion, too, I held the bible in front of me, and he ordered it brought to him and examined it at length.) (29.20).

Later, nearly the same scene is reported once again by William, on whom the unique power of the visual is not lost: "Et cum vidisset nos tenentes biblias coram pectore fecit sibi afferri ut videret, quas multum diligenter respexit" (Seeing us clasping the bibles to our breasts, he [Mangu] had them taken to him so that he could see them and inspected them with great care) (29.28).[32]

Not only do pictures and visuality work to reach William's audience where language otherwise falters, but these visual scenes reach their targets in a very particular way. For in each of these illustrative scenes or visual tutorials, we find the subject-viewer of the scene, William, represented as an object within the frame of description. In the passage above, William is seen gripping the breviary and the Bible before an observing Mongol emperor. In the illustration scenes where visual language supplemented William's otherwise "loss for words," William in a like manner makes his own subjectivity and emotions part of the message, locating himself as an inextricable part of the scene he is setting: "I felt as if a great city were on the move towards me"; "I was struck with awe"; "which I could describe to you only by drawing—and indeed I should have drawn everything for you had I known how to draw." Alongside the eyewitnessed, visual empiricism on which William insists, we have scenes that expose the very subjectivity of the eye as it is witnessing. Alongside descriptions of alien practices, we find scenes that mix self and other, subject and object, within the very same frame of description, quietly disrupting any notion of their clear separation.

And, of course, the notion of their separation is one on which modern ethnographic practice is founded, as its various critics have argued. Timothy Mitchell has characterized the work of the ethnographer's eye upon colonial Egyptian lands and subjects as one operating from a stable viewpoint outside the frame, such that the viewer-ethnographer is entirely absent from the production of the descriptive scene, and has instead assigned himself a space of his own invention from which he can safely gaze without being gazed at in return.[33] Mary Louise Pratt has similarly characterized the work of travelers' "imperial eyes" upon eighteenth-century African landscapes: "Unheroic, unparticularized, egoless, the eye seems able to do little but gaze from a periphery of its own creation."[34] The systematic removal of the trace of the traveler-ethnographer from the scene of his description, Mitchell, Pratt, and others suggest, creates the fictional effect of "objectivity" and the objectness of those being gazed at.[35] This removal is, moreover, integral to the denial of coevalness, or the denial of the simultaneity of ethnographer-subject's time and native-object's time, which furthers the object-other's spatial distancing from the observing ethnographer— in short, for processes of objectification and dehumanization.[36]

These processes are not consistent with the work of incorporation that characterizes the conversion aim and salvational discourse, and as we might expect, William's ethnographic practice works in a very different way. William incorporates the spatial and temporal coordinates of the self within the scene of looking in a way radically at odds with the construction of a stable viewpoint outside the frame or a ubiquitous and yet invisible gaze that is unreturnable by the viewed object. William's ethnographic practice and poetics is, instead, like those of the other authors of this study, characterized by deixis, self-reflexive utterance that routinely refers back to the body of the speaker and includes information about the spatial and temporal relation of the speaker to his objects of description.[37] William's landscape, far from being stripped of natives and of their various activities— "fetching water, carrying baggage, driving oxen, stealing brandy, guiding, interpreting"[38]—as critiqued by Pratt, is precisely peopled with such activities: Mongols translating, if imperfectly, hoarding and stealing food, making comos, defecating publicly, and indeed driving oxen. William's emotions—"states of confusion, violent feelings or acts, censorships, important failures, changes of course and excessive pleasures,"[39] which would be excised from official, professional ethnographic accounts in the modern era—suffuse his ethnographic account. We have already glimpsed a few of these—awe, amazement, feelings of inadequacy as a painter—but his text offers many more, as when on more than one occasion his frustrations mount such that he calls for the destruction, in the form of crusade, of the very people he has journeyed so far to save. A final way in which William's ethnographic poetics reflects deixis is perhaps the most striking: his depiction of himself in the gaze of his Mongol hosts, in a number of disorienting scenes of self-objectification in the text. Perhaps the aesthetics of incorporation are nowhere more on display than in these disturbing scenes, which, far in excess of mixing subjects and objects in a single frame, trouble the presumption of their distinct and differing vantage points.

SEEING AS OTHER (IN OCULIS EORUM): THE MISSIONARY'S GAZE

William's keen gaze renders him as sensitive to how he is being seen by those around him as to what he is himself seeing in the course of his mission. His sensitivity to the gaze of others upon him and his Christian cohorts is evidenced in several passages. In Sartach's territory, William and colleagues are ordered to arrive at court bearing Louis's letter, their liturgical items, and books, as Sartach "wished to see them": "Quod et fecimus, honerantes bigam unam libris et capella, et aliam pane et vino et fructibus. Tunc fecit omnes libros et vestes explicari. Et circumstabant nos in equis multi Tartari et christiani et sarraceni" (We obeyed, loading up one wagon with the books and the ornaments and another with bread, wine and fruit. Then he [Coaic] had all the books and vestments displayed, while a great many Tartars, Christians and Saracens surrounded us on horseback) (15.5). Before Sartach himself, "et levaverunt filtrum quod pendet ante hostium, ut posset nos videre" (they lifted up the felt hanging in front of the doorway so that he could see us) and after some questioning regarding the liturgical items, "Postea fecit circumstantes nos retrahere se, ut plenius posset videre ornamenta nostra" (Then he made the people standing round us draw back, so that he could have a better view of our finery) (15.6–7). Upon dismounting at the court of Mangu, William and company are exposed to immediate scrutiny: "Et cum circumdarent nos homines et respicerent nos tamquam monstra, maxime quia eramus nudis pedibus, et quererent si nos non indigeremus pedibus nostris, quia supponebant quod statim amitteremus eos, ille Hungarus reddidit eis rationem, narrans eis conditiones Ordinis nostri" (People gathered round us, gazing at us as if we were freaks, especially in view of our bare feet, and asked whether we had no use for our feet, since they imagined that in no time we would lose them. And this the Hungarian explained to them, telling them the rules of our Order) (28.4). Franciscans at the court of Mangu, William shows us in such scenes, are a source of wonder and consternation, requiring humanization and cultural contextualization lest they themselves be taken as tamquam monstra to those eagerly regarding them.[40] In doing so, William registers his awareness of what a strange sight he and the members of his order make as guests in a Far Eastern empire with few diplomatic ties to the Latin West, where Christianity competes from a marginal position with several other faiths, both monotheistic and nonmonotheistic. Clear-eyed about this marginality, he knows he must greet and welcome rather than shun the gaze of uncomprehending and mocking outsiders if he is to attract them to the faith he preaches; this is the sort of regard on the faith that William must seek if he is to be a successful missionary in Mongolia.

But as we also glimpse from the scenes above, the gazes of Mongolians upon the strangeness and differences of Latin Christians are often uncomfortable and destabilizing for the Christian self. Nowhere is this uneasy dynamic of the Mongols' at-once disorienting and welcome gaze upon Christian missionaries more acutely evident than at William's appearance at Baatu's court. Having characterized his entrance into the pavilion of Baatu with the threshold language marking "other world" entries ("and when I came among them I really felt as if I were entering some other world"), William completes the scene with a picture of his own alterity in the eyes of his Mongol hosts: "Tunc duxit nos ante papilionem, et monebamur ne tangeremus cordas tentorii quas ipsi reputant loco liminis domus. Stetimus ibi nudis pedibus in habitu nostro discoopertis capitibus, et eramus spectaculum magnum in oculis eorum" (Then he conducted us before the pavilion, and we were warned not to touch the tent-ropes, which for them represent the threshold of the dwelling. We took up our stand there, with bare feet, wearing our habits but with our heads uncovered, and presented quite a spectacle in their eyes) (19.5, trans. adapted). William here shows himself able to step into the viewpoint of his Mongol hosts and project himself in their eyes—in oculis eorum—anticipating an ethnographic description that will be highly mediated by the other's gaze and so composed in light of another's word. William extends himself much further still in the course of this imperial interview. After being ordered to speak and advising Baatu that he be "absolutely sure that you will not possess the things of Heaven without having become a Christian—For God says, 'He that believeth and is baptized, shall be saved: but he that believeth not shall be condemned'"—William is answered with "a slight smile" by Baatu and the laughter of the Mongols in attendance, who, he says, "inceperunt plaudere manus deridendo nos" (began to clap us in derision) (19.7). His interpreter is palpably uncomfortable and afraid; William reassures him and forges on, waiting for the restoration of silence. After some more questions, including ones regarding his and his colleagues' names and the status of his country vis-à-vis war with the Saracens,

> Tunc fecit nos sedere et dare de lacte suo ad bibendum, quod ipsi valde magnum reputant, quando aliquis bibit cosmos cum eo in domo sua. Et dum sedens respicerem terram, precepit ut elevarem vultum, volens adhuc nos amplius respicere vel forte pro sortilegio, quia habent pro malo omine vel signo vel pro mala pronostica quando aliquis sedet coram eis inclinata facie quasi tristis, maxime cum appodiat maxillam vel mentum super manum.

> (Then he made us sit down and had us given some of his milk to drink—they make much of it when someone drinks *comos* with him in his own dwelling. While I sat gazing at the ground, he ordered me to raise my face, as he wanted to have another look at us—or possibly with witchcraft in mind, since they view it as a bad omen or sign, or foreshadowing evil, when someone sits in their presence with his head lowered as if he were sad, and especially when he leans his cheek or chin on his hand.) (19.8).

In this stunning scene, we find encapsulated the complex dimensions of the uneasy and precarious dynamic of vision in the context of preaching and conversion. William portrays his sadness—another emotion anchoring himself deictically in the scene—after what has been a cruel and unsuccessful exposure to multiple would-be converts at the court of Baatu. But the very means by which he delivers this self-portrait shows up the complex layering of perspectives in the scene: we know he is sad from his depiction of himself as "sedens respicerem terram" ([sitting] gazing at the ground) —a gaze upon William from an external viewpoint. It soon becomes evident that the viewpoint William is occupying is that of Baatu, who "precepit ut elevarem vultum, volens adhuc nos amplius respicere" (ordered me to raise my face, as he wanted to have another look at us). But William's sadness is embedded in further mediated gazes: "or possibly [Baatu ordered me] with witchcraft in mind, since they view it as a bad omen or sign . . . when someone sits in their presence with his head lowered as if he were sad." William, William tells us, is possibly provoking Baatu to order him to raise his head, because Mongols do not appreciate it, for reasons not entirely known to William, when someone lowers the head in their presence, especially while leaning cheek and chin on the hand, as we might guess William was doing before being directed to stop. We have here a picture of William, abject from sadness before the gaze of Baatu, from the viewpoint of his Mongol host, a picture that is only completed—the head leaning on the hand—within a note about Mongol superstitions.

William is clearly objectifying himself here in the eyes of the Mongol other—what better way than to freeze himself into an instantaneous image (which would have disappeared forever, had he not, like a photograph, caught and "developed" it for our viewing pleasure)? But much more is at work in this representational strategy. For it is William who is doing the portraying, and just as he is not held back by derision at court, neither will he seemingly allow himself to be held back by his apparent emotional distress in this scene from continuing with the work of conversion by gleaning whatever cultural information about Mongol customs he can in the process. We learn that Mongols view the offering of comos as a meaningful gesture of hospitality, and that some form of superstition attaches to assuming the bodily position William has inadvertently assumed before a Mongol emperor. William is still the subject-ethnographer here, even if he is also an object in his own depiction. And he has authored a highly complicated and mediated descriptive scene, which is more like a set of pictures within pictures than a linear narrative. His memorable self-portrait reaches us as an image of an image of an image: his words provide King Louis with a picture of his goings-on at Baatu's court, which contains within it a picture of Baatu's gazes on William, which is itself rendered, through William's ethnographic intervention, as a picture of William in an abject pose, staring at the ground.

At no point does William the missionary-ethnographer turn away from a gaze, even when it alienates him from himself or renders him a fixed object-as-image. In this dynamic, perspectival dance, it is finally impossible to say who has the final look, or occupies the privileged vantage point. Instead of a single, dominant gaze, we have a series of competing and reciprocal ones—William has prepared us for as much at the outset of this interview when he notes that "respexit ergo nos diligenter et nos eum" (he [Baatu] regarded us with a keen gaze, as we did him) (19.6). The flow of force is also reciprocal: William may be objectified by the Mongols, but in never ceasing to note important cultural information, he returns the favor, collecting valuable knowledge about these would-be Christians for future, if not present, use. Neither William nor his hosts are entirely fixable or objectifiable; rather, according to William's representation, the two participate in a dialogic contest of agency and passivity, seeing and being seen, in which either one may occupy either position at any given moment.

William's uncomfortable and disorienting acts of self-objectification—striking though they may be as representational practice—may be grounded in a clear cultural and referential system, again that of the conversion aim. For the scene above enacts in practice what was being theorized in Europe with regard to the reflexivity of the conversion endeavor, complete with its visual manifestations. In such Dominican and Franciscan preaching manuals as the *Liber de eruditione praedicatorum* (c. 1263) of Humbert of Romans, thirteenth-century preachers were being taught to regard themselves as public display objects and to see themselves as they were being seen—not only in the eyes of God, as the tradition of *speculatio* had held for Benedictines and Cistercians, but increasingly in the eyes of their fellow human beings. In this task, Dominican and Franciscan training books routinely urged "the adaptation of the preacher's self-presentation (of his gait, his demeanour, even of his vocal inflections and vocabulary) to the demands and needs of his audience."[41] Aron Gurevich similarly suggests that audience-adaptive preaching was emphasized throughout the medieval period, within local European settings: "Preachers, who strove to penetrate the mind of each listener, could achieve this only by adapting to their audiences."[42] (Indeed so self-consciously delineated and increasingly codified would the art of preacherly gesture and gesticulation become that art historians like Michael Baxandall have located in late medieval preaching manuals subtle and precise clues to the gestural vocabulary of Renaissance masters such as Leonardo and Boticelli.)[43] Likening the preacher to a host who must prepare a meal for his guests, Humbert of Romans offers hundreds of sample sermons to suit different occasions, and lists over seventy discrete types of audiences, divided according to age, gender, class, education, and type of sin, among other categories. Considerable flexibility of message may be required to reach some audiences, he warns: "There is no single exhortation which is suitable for everyone, because men are not all held by the same kind of morals. Often, what helps one man harms another."[44] Although Humbert does not address the problem of non-Christian audiences like the ones William encounters abroad, his fellow Dominican, Thomas Aquinas, does so in the *Summa Contra Gentiles*, written to aid conversion in multiconfessional Spain. Noting in book 1.2 the difficulty of answering those who "do not agree with us in accepting the authority of any Scripture, by which they may be convinced of their error," Aquinas recommends the following set of audience-dependent approaches: "Thus, against the Jews we are able to argue by means of the Old Testament, while against heretics we are able to argue by means of the New Testament. But the Mohammedans and the pagans accept neither the one nor the other. We must, therefore, have recourse to the natural reason, to which all men are forced to give their assent. However, it is true, in divine matters the natural reason has its failings."[45] Different texts and rhetorical strategies may be needed for different religious groups, Aquinas advises the missionary. But as Humbert of Romans notes, and William of Rubruck surely appreciated, preachers must not rely solely on words; rather, preachers must strive for salvation "in any way they can. And sometimes this is achieved better by good conduct than by words."[46] William's final interview before Mangu, in which the latter chastises wayward Christians and exempts only William on the basis of his consistently exemplary conduct, reveals the extent to which William took seriously the power of his example among the Mongols.

Thirteenth-century preachers were further admonished to remember that all settings were potential preaching settings, and thus the work of adaptation to others was never complete. The preacher was thus to regard himself as a thoroughly public being, always in the public eye, under the many gazes of potential converts and confessors, as well as the ubiquitous gaze of an all-knowing God. Authors of manuals for novices, such as the thirteenth-century Franciscan David of Augsburg, similarly cautioned: "At no time should you ever be careless or secretive, rather you should always maintain yourself with discipline and chastity in sight, taste, touch and in everything else, as if you were being watched by someone."[47] The gazes of the preacher and the convert are reciprocal: "raised above the crowd," the preacher occupies a privileged vantage point for both observing and being observed. Visible to all, he is subject to the scrutiny of all, finally, even to his own. When alone, Humbert of Romans writes, the preacher must make of himself his own audience in order to test the honesty of his self-presentation.[48]

The gazes of preachers in the service of God's work feature considerable disorientation to the preacher-self, then, requiring the destabilizing ability to see the self as other, in two ways—seeing how one is being seen from without, in public display, and learning to scrutinize one's self as one would any other. Indeed, given such a regime of inspection and introspection, the self of the preacher is thoroughly other mediated, much like William's portrait of himself leaning on his hand at the court of Baatu. The successful preacher must remain "other oriented," that is, ever ready to adapt to the demands of ever-new and differing audiences he comes upon in the course of his travels. Whereas the goal for earlier monastics had been assimilation of self to order, the goal of the preaching friars was far more open-ended, and involved adaptation to a limitless variety of preaching settings.[49] The requirement of such constant adaptation and improvisation on the part of preacher toward his audience and setting means that, in practice, the work of conversion requires more extension of self toward other, and more disorientation for the self, than theories of conversion tend to stress.[50]

This great self-extension toward the other can be shown, moreover, to have been highly productive from an ethnographic viewpoint, pushing its most faithful practitioners into fully unscripted terrain, where new modes of thinking and writing about the other could and did emerge, as well as new self-recognition. William's travels and notes certainly confirm this. We have already observed William's willingness to see as others see at the court of Baatu, and the intersubjectivity of his description of his interview at that court. The same ability accounts for much of William's success at the famous debate between the faiths at Caracorum, where he engages in the rhetorical equivalent of "seeing as other" and thereby demonstrably pushes European understandings of both self and other well beyond their usual limits. There, William appeals to the "natural reason" of Buddhists and Muslims in ways Aquinas might have approved, but in doing so, displays remarkable strategic flexibility in the way he positions Christianity among these other faiths. In pre-debate practice with his fellow

Christians, the Nestorians, William asks "qualiter vellent procedure" (how they wished to proceed), and when the Nestorians there recommend debate with the Saracens first, William responds, "This would not be a good method, . . . since the Saracens agree with us in saying that there is one God and therefore provide allies with us against the *tuins*." Between monotheistic and nonmonotheistic non-Christians, monotheistic non-Christians such as the Saracen Muslims are Christianity's allies. Already an improvised system of flexible, audience-dependent and contingent affiliation comes into view. (And one, indeed, that proves efficacious at the debate: William purposefully opens with the nature of God, and by the time he is through with the tuins, the Saracens declare they no longer want to debate him.) But William stretches himself much further in the course of these preparations:

> Quibus dixi: "Experiamini qualiter vos habebitis contra eos. Ego assumam partem tuinorum, et vos sustinete partem chiristianorum. Ego sum de illa secta, ponatur ita quod dicunt quia Deus non est, probate quod Deus sit." Est enim quedam secta ibi que dicit quod quelibet anima et quelibet virtus in qualibet re est Deus illius rei, et quod non sit aliter Deus. Tunc nestorini non sciverunt probare aliquid, nisi solum narrare quod Scriptura narrat. Dixi: "Ipsi non credunt Scripturis, si vos narretis unum, et ipsi narrabunt aliud." Tunc consului eis quod permitterent me primo convenire cum eis, quia si ego confunderer, adhuc remaneret eis locus loquendi; si ipsi confunderentur, ego postea non haberem auditum. Acquieverunt.
>
> ("Let us rehearse", I suggested, "to see how you will handle yourselves against them. I shall take the part of the *tuins* and you maintain the Christian view. Now I belong to their sect, and let us assume that they deny the existence of God: prove that he does exist". (For there is a sect there which asserts that any soul or any power in anything is the god of that thing, and that God does not exist otherwise.) But at this point the Nestorians were incapable of proving anything, but could only relate what Scripture tells. "They do not believe in the Scriptures", I said: "if you tell them one story, they will quote another." Then I advised them to let me be the first to meet them [the *tuins*], since should I be worsted they would still have an opportunity to speak, whereas if they were worsted I should not receive a hearing afterwards; and they agreed). (33.11)

What first strikes us is William's idea of rehearsal by role play: he will be the Buddhist, the Nestorians the representative Christians. This role play suggests, however inadvertently, that religious identities are not fixed or absolute subject positions, but are rather object-like, capable of being occupied or vacated as need be. Such a religious subject will likewise be capable of flexible movement between different subject positions. The provisional flexibility of subjectivity having been established, William demonstrates that the belief systems of the other can be, indeed must be, wholly assumed as one's own in order to be answered persuasively—the necessity of dialogic engagement with alternative viewpoints.[51] Critiquing the Nestorians for being unable to reach outside scripture in order to prove the existence of God and therefore "incapable of proving anything," William points out (much like Aquinas) that the scriptures are mere fictions from the viewpoint of those outside the Christian tradition—"si vos narretis unum" (if you tell them one story)"—worse, fictions without inherent primacy over others in the context of multifaith debate—"et ipsi narrabunt aliud" (they will quote another). Christians must extend themselves beyond the stories of scripture that form the core of their beliefs—to see, in short, in light of another's word— if they are to convince those who do not already believe those stories. Difference exists and must be met on its own terms, not those of the self; the inherited script of Christianity will not suffice. This simple yet profound realization on William's part is impossible without his performing the uncomfortable and disorienting maneuver of stepping outside his own shoes, beyond his own vantage point upon the world, beyond his Christian subjectivity. The skill that allows him to so deftly strategize how to reason at this interfaith debate is the same one William strategically exhibits before the imperial eyes of various Mongol rulers: an externalization of his own subjectivity, and the occupation of viewing positions not his own, in the service of the conversion aim. These uneasy and disorienting skills are, we see from contemporary literature, paradoxically, part of a successful preacher's repertoire. The resulting literary record of such uneasy preaching skills practiced abroad is the strikingly dialogic ethnography of William of Rubruck's *Journey*, composed as much in light of an other's gaze as in William's own.

In the course of his travels, William adapts to his environment in ways that he probably never imagined he would at the outset, but that are either expedient for his wider aim or that occur unwittingly.[52] While thus far I have been suggesting that William's uncomfortable self-othering before Mongol audience has been a self-consciously chosen step toward the greater good of conversion, the missionary's work of openness and adaptation to the world leads to some rather heterodoxic practices and results that the faithful William could not have desired or willed. William's tolerance of the Armenian monk's many misrepresentations of the Christian message—together with his attendance before idolatrous practices and use of soothsayers—in exchange for this monk's language skills has already been noted. And while William upbraids Nestorian Christians for their mixing of Christianity with local practices and beliefs such as polygamy, in practice, he himself participates in a number of ceremonies at which the Christian faith becomes altered and adapted to local needs. For instance, at the court of Mangu, William describes being forced to participate in a drinking ceremony in which Christian blessings are occasionally inserted: "The lady held the full cup in her hand, and on her knees asked for a blessing. The priests all chanted in a loud voice, while she drained the cup. My colleague and I were also obliged to sing at another juncture when she wanted to drink" (29. 22). Elsewhere, William notes the obligation of Christians to participate in the consecration of white mares in a herd, a Shamanistic ritual (35.4). William accommodates himself to expectations when he prays that Christ grant Mangu a long life, for, as he notes, "they like one to pray for their lives," and indeed it is shortly thereafter revealed that all the different religious leaders in Mongolia obligingly do the same (28.16, 29.15). William even adopts local customs in circumstances having little to do with religion, but which nevertheless underscore the considerable adaptability required for missionary work abroad: he dresses in Mongol clothing, he accepts gifts against the rule of his order where to do otherwise would be insulting, he takes to drinking and even liking comos, and he ends his report by recommending the sparseness of the Mongol diet for increased fitness and mobility of troops. These unscripted, culturally syncretizing actions—undertaken by a most religiously anchored subject—again speak to the powerful forces of disorientation and reorientation that worked on medieval Europeans as they engaged with other words and other worlds in dialogic contact zones such as thirteenth-century Mongolia.

At one moment in his narrative, William expresses considerable anxiety about whether he should attend a ceremony involving idolatrous practices at Mangu's court. Revealing the complex calculus behind the accommodation and adaptation of the preacher, he writes:

> Ego multum deliberabam de me quid deberem facere vel ire vel non
> ire, et timens scandalum si discederem ab aliis christianis, et quia
> ipsi Chan placebat, et timens ne bonum impediretur quod sperabam
> me posse optinere, eligebam magis ire quamvis viderem facta eorum

> plena sortilegiis et ydolatria. Nec aliud ibi faciebam nisi orare pro tota ecclesia alta voce et etiam pro ipso Chan ut Deus dirigeret eum in viam salutis eterne.
>
> I reflected a good deal as to what I should do myself, whether to go or not. But since I was afraid that dissociating myself from the other Christians would cause a scandal, and since it was the Chan's will, and since I feared lest any advantage might be thwarted which I hoped to gain, I chose to go, even though I should be observing them engaging in practices that were riddled with superstition and idolatry. And all I did there was pray out loud for the whole church, and also for the Chan, that God would direct him in the path of eternal salvation. (30.8)

As Dallas Denery has noted, "wandering through and preaching in the world, and yet not a part of the world, the friar faced something of a dilemma. He needed to regulate his appearance, his self-presentation, so as to . . . edify those around him, without being contaminated by them."[53] The above scene nicely captures this dilemma. William here connects his fear of exposure to corrupting practices to the act of observing them, in so doing reflecting an anxiety about vision characteristic not of the perspectivist tradition of Roger Bacon but of moralizing approaches to vision epitomized in the *De oculo morali* (c. 1260–1306) of Peter of Limoges. In this highly popular treatise, Peter of Limoges stresses the need for active, internal censoring on the part of the subject-viewer if he is to avoid the harmful moral effects of external visual stimuli before him.[54] The fear expressed by such cultural documents as the *De oculo morali* is that of the power of vision to seduce the self away from the self, a testament of the consciousness of the power, equally, of worldly contamination of the self and of the seen upon the seer, in thirteenth-century society. Wandering preachers were particularly, perhaps uniquely, vulnerable to such dangers, and indeed Humbert of Romans advised that a preacher "wash away any defilement that he has incurred and repair anything that has got broken" in the process of preaching,[55] a ritual cleansing of self (or "lif") also performed, as we will see, by the "pilgrim" John Mandeville upon his return home after exposure to so much worldly *dyursety*.

In the *De oculo morali* and in William's testimony above, the fear of the effect of the world upon the self is expressed as the consciousness of the dangers of seeing in the world, of seeing "as other" in precisely the way that preaching, at the same time, requires. The power of vision in the context of preaching was understood to cut both ways in the thirteenth century, that is, to attach equally to seer and seen, subjects and objects of the conversion aim. This understanding returns us to the differences of the premodern ethnographic gaze from its modern counterpart, and of the power relations of cultural information gathering in the interests of conversion on the one hand and of colonization and empire on the other. William's mission is part of a larger set of missions, including especially John of Plano Carpini's, conceived as part of a *defensive* strategy—whether, as Bacon would have it, to prevent dangers to European travelers in Asia, which could be avoided through knowledge, or according to the thinking of Innocent IV, to assess the nature of the threat at Europe's eastern door—rather than as part of an offensive strategy in the service of colonization, which might properly be termed a medieval "Orientalism."

Thirteenth-century relations between Latin Christendom and Mongolia were marked not by an imperial-colonial relationship but by the uneasy tensions existing between those who were neither friends nor foes. Such uneasy relations are well demonstrated by the letters that passed between Guyuk Khan and Innocent IV in 1245–46, nearly a decade before William's mission. Innocent IV initiated the exchange, writing two bulls to the Mongol emperors. The first of these explains the notion of papal responsibility for the salvation of all and announces on this basis Innocent's sending of Laurence of Portugal among others on a mission to Mongolia, asking for their safe conduct and benevolent treatment. The second letter, written only a week later, asks the same reception of Carpini, but adds that "we are driven to express in strong terms amazement that you, as we have heard, have invaded many countries belonging both to the Christians and to others and are laying them waste in horrible desolation, and with a fury still unabated you do not cease from stretching out your destroying hand to more distant lands, but, breaking the bond of natural ties, sparing neither sex nor age, you rage against all indiscriminately with the sword of chastisement." Innocent follows this by asking that "you desist entirely from assaults of this kind and especially from the persecution of Christians," and upon "profitable discussions with them concerning the aforesaid affairs, especially those pertaining to peace, [you] make fully known to us through these same Friars what moved you to destroy other nations and what your intentions are for the future."[56] Guyuk Khan answers a year and a half later, in terms that no doubt did little to appease Innocent IV's concerns. As for Innocent's prayers that "I might find a good entry into baptism, . . . This prayer of thine I have not understood. . . . Though thou [likewise] sayest that I should become a trembling Nestorian Christian, worship God and be an ascetic, how knowest thou whom God absolves, in truth to whom He shows his mercy?" And as to the charge of unjust conquests on the part of Mongols, Guyuk answers: "These words of thine I have also not understood. The eternal God has slain and annihilated these lands and peoples, because they have neither adhered to Chingis Khan, nor to the Khagan [the supreme leader], both of whom have been sent to make known God's command, nor to the command of God. . . . How could anybody seize or kill by his own power contrary to the command of God?" Guyuk ends by asking for what he seeks: "Now you should say with sincerest heart: 'I will submit and serve you.' Thou thyself, at the head of all the Princes, come at once to serve and wait upon us! At that time I shall recognize your submission."[57]

The tensions embodied in the epistolary exchange are considerable; indeed, the agendas of the Mongols for political submission and the Latin Christians for the expansion of Christendom largely speak past each other. Such tension is evident in William's Mongolia as well, where William notes bitterly that the Mongols "iam in tantam superbiam sunt erecti, quod credunt quod totus mundus desideret facere pacem cum eis" (have reached such a level of arrogance that they believe the whole world is longing to make peace with them) (28.3), where he has trouble convincing anyone of the primacy of the Christian message in matters of salvation, and from whence he is finally cast out unceremoniously without a return invitation—the ultimate symbol of the failure of Christian aims vis-à-vis the Mongols.[58] And what of Mongol aims for western European submission? While the Mongols of William's day had not yet acted on such desires, they do occasionally evince a suggestive curiosity regarding William's homeland. At Mangu's court, the court secretaries "inceperunt multum inquirere de regno Francie, utrum essent ibi multi arietes et boves et aqui, ac si statim deberent ingredi et capere omnia; et multociens alias oportebat me facere magnam vim in dissimulando indignationem et iram, et respondi: 'Multa bona sunt ibi que vos videbitis si contingat vos illuc ire'" (began to ask us numerous questions about the kingdom of France: whether it contained many sheep, cattle and horses—as if they were due to move in and take it all over forthwith. On this as on many other occasions I had to exercise great self-control in order to conceal my indignation and fury, and I replied: "It contains many fine things, which you can see for yourself if you happen to go there") (28.19). Ever welcoming of opportunities to promote the faith, no matter how personally uncomfortable the circumstances, William works to contain his anger before the "imperial eyes" being cast by Mangu's court secretaries on western Europe.

In the text of William of Rubruck's *Journey*, instead of a European imperial gaze upon the eastern peoples whom the text scrupulously describes, we find neither objectified Mongols nor viewing subjects entirely distinct from their viewed objects. The reciprocal gazes of conversion and its work of incorporation ideally require much the opposite: the humanization of would-be converts, and conversely, the making of a public display object out of a preacher who must extend himself, whatever the subjective risks, toward the other—an ever-changing audience—in the name of salvation.[59] Critics of the gaze of European empire, of its ethnographers, or of the state's panoptical control of its modern subjects all assume the modern gaze's dehumanization of its object through an imposition of domination upon it. As Jean-Paul Sartre, an early theorist of the gaze, characterized the modern visual regime: "the one who casts the look is always the subject and the one who is targeted is always turned into an object. . . . [O]bjectification is the *telos* of the look."[60] But as we see in William's ethnographic account of Mongol culture, in a visual regime governed by the conversion aim, incorporation rather than objectification may well be the telos of the look, with rather different results. Unlike the objectification of humans under an invisible ethnographer's eye that we find in later "scientific" ethnography, the gazes of William's missionary-ethnography suggest a greater fluidity and dialogue in the relation between the viewers and viewed, the subjects and objects, of ethnographic encounter in the premodern era, and the intersubjective nature of cultural knowledge production in this still precolonial era of European contacts with Asia and its inhabitants.

Another way we can approach the problem of the premodern "gaze" is by considering the interaction of subjects and objects according to the visual understandings of the period, embodied in the contemporary science of optics. Here again, Roger Bacon provides invaluable information. Bacon's theory of the multiplication of species—according to which vision works by the eye's reception of "species" of light and color emanating outward from objects toward the eye—establishes a continuity, indeed an identity, between seer and seen: "Transformed into an extension of the eye itself, assisting the visible object's species as they multiply themselves to the eye, the medium actually unites the eye with its object. . . . Physical and psychological processes unite to form something like a continuous and uninterrupted 'optical medium' between the one who sees and what is seen."[61] The eye itself, then, according to Bacon and other perspectivists, is "sentient" and endowed with "the active potential to assimilate itself to the visible object as sensed and cognized" and therefore "become[s] what it sees even as it sees what it sees."[62] This is a far cry from the disembodied instrument that René Descartes, writing his *Optics* (c. 1637) some four hundred years later, would make of the eye. Descartes's eye would not interpret or fuse with its objects, but merely transmit information in the form of neural impulses.[63] In the final chapter, we will observe the turn in fourteenth-century theories of vision away from the perspectivists' confidence in the efficacy of vision towards an emphasis on visual error and corruption, coupled with a diminished confidence in the accuracy of man's understanding of things earthly and divine. Before the new perspective of the Renaissance, the so-called Renaissance rediscovery of linear perspective, and its renewed and secularized confidence in men's judgment of other men and other cultures, William of Rubruck's *Journey* provides us with a window into a visual culture according to which only God escaped the network of reciprocal gazes implicating all men, making them ever the objects of others' gazes as much as subjects of their own.

CHAPTER 4

Casting a "Sideways Glance" at the Crusades

The Voice of the Other in Joinville's Vie de Saint Louis

As one indication of the historical connections between the crusading and missionary endeavors,[1] the biography of William of Rubruck's sponsor on mission, King Louis IX, serves as one of the great crusade chronicles of the medieval period. It is in many ways atypical of the crusade chronicle genre, certainly at the genre's outset. Chronicles of the First Crusade, and the many chansons de geste that emerged from its spectacular events, reflect little or no ethnographic interest in the Muslim other, whose defeat they describe in epic and ideologically driven terms as sanctified by God. This early crusading literature, whether it be the chronicle of Fulcher of Chartres or the *Chanson de Roland*, is marked by a high degree of both ignorance and intolerance of Muslims (as well as Jews and Oriental Christians) and their religion. A crusade that became infamous for Christian cannibalism of "Saracen" bodies during the siege at Ma'arrat al-Numan, after all, hardly set a hopeful early standard for humanization of the enemy. But successive crusades brought changes to this monologic, dehumanized view of the enemy. First we see a greater personalization of the enemy: Salahadin's recapture of Jerusalem in 1187, which prompted the Third Crusade led by Richard the Lion-hearted of England, made Salahadin a household name, and the subject of numerous depictions in European vernacular literature. His enduring significance for both crusading and chivalric culture, as we will see, had in no way faded by the time of King Louis's and Joinville's arrival in the Levant. With successive crusades, all after the first ending in military losses or the inability to secure Jerusalem,[2] we also see a coming apart of the grand, epic narrative that justified itself by God's will. Lack of success was, of course, already a sign of divine disfavor, but events such as those of the chaotic Fourth Crusade, in which Christians sacked Constantinople, an Eastern Christian capital, muddied the clarity of the crusading mission still further. At the same time, as this chapter will show, generations of commingling with the enemy in the Latin Kingdom and its environs brought greater everyday exposure to, interest in, and knowledge of Arab cultural life, setting the stage for an empirical ethnography such as Joinville's to emerge.

Jean de Joinville, seneschal and companion to King Louis IX during the Seventh Crusade, recorded his account of those events in his famous *Vie de Saint Louis*: "ce que je vi et oy par l'espace de sis anz, que je fu en sa compaignie ou pelerinaige d'outre mer" (what I saw and heard both in the course of the six years in which I was on pilgrimage in his company oversea) (10/167).[3] The text now serves as a rich primary source for the ill-fated Seventh Crusade in Egypt from 1248 to 1250 and Louis's stay in the Latin Kingdom thereafter, including the initial, easy capture of Damietta in June 1249; the bold decision to march on Cairo and ensuing difficulties in navigating the Nile and its tributaries on route; the stalemate and then siege at Mansourah, leading to widespread disease and starvation in Louis's camp; Louis's forced retreat back toward Damietta; his and his troops' surrender and capture in spring 1250; and the lengthy negotiations that followed for the full release of Louis himself and his troops, which, together with the fortification of the Frankish coast, occupied Louis in the Latin Kingdom until 1254. The text also captures a dramatic moment in Egyptian history, namely the end of the Ayyubid dynasty in Egypt: Joinville reports on the death of the Ayyubid sultan al-Salih in late 1249, the succession of his son Turan-shah to the throne, and the coup that rendered the Mamluks the new masters of Egypt.[4]

But the *Vie* can hardly be simply regarded as a crusader chronicle. Indeed its generic multiplicity and complexity is a leitmotif of its textual criticism.[5] For Joinville produced the *Vie* upon the request of Queen Jeanne de Navarre to write a book of "des saintes paroles et des bons faiz nostre roy saint Looys" (the pious sayings and the good deeds of our King Saint Louis) (2/163), thus invoking a second thirteenth-century genre, hagiography.[6] Add to these the facts of composition, that he had his observations written down as an octogenarian some fifty years after their occurrence, and a third genre, the memoir, emerges.[7] For some critics, the novel humanism of this hagiographical narrative moves the text toward biography,[8] while for others, Joinville's choice to locate himself in some 73 percent of his text's paragraphs[9] shifts it toward autobiography.[10] Finally, it must be said that if the *Vie* is overly focused on the author's self, it is also unusually focused on the other. As his readers discover, Joinville is often concerned to evoke the particularity of Levantine Muslim lifeways and perspectives, moving the text toward still another nascent medieval genre, ethnography.

Recent criticism has begun to attend to the nature of the *Vie*'s ethnographic dimensions, its many descriptions of and attentions to various Saracen groups encountered by Joinville during the crusade and a lengthy stay in the Latin Kingdom thereafter.[11] Joinville openly anticipates and engages his French public's desire for specialized knowledge about exotic life and customs of the Muslim inhabitants in Outremer, such as when he announces, regarding the palace of the sultan of Iconium, "Ferrais est cil qui tient les paveillons au soudanc et qui li nettoie ses maisons" (Now a *ferrais,* I would have you know, is a servant who looks after a sultan's pavilions and keeps his houses clean) (78/200). In the course of his crusader account, Joinville offers extensive ethnographic excurses on the pastoral lifeways of the Bedouins, the origin of the Assassin sect, the elaborate Mamluk system of recruitment, the origins of Islam's Shii-Sunni split, and the rise of the Mongol Empire, which occurred in Joinville's lifetime. Furthering the ethnographic function of his text is Joinville's decision to describe numerous aspects of Muslim cultural and religious belief in Muslim voice, citing the direct and indirect speech of Muslims in a variety of recorded dialogues with the other—negotiations, the swearing of oaths, and interviews. If it has long been observed that the *Vie de Saint Louis* is a particularly "conversational" text, it has not been observed enough that it rings with the voices of Latin Christendom's would-be enemies, the Muslims of the Holy Land and wider Levant.[12]

In what follows, I analyze the *Vie de Saint Louis*'s manifold representations of Muslim speech, custom, and perspective as evidence of past and continuing Franco-Islamic dialogues in the crusading theater. Joinville's text is woven with multiple instances of a shared set of Christian-Muslim cultural references, customs, and vocabulary testifying, from the vantage point of the Seventh Crusade, to decades of sustained and layered crusader contacts with the putative enemies, official crusader ideology notwithstanding. Such previous contacts in turn provide the foundation for continuing dialogues as cited in the

Vie, which, I will show, work to cast an unofficial "sideways glance," in Mikhail Bakhtin's terms, on official Latin Christian viewpoints on the Muslim other, opening the text to the unfamiliar and unsettling perspectives of that other and rendering the *Vie de Saint Louis* an ethnography composed in light of another's word. Current literary critical approaches to the *Vie de Saint Louis* and other texts of Eastern description have tended to view representations of Muslim encounter statically and one-directionally, as a mirror for European approaches to the East,[13] problematically leaving the European self untouched and unchanged by the other in the exchange. A two-way, dialogic approach to precolonial medieval European texts of Eastern encounter, such as I take in this chapter and in the book as a whole, insists rather on the inevitable reorientations of both self and other in the contact zone, finding in the *Vie* as much a record of the destabilizing effects of premodern Eastern encounters on the European self as a stable record of premodern approaches to the East. The decentering effects and affects of encounter in the *Vie* are visited primarily on the author-narrator himself, and Joinville's deictically anchored presence in the text ensures that we too, the *Vie*'s readers, are able to perceive these unsettling effects on his person. A dialogic reading such as this one insists, moreover, on the irreducibility of the other to a mere image or fantastic projection of the self, and also on the stubborn difference of the other's alternate perspectives and the ability of these to alter the textual environments in which they are placed. In taking this approach, my reading aligns itself with recent currents within postcolonial medievalist scholarship that similarly emphasize the impact of Europe's external and internal others on medieval European identity and canon formation.[14]

Outside the interests of vernacular literary criticism, a dialogic approach to the *Vie de Saint Louis* necessarily enters into debate with crusader historiography. For if Joinville's record of the Seventh Crusade is the culmination of decades of previous crusading contacts, historians of the Crusades are still far from consensus on the nature of those contacts and of Outremer society itself. Against an earlier generation of historians, and against some of the most basic and enduring myths of the Crusades, recent Crusades studies from a wide array of disciplines have been generating a picture of Outremer as a zone of everyday contact, connectivity, and dialogue with its Islamic Levantine neighbors, out of which new and syncretic cultural forms and understandings were produced—what we might call, in short, a medieval "contact zone." I begin with a brief sketch of Outremer society as a medieval contact zone, which will act as background and frame to my reading of the *Vie de Saint Louis*.

TOUCHED BY ISLAM: OUTREMER IN ITS LEVANTINE CONTEXT

Chroniclers and participants of the First Crusade forged a myth that far outlasted their bold settlement of a society "outre-mer," one that still holds considerable sway in popular culture and historiography of the Crusades: that of the Latin Kingdom as the repossession of Christian Holy space from the Infidel, and thereafter a continuing military and civilizational frontier against hostile Muslims—"a two-dimensional myth of conquest and battle," in Christopher Tyerman's words, without regard for "temporal realities, political compromises and social exchange."[15] This ideologically guided, epic narrative of crusading was one that medieval Europeans, looking at the Latin Kingdom from across the sea, expected to have reflected back to them, and already in the twelfth century, writers living in Outremer had to work to meet the expectation. The Latin Kingdom's most significant local historian, William of Tyre, bemoaned Latin difficulties in countering Salahadin's gathering strength in the 1170s as evidence of a diminishing battle readiness and religious devotion among successive Outremer inhabitants. Calling his fellow Latin Kingdom inhabitants "populus vero Orientalis"—people, in effect, of the Orient—William effectively mourns the effects of too many years of peace on the frontier character.[16] James of Vitry similarly derided easternized Latins for their newly acquired softness, for preferring "baths to battles."[17] A gap had clearly opened between the heroic founding fathers and those settlers who remained behind in the Latin Kingdom, in Ronnie Ellenblum's assessment, "to live, raise families, build homes, acquire estates, and not merely to die in the name of God,"[18] and between their narratives—epic clash of religions, on the one hand, and everyday interreligious accommodation and coexistence, on the other.

This discrepancy in medieval historical interpretation of the crusade finds its counterpart in modern historiographical debates between those who see the crusading expeditions and settlements primarily through the prism of Franco-Muslim hostility and those who see in the life of the Latin Kingdom evidence of significant Franco-Islamic interconnectivity, dialogue, and transculturation in spite of religious difference. The debate about the proper characterization of the Latin Kindom's relation to its subject and neighboring Muslims has its roots in the early twentieth century, when French historians posited the emergence of a unique synthesis in Outremer, a "Franco-Syrian nation." In this nation, Franks ruled over their Muslim subjects with tolerance and became themselves thoroughly Orientalized of custom—enjoying Oriental baths, adopting Arab textiles and dyes in fashion, sporting beards and hair scarves, decorating homes in Eastern styles, hiring dancing girls for entertainment, and adopting a Levantine Muslim diet.[19] In the 1950s, "segregationists" led by R. C. Smail and Joshua Prawer countered this harmonious picture: Prawer likened the Latin Kingdom to early European colonialism, while Smail asserted that a persistent state of war permeated the Latin settlements' relations with both internal and neighboring Muslims.[20] While the "segregationist" account offered an important corrective to the idealism of the French model, it risked the inadvertent reenactment of the crusader myth's frontier ideology, or its present-day, more sweeping Orientalist counterpart, the "clash of civilizations."

Scholarship of the Crusades has in recent years largely moved away from the segregationist account, toward an acknowledgment of Outremer's connectivity with its Levantine setting, to varying degrees, in nearly all major arenas of settlement life, from politics, to economy, to religion,[21] without, notably, any necessary idealization of the harmonious nature of such contacts. In trade, scholars have shown, the Latin Kingdom assumed a lucrative middle position between Europe and existing Islamic networks,[22] benefited from the broader Levantine trade,[23] and modeled its local coinage on the Muslim dinar of the Fatimids, complete with Arabic inscription and blessings to Allah.[24] Politically, the notion that the Latin Kingdom was engaged in a permanent state of war with its neighbors has come under substantive challenge and revision by prominent European scholars of the crusade and their Islamic counterparts, who have shown, rather, that for most of the Latin Kingdom's duration realpolitik, local alliances, and unsteady coexistence typified relations between the Latin East and its Muslim neighbors.[25] The practical business of everyday commerce, in any case, seems to have proceeded irrespective of states of war or truce between the Latin Kingdom and its neighbors, as attested by Ibn Jubayr, the twelfth-century Andalusian visitor to the Latin Kingdom: "One of the astonishing things that is talked of is that though the fires of discord burn between the two parties, Muslim and Christian, two armies of them may meet and dispose themselves in battle array, and yet Muslim and Christian travelers will come and go between them without interference."[26] Ibn Jubayr's point is underscored by the fact that he is writing at the peak of Salahadin's jihadist countercrusade in the 1180s, when Franco-Muslim tensions were running high. The distinctly syncretic nature of the Latin Kingdom's religious life has also been widely remarked on.[27] A variety of sources attest to unofficial syncretic and accommodational religious practices. Among these sources are the memoirs of Usamah ibn-Munqidh (1095–1188), a member of a patrician family in Shayzar in northern Syria who had frequent diplomatic and informal contacts with Franks during his lifetime. Usamah's account of a certain unpleasant encounter he had while praying at the al-Aqsa Mosque in Jerusalem testifies not only to forms of everyday accommodation between worshippers sharing holy sites in cities like Jerusalem but also to the palpable tensions that such accommodations could provoke. Writing with characteristic wit and high cultural self-regard, Usamah begins by making his oft-quoted observation, "Everyone who is a fresh emigrant from the Frankish lands is ruder in character than those who have become acclimatized and have held long association with the Moslems." He illustrates by anecdote:

> Whenever I visited Jerusalem I always entered the Aqsa Mosque, besides which stood a small mosque which the Franks had converted into a church. When I used to enter the Aqsa Mosque, which was occupied by the Templars [*al-dawiyyah*], who were my friends, the Templars would evacuate the little adjoining mosque so that I might pray in it. One day I entered this mosque, repeated the first formula, "Allah is great," and stood up in the act of praying, upon which one of the Franks rushed on me, got hold of me and turned my face eastward saying, "This is the way thou shouldst pray!" A group of Templars hastened to him, seized him and repelled him from me. I resumed my prayer. The same man, while the others were otherwise busy, rushed once more on me and turned my face eastward, saying, "This is the way thou shouldst pray!" The Templars again came into him and expelled him. They apologized to me, saying "This is a stranger who only recently arrived from the land of the Franks and he has never before seen anyone praying except eastward." There upon I said to myself, "I have had enough prayer."[28]

Local Templars here play the role of the more civilized, acclimated Franks, as well as Usamah's "friends," voluntarily extending him praying privileges at the Temple of the Lord, so creating an informal dual-use religious site out of the Temple. Similarly, in Acre, Ibn Jubayr attests, part of a converted mosque was reserved for use by Muslims;[29] in Homs, the largest church was used by both Christians and Muslims in the eleventh century,[30] and in Hebron, Jews and Muslims were permitted, on payment of a sum, to worship at the Tombs of the Patriarchs inside a Frankish cathedral.[31]

Finally, the Latin Kingdom's material culture and arts have provided scholars with the most ostensible evidence of syncretism across East-West, Christian and Islamic tradition and theme.[32] In the "minor arts" and in manuscript illumination, art historians have been pressed to account for the production and consumption of art objects of evident Islamo-Christian hybridity, such as Christian manuscript illuminations featuring Muslims, and a range of thirteenth-century Islamic domestic and luxury art pieces in metalwork, glasswork, and pottery featuring overtly Christian themes and images.[33] Against a former view of these hybrid arts as atypical curiosity or problem pieces, scholars like Maria Georgopoulou have insisted that such pieces are "indicative of a far wider production than previously thought,"[34] likely aimed at a range of local consumers including Franks, local Oriental Christians, elite Muslims, crusaders, and European visitors,[35] and emerging from heterogeneous Levantine sites of production that "more often than not transcended ethnic or religious boundaries."[36]

These recent Crusades studies, emerging from a range of disciplines, overturn the easy categorization and appropriation of the Latin Kingdom as a "European" space, and urge its revision as a space interconnected with its wider Islamic-Levantine setting, a view eclipsed by the founding myth of the Crusades. If the belief in this official image of the Crusades was common among participants of the First Crusade and later recruits from Europe, it was harder to find, in Usamah's words, among Frankish immigrants long acclimatized to life in the East. In an analogous fashion, while the founding crusading myth is amply attested in the chronicles of the First Crusade, it is harder to locate in later generations of crusade chronicle, in which it becomes increasingly diluted and uncertain,[37] culminating in the record of dialogic, cross-confessional encounters we find in *Vie de Saint Louis*. A text of war, the *Vie de Saint Louis* indeed attests to the surprisingly manifold possibilities of engaged intercultural and religious dialogue in the least ideal, and most unexpected, of human circumstances.

RECORD OF A HYBRID PAST

Joinville, we know, accompanied Louis IX during not just the crusade in Egypt but also for a further, negotiation-filled four-year stay in the Latin Kingdom's capital of Acre, providing him ample opportunity to observe the modes of religious convergence and cultural interanimation we have been surveying. While we might expect to find little representation of cross-cultural encounter during Joinville's depictions of the military phase of the campaign, we instead find plenty at this opening juncture. Indeed it is here that readers see the result of decades of Frankish-Islamic engagement through previous crusader contacts in the existence of a working, syncretic Islamo-Christian culture on the ground. Frankish leaders from prior crusades have, according to Joinville, entered the Arab cultural vernacular. The reputation of Richard the Lion-hearted, English leader of the Third Crusade, is so fearsome locally that Arab mothers discipline their children with threats of his reappearance: "Taisiez-vous, vez-ci le roy Richart!" (Be quiet . . . King Richard's here) (44/183, trans. adapted). Frederick II, king of Sicily and Holy Roman emperor, enjoys apparent esteem in the Levant. The grandson of the great patron of Arabic knowledge in twelfth-century Sicily, Roger II (under whose patronage al-Idrisi wrote his remarkable geography, *Kitab al-Roger*, or the *Book of Roger*), Frederick, like Roger before him, read and spoke Arabic, and continued his tradition of patronage for Islamic learning, especially in the sciences. But local Egyptians and Levantines knew him through crusader contact, as the leader of the Sixth Crusade who parlayed with the Egyptian sultan al-Kamil for five months and so negotiated the peaceful transfer of Jerusalem to Christian hands without any military engagement.[38] Frederick exploited the cosmopolitanism of his Mozarabic Sicilian milieu to good effect during these negotiations, garnering respect among the local population for his tolerance, and knowledge, of Arabic and Islam; he even consulted al-Kamil on questions of Islamic philosophy, geometry, and mathematics.[39]

References to Frederick II pepper Joinville's narrative. While in captivity, Joinville learns personally of the benefits of being affiliated with the beloved emperor. Asked directly by the admiral holding him about his relation to the emperor, he answered, "et je li respondi que je entendoie que madame ma mere estoit sa cousine germainne; et il me dist que de tant m'en amoit-il miex" (I had reason to believe that my lady mother was his first cousin; whereupon the admiral remarked that he loved me all the more for it) (178/245). During the military campaign, Joinville notes hybrid insignias borne on the armor of Fakhr ad-Din, the Ayyubid sultan's vizier, that combine the arms of the sultanates of the East with the most powerful titular head of the West: "En sa baniere portoit les armes l'empereour qui l'avoit fait chevalier. Sa baniere estoit bandée: et l'une des bandes estoient les armes l'empereour qui l'avoit fait chevalier; en l'autre estoient les armes le soudanc de Halape; en l'autre bande estoient les au soudanc de Babiloine" (On his banner, which was barred, he bore on one bar the arms of the emperor [i.e., Frederick] who had made him a knight, on another the arms of the Sultan of Aleppo, and on the third the arms of the Sultan of Cairo) (108–110/214]). Frederick II had knighted the vizier between 1226 and 1229 during the negotiations of the Sixth Crusade, at which Fakhr al-Din represented al-Kamil.[40] (The knighting of the sultan's vizier by a Frankish leader does not stand alone in crusader lore: Richard was reputed to have knighted Salahadin's nephew, the son of al-Adil, during the Third Crusade, and numerous stories of Salahadin's knighting by Christian knights circulated throughout Europe in the twelfth to thirteenth centuries in such chronicles as the *Itinerarium Peregrinorum* [c. 1191–92], the pseudo-*Ernoul*, and the *L'Ordene de Chevalerie*.)[41]

Years of crusade had also established certain uses and customs of waging war in the Holy Land among the crusaders as well as between crusaders and Muslims. Joinville describes one of "les bones coustumes anciennes" (92), or good old customs, the division of the spoils of a captured city. Having captured Damietta, King Louis hands over the spoils to a certain Jean de Valery to apportion as he thinks best; Jean de Valery protests that to do so would run counter to "les bonnes coustumes de la Sainte-Terre" (92), according to which:

> Quant l'on prent les cités des ennemis, des biens que l'on treuve dedans, li roys en doit avoir le tiers, et li pelerin en doivent avoir les dous pars. Et ceste coustume tint bien li roys Jehans quant il prist Damiete; et ainsi comme li ancien dient, li roy de Jerusalem qui furent devant le roy Jehan, tindrent bien ceste coustume. (92)

> (Whenever a city belonging to the enemy is captured the king takes a third of all the goods found in it, and the other Crusaders two thirds. This custom was duly respected by King Jean [of Jerusalem] when he took Damietta [in the Fifth Crusade], and also, as old chroniclers tell us, by all the kings of Jerusalem before his day.) (207)

When the king institutes his own, new way, "mainte gent se tindrent mal apaié de ce que li roys deffit les bones coustumes anciennes" (many people were displeased that his Majesty had chosen to ignore such a good old custom) (92/207). Other crusading customs include "la coustume entre les Crestiens et les Sarrazins, que quant li roys ou li soudans meurt, cil qui sont en messagerie, soit en paennime ou en crestientei, sont prison et esclave" (the custom between Christians and Saracens that whenever a king or a sultan dies those who are acting as envoys at the time, whether it be in a Christian or pagan land, are held as prisoners and slaves) (198/255).

Many of the "old" Islamo-Frankish customs of the Latin Kingdom recorded in the *Vie*, then, center around or emerge from contacts of war. Indeed it is through military campaigning that Joinville encounters some of his ethnographic objects of description, such as the Bedouins, whose nomadism, clearly drawn from developmental anthropology (see Chapter 1), Joinville sketches only upon their raid of crusader camps: "Li Beduyn ne demeurent en villes, ne en cités, n'en chastiaus, mais gisent adès aus chans" (These people do not live in villages, or cities, or castles, but sleep always out in the open fields) (138/227). But the *Vie* also reflects notable examples of hybrid customs outside the theater of war. While in Caesarea after the war, Joinville refers to Frankish modes of living conducted "selonc la coustume dou païs" (according to customs of that land), by which we find he means the Islamic Levant, where the knights in his battalion "mangeoient li uns devant l'autre . . . et séoient sur nates à terre" (ate facing each other, seated on mats on the ground) (276/291). The daily customs of the Latin Kingdom in Caesarea have blended with those of the Islamic Levant to create customs foreign to European eyes. A process of transculturation has taken place in the Latin Kingdom's past that we are here left to imagine. Elsewhere in the *Vie de Saint Louis*, however, Joinville provides a window into processes of Franco-Islamic improvisation and syncretism in the thirteenth-century Levant to which he was witness and participant.

IMPROVISATION AND TRANSCULTURATION IN THE CRUSADING CONTACT ZONE

King Louis engaged in substantive diplomacy with local actors from 1250 to 1254, a period in which he acted as all but official ruler of the Latin Kingdom from its capital in Acre, negotiating for the release of his remaining troops and working to shore up the defenses of the crusader coastal cities. The king's diplomacy with Mamluks as well as their Ayyubid enemies in Damascus resulted in a fifteen-year truce with the former and a two-year truce with the latter.[42] In this time, Louis also received envoys from the legendary leader of the so-called Assassins or Isma'ilis, the Old Man of the Mountain. As Joinville reports, the Old Man's envoys paid King Louis court, leaving him a number of items of tribute, including their lord's shirt, "comme la chemise est plus près dou cors que nus autres vestemens" (as the shirt is closer to the body than any other garment) and "son anel . . . et li manda que par son anel respousoit-il le roy; que il vouloit que dès lors en avant fussent tuit un" (his own ring . . . with this the message that by this ring he joined himself in close alliance with the king, wishing from that time onward that they should be united, as if they were wedded to each other) (250/278). In addition to partaking in a symbolic political marriage, King Louis and the Old Man traded costly gifts, a form of cultural exchange now coming into view as a fruitful source of study by art historians:[43]

> Entre les autres joiaus que il envoia au roy, li envoia un oliphant de cristal mout bien fait, et une beste que l'on appelle orafle, de cristal aussi, pommes de diverses manieres de cristal, et jeuz de table et de eschiez; et toutes ces choses estoient fleuretées de ambre, et estoit l'ambres liez sur le cristal à beles vignetes de bon or fin. . . . Li roys renvoia ses messaiges au Vieil, et li renvoia grant foison de joiaus, escarlates, coupes d'or et frains d'argent. (250)

> (Among other costly gifts the Old Man sent the king he included a very well-made figure of an elephant, another of an animal called a giraffe, and apples of different kinds, all of which were of crystal; with these he sent gaming boards and sets of chessmen. All these objects were profusely decorated with little flowers made of amber, which were attached to the crystal by means of delicately fashioned clips of good fine gold. . . . The king sent the envoys back to the Old Man, and with them a great quantity of jewels, pieces of scarlet cloth, cups of gold, and horses' bits of silver.) (278–79)

These gifts echo an earlier gift exchange between Louis and envoys sent to him from Mongolia,[44] who visit Louis in Cyprus before the launch of the crusade: "Et par les messaiges, envoia li roys au roy des Tartarins une tente faite en la guise d'une chapelle. . . . Et li roys, pour veoir se il les pourroit atraire à nostre créance, fist entaillier en la dite chapelle, par ymaiges, l'Anonciacion Nostre-Dame et touz les autres poins de la foy" (By these men his Majesty sent the King of the Tartars a tent arranged for use as a Chapel. . . . Moreover, in the hope of making our religion appear attractive to the Tartars, the king had ordered for this chapel a series of little figures carved in stone, representing the Annunciation of our Lady, and all other subjects relating to the Christian faith) (74/198). The envoys in turn bear with them a letter conveying Guyuk Khan's wishes for Louis's success against their common adversaries in the Near East, a contact that encourages Louis to send the first of his missions to Mongolia, led by the Dominican Andrew of Longjumeau. Word of the Tartars' (in fact, Guyuk's widow's) response to the mission—demand for submission as tributaries to the khan—reaches Louis while he is in Caesarea. Joinville thereupon relates his "bitter regret" of the mission, but Louis is moved by news of a Mongol prince's conversion to Christianity to launch another mission before leaving the Latin Kingdom, that of William of Rubruck in 1253.

These diplomatic meetings show how formal negotiations can lead to new ideas borne of cultural cross-pollination and contact—new words ("a kind of animal called a giraffe" [*orafle*]), new artistic techniques ("flowers attached to crystal . . . by means of delicately fashioned clips of find gold"), new strategies of engagement (such as mission), and new techniques suited for missionizing nomadic populations (a movable tent-chapel). A form of cultural exchange in themselves, Louis's negotiations reveal the work of improvisation, adaptation, and recombination typical of cultural contact zones.[45] The unpredictability and novelty of heterogeneous cultural collisions in the contact zone can be felt even by their participants, as is illustrated by two episodes describing circumstances around the release of Louis's captive lords.

In negotiating ransom terms with the Mamluk emirs, King Louis asks for assurance that upon payment of five hundred thousand livres in French currency, his captive forces would be set free. Having received such assurance, Louis relays that he would willingly pay the ransom for release of his people, and, moreover, surrender Damietta for his own person, "car il n'estoit pas teix que il se deust desraimbre à deniers" (since it was not fitting for a man of his high rank to purchase his liberty with money) (186/250). "When all this was reported to the sultan," Joinville continues, "he exclaimed: 'Par ma foy! larges est li Frans quant il n'a pas barguignié sur si grant somme de deniers. Or li alés dire, fist li soudans, que je li doing cent mile livres pour la reançon paier'" (By Allah! this Frank is a very generous-minded man not to have haggled over paying so great a sum! So go and tell him I'll let him off a hundred thousand *livres* of the ransom money) (186/250).

Haggling is, it appears, culturally mandated even in ransoms for life in the Levant. And when the time comes for Joinville himself and a number of lords to be released at last from captivity, Joinville recounts conditions of release according to which their captors' hospitality is nonnegotiable:

> Aussi comme Diex vout, qui n'oublie pas les siens, il fu acordei, entour soleil couchant, que nous seriens delivrei. Lors nous ramena l'on, et mist l'on nos quatre galies à terre. Nous requeismes que on nous lessast aler. Il nous dirent que non feroient jusques à ce que nous eussiens mangié: 'Car ce seroit honte aus amiraus, se vous partiés de nos prisons à jeun.' Et nous requeismes que on nous donnast la viande, et nous mangeriens.... Les viandes que il nous donnerent, ce furent begniet de fourmaiges qui estoient roti au soleil, pour ce que li ver n'i venissent, et œf dur cuit de quatre jours ou de cinc; et pour honnour de nous, on les avoit fait peindre par dehors de diverses colours. (204)

> (But God, who does not forget His own, so willed that, round about sunset, it was agreed that we should be released. So we were brought back and our four galleys drawn up alongside the bank. We demanded to be allowed to go, but the Saracens said they would not let us leave until we had had a meal, for, said they, 'Our emirs would be shamed if you left our prisons fasting.' So we told them to bring us some food, and we would eat. The food they gave us consisted of cheese fritters, baked in the sun to keep them free from maggots, and hard-boiled eggs cooked three or four days before, the shells of which, in our honour, had been painted in various colors.) (257)

Each episode couches stereotypically Arab cultural customs—bargaining, hospitality—within a captivity negotiation, a juxtaposition that illustrates the unlikely cultural collisions of contact zones and makes humor out of the materials of ethnography and war.

Perhaps the most unexpected plot turn takes place upon the assassination of the last Ayyubid sultan, Turanshah, by the Mamluks. Apparently, the Mamluk emirs are so impressed with Louis himself that "dès que li soudans fu occis, en fist venir les estrumens au soudanc devant la tente le roy, et dist-on au roy que li amiral avoient eu grant vouloir et consoil de li faire soudanc de Babiloine" (Very shortly after the sultan's death the insignia of his office had been placed before the king's tent, and he had been informed that the emirs, having met in council, had expressed a great desire to make him Sultan of Egypt) (200/255), Joinville relates. The offer does not materialize of course, and historians now take it as a joke.[46] Louis, however, treats the offer with his characteristic seriousness: "Et il me demanda se je cuidoie que il eust pris le royaume de Babiloine, se il li eussent presentei. Et je li dis que il eust mout fait que fous, á ce que il avoient lour signour occis; et il me dist que vraiement il ne l'eust mie refusei" (The king asked me if I thought he would have taken this kingdom if it had been offered to him. I told him that if he had done so he would have acted very foolishly, seeing that these emirs had killed their former lord. He told me, however, that in fact he would not have refused it) (200/255). If we must strain to imagine Louis as the next sultan of Egypt, as if to assist the imagination, Joinville offers us the following visual aid. On his way to Christian Acre, Louis "ne trouva onques que sa gent li eussent riens appareillié, ne lit, ne robes" (had found that his people had got nothing ready for him, neither bedding or clothing) (220/265). So the king dresses himself in clothes given by the sultan, "de samit noir, forrei de vair et de griz; et y avoit grant foison de noiaus touz d'or" (of black satin, lined with miniver and grey squirrel's fur and adorned with a vast quantity of buttons, all of pure gold) (220/265).

Other instances of cultural dialogue in the *Vie* have a distinctly more serious edge, revealing the way in which the *Vie*'s many citations of the voices of the other work to cast an unofficial sideways glance on the Latin Christian perspectives with which they are brought into dynamic dialogue. In doing so, they move the text beyond a single-point Latin Christian perspective into the unscripted possibilities and dangers of writing in light of another's word. It is to the examination of these cited Muslim voices, and their material effects on their textual and social environment, that I turn in conclusion.

THE CRUSADES VIEWED WITH "A SIDEWAYS GLANCE": THE VOICE OF THE OTHER IN THE *VIE DE SAINT LOUIS*

Unlike the gaze-filled terrain of William of Rubruck's *Journey*, Joinville's *Vie de Saint Louis* provides comparably little narration of the operation of gazes of either the self or the other amid crusade. Joinville's attention to the gaze is focused in the early military phase of the crusade. The following excerpt, taken from the description of landing in Egypt, exemplifies a pervasive storytelling technique in this section of his narrative:

> Si tost comme il nous virent à terre, il vindrent, ferant des esperons, vers nous. Quant nous les veismes venir, nous fichames les pointes de nos escus ou sablon, et le fust de nos lances ou sablon et les pointes

vers aus. Maintenant que il virent ainsi comme pour aler par mi les
ventres, il tournerent ce devant darieres et s'en fouirent. (86)

(No sooner had they seen us land than they charged toward us, spur-
ring hotly. As for us, when we saw them coming, we struck the sharp
ends of our shields into the sand and fixed our lances firmly in the
ground with the points towards the enemy. But the moment they saw
the lances about to pierce their bellies, they wheeled round and fled.)
(203)

Here Joinville relates military confrontation in the form of reciprocal, incomplete gazes exchanged between enemy forces. Elisabeth Gaucher has aptly described the readerly effects of this narrative strategy: Joinville "imposes his own vision of events, often partial, and we live the point of view of a combatant engaged in a complex strategy, who cannot grasp it in its totality; above all, the crusade proceeds according to a series of micro-stories, in which the lighting moves from one detail to another, without a general perspective."[47] Rather than a distant gaze from an impersonal vantage point untethered to the frame of description, we have here a series of personal, engaged, partial, and incomplete perspectives emanating from an eyewitnessing author viewing the scene as its central participant. Joinville's gazes—incomplete, subjective, and grounded in deictic self-reference—are much like Gerald's then, and we can assume that like Gerald, his ethnographic poetics were shaped by the historiographical tradition to which he belonged, and which similarly emphasized the accrual of "impartiality" only through multiple, partial gazes.[48]

What we cannot anticipate from the above description is the extent to which Joinville's ethnographic perspectives will dialogize and fuse with those of the Muslim other in his crusading account—the extent to which he will narrate an ethnography composed in light of another's word. For this dialogic ethnography emerges only as military engagement slides into more intimate contacts between self and other in the text, including lengthy diplomatic negotiations and more informal forms of communication between Europeans on crusade and Muslims. A text that privileges and attends to conversation over and against visual apprehension (in a direct contrast with William of Rubruck's representative mode) would seem to preclude further study of its ethnographic gazes. But as Bakhtin reminds us in "Discourse in the Novel," words, too, bear gazes, or "ideological points of view, approaches, directions and values."[49] In particular, heteroglossic utterance, or the voice of the other with which Joinville's text is replete, casts its own unofficial, decentering "view" or rather sideways glance upon official speech wherever and whenever the two come into dynamic contact.[50] In such linguistic contact zones, official discourse becomes dialogized, infused with the difference of the other's voice—as does human subjectivity, thus shifting perception and identity[51]—making possible, as we will see, new and unscripted modes of ethnographic thinking and writing, as well as a new, and sometimes uneasy, self-consciousness.

The disorienting effects of heteroglossic utterance and worldview on official European perspectives and subjectivity are dramatized throughout Joinville's text, but are especially visible in the dramatic center of the book, describing the capture, captivity, and eventual negotiated release of the crusader lords, including Joinville. In one significant citation of the other's word and worldview, Joinville elaborates upon the swearing of oaths on which the truce with Louis was to be sealed by the emirs:

> Li sairement que li amiral devoient faire au roy furent devisié, et furent tel: que se il ne tenoient au roy les couvenances, que il fussent aussi honni comme cil qui par son pechié aloit en pelerinaige à Mahomet, à Maques, sa teste descouverte. . . . Li tiers sairemens fu teix: que se il ne tenoient les couvenances au roy, que il fussent aussi honni comme li Sarrazins qui manjue la char de porc. Li roys prist les sairemens desus diz des amiraus à grei, parce que maistres Nicholes d'Acre, qui savoit le sarrazinnois, dist que il ne les pooient plus forz faire selonc lour loi. (196)

> (The oaths which the emirs were to swear to the king were arranged, and were to this effect: that if they did not observe their covenant with the king they should be held as dishonoured as a man who, in penance for a sin he has committed, goes on a pilgrimage to Mahomet of Mecca, with his head uncovered. . . . Their third oath was as follows: that if they broke faith with the king, they were to incur the same disgrace as a Saracen who has eaten pork. The king was satisfied with these oaths I have just mentioned, because Nicole d'Acre, a priest who knew their language, assured him that according to their law they could have devised no oaths that were stronger or more binding.) (254; trans. adapted)

Joinville here not only explains, contextualizes, and domesticates these Muslim oaths to augment his reader's ethnographic knowledge of the other, but in the process of decoding them, he necessarily validates them as part of a religious belief system with its own integrity and logic.[52]

Other instances of interfaith interaction indicate even more conscious and overt Christian dialogue with the Muslim faith, such as when Joinville tells how Brother Yves Le Breton, a friar familiar with Arabic, "found a book by the head of the Old Man's bed in which were written many of the things our Lord had said to Saint Peter while he was on earth": "Et freres Yves li dist: 'Ha! pour Dieu, sire, lisiés souvent ce livre; car ce sont trop bones paroles.' Et il dist que si fesoit-il: 'Car j'ai mout chier mon signour saint Pere'" ("Ah! My lord," said friar Yves, "For God's sake read this book very often, for these are very good words." The Old Man replied that he did in fact read it very often, "Because," said he, "Saint Peter is very dear to me") (252/279, trans. adapted). The scene provocatively plots Latin Christians' collision with the central role of Christian saints within Islam, an opening of perspective that is met with evident surprise ("Ah!") by Brother Yves and in all likelihood by Joinville's audience back home. But the apparent opening is followed by feelings of unease, for if Brother Yves believes he has through his discovery identified a point of entry into a foreign religion whose adherents may be more easily converted on that basis, his error is soon pointed out to him: the point of entry is already occupied by Islamic thought, Saint Peter already dear to the Old Man, Islam already in dialogue with Christian belief. This subtle lack of alignment in perspectives turns to more overt unease when the Old Man goes on to place Saint Peter within an apparent (if garbled) theory of the transmigration of the souls of the prophets.[53] The friar attempts to correct the unorthodox and "mistaken" belief to no avail ("but the Old Man would not listen"),[54] and the religious encounter that began with the hopeful discovery of shared saints ends on the sobering note of the stubborn alterity of the other's perspective. Perhaps the sole by-product of the exchange for Brother Yves is the difficult self-recognition of his mistaken assumptions, an opening of Latin Christian perspective to its own limitations.[55]

What is clear is that such unofficial, sideways glances of the other upon the self effect shifts in Europeans' self-perceptions around their own beliefs. Reporting on the Bedouin belief in the preordained moment of death, Joinville chooses to couch the Bedouin belief in an analogy to certain Christians he knows: "J'ai veu en cest païs, puis que je reving d'Outremer, aucuns desloiaus crestiens qui tenoient la loy des Beduyns, et disoient que nulz ne pouoit morir qu'à son jour" (In our own country, since I returned from the land oversea, I have come across certain disloyal Christians who follow the Bedouin faith in holding that no man can die except on the appointed day) (140/228). Joinville here dissipates the distance of alien viewpoints held by certain Muslims "oversea" by finding the same opinions in nearby Christians at home. The fact that he discovers such local resonances with Muslim faith after his return from crusade further suggests a subtle shift in his cognitive horizons through his personal experiences and exposure to Muslims abroad.

That Joinville himself is changed, his subjectivity shifted, through contact with the other abroad is nowhere more suggested than in his narration of his own dramatic capture and release at the center of the *Vie*'s crusade account, on which I focus for the remainder of the chapter. The events begin with his ship's seizure and capture by the sultan's men, led by Turanshah, son of the recently deceased al-Salih, himself soon to be assassinated in a Mamluk coup. Just as his ship is boarded by the enemy, "Lors m'envoia Diex un Sarrazin qui estoit de la terre l'empereour" (God sent me a Saracen from the Emperor of Germany's land) (174/243), an abettor who swims across the stream and boards Joinville's ship. He tells Joinville that he must act quickly if he wants to live and directs him to jump across onto the prow of the adjacent ship, throwing him a literal lifeline. Once on board the enemy ship, Joinville is thrown to the ground and nearly killed by some 280 men, "car cil qui m'eust occis cuidast estre honorez. Et cis Sarrazins me tenoit touz jours embracié, et crioit: 'Cousin le roi!'" (for any man who killed me would have thought to win honour by it. But the Saracen still held me in his arms, and cried: "He's the king's cousin!") (176/244), thus saving the author's life a second time. From this period henceforth, Joinville refers to the man as "mon Sarrazin," my Saracen, with what we may deem both affection and a possessiveness born of desperate circumstance, marking another shift in Joinville's perspective as a result of this dramatic encounter.

Once in captivity, Joinville is dining with the admiral of the galleys from which he has just been rescued (having told him of his relation, however distant, to Frederick II, as we saw, and been warmly received for it), when another scene of provocative cultural encounter takes place:

> Tandis que nous mangiens, il fist venir un bourgois de Paris devant nous. Quant li bourgois fu venus, il me dist: "Sire, que faites-vous?" "Que faiz-je donc?" feiz-je. "En non Dieu," fist-il, "vous mangiez char au vendredi!" Quant j'oï ce, je boutai m'escuele arieres. Et il demanda à mon Sarrazin pourquoy je avoie ce fait, et il li dist; et li

amiraus li respondi que jà Diex ne m'en sauroit mal grei, puisque je
ne l'avoie fait à escient. (178)

(While we were dining he summoned a citizen of Paris to appear
before us. When the man arrived he said to me: "My lord, what are
you doing?" "Why, what can I be doing?" said I. "In God's name,"
he replied, "You're eating meat on a Friday." As soon as I heard this
I put my bowl behind me. The admiral [emir] asked my Saracen why
I had acted thus, so he told him. The admiral replied that God would
not hold what I had done against me, seeing that I had not realized I
was doing wrong.) (245)

Joinville's unfamiliar surroundings have no doubt distracted him from his usual practices. What is striking is his narrative framing of the vignette, which ends by casting the Muslim view on his actions, that is, the intention of the faithful is what will be affirmed in God's eyes. Joinville frames the scene such that his actions are ultimately not glossed, or interpreted, but *heteroglossed* and defamiliarized—and indeed the alternative viewpoint of the other takes its place as the point of Joinville's story.

This scene is shortly followed by another of singular dramatic force and dialogic resonance:

Le dymanche après, li amiraus me fist descendre et tous les autres
prisonniers qui avoient estei pris en l'yaue, sur la rive dou flum. Ende-
mentieres que on trehoit mon signour Jehan, mon bon prestre, hors de
lat soute de la galie, il se pausma; et on le tua et le geta l'on ou flum.
Son clerc, qui se pasma aussi . . . fu mors, et le geta l'on ou flum. Tan-
dis que l'on descendoit les autres malades des galies où il avoient estei
en prison, il y avoit gens sarrasins appareilliés, les espées toutes nues,
que ceus qui chéoient, il les occioient et getoient touz ou flum. (178)

(On the following Sunday, by the emir's orders, I and all the others
taken prisoner on the water were landed on the river bank. While
they were taking Jean, my good priest, out of the hold of the galley,
he fainted. The Saracens killed him and threw his body into the river.
His clerk . . . also fainted . . . they killed him too, and cast his body
into the stream. While the rest of the sick were being landed from
the galleys in which they had been held prisoner, there were Saracens
standing by, with their swords ready drawn, to deal with all those
who fell as they had dealt with my priest.) (245)

Joinville's response to these direst of circumstances shows that he has kept his wits about him: "Je lour fis dire, à mon Sarrazin, que il me sembloit que ce n'estoit pas bien fait; car c'estoit contre les enseigne-mens Salehadin, qui dit que l'on ne devoit nul home occire, puis que on li avoit donnei à mangier de son pain et de son sel" (I sent my Saracen to tell them that I thought this a very wrong thing to do, because it was contrary to the teachings of Saladin, who has said you should never kill a man once you had shared your bread and salt with him) (178, 180/245). Joinville is citing from the lessons of crusader history: specifically, those of the famous Rainald of Chatillon episode of the Third Crusade, which takes place directly after the Battle of Hattin in 1187 at which Frankish forces led by Rainald and then-king of Jerusalem Guy of Lusignan were cut off from their water supply and encircled by fire set by Salahadin's troops. Salahadin, having captured both Rainald and Guy and had them brought to his tent, freely offers water to the thirsty Guy, but refuses the offering to Rainald. He in no way means to spare the life of the one who had so often used his position at al-Kerak to harass Muslim caravans passing between Syria and Egypt, plundering goods and imprisoning pilgrims in spite of existing truces.[56] But if Joinville here precisely recalls and applies the potentially lifesaving teachings, and indeed customs,[57] of the other at this desperate moment, his interlocutor, the admiral, is not so exacting or compassionate an interpreter of the same teachings. The admiral responds to Joinville's plea by claiming "que ce n'estoient pas home qui vausissent riens, pour ce que il ne se pooient aidier pour les maladies que il avoient" (that the men in question did not count, because the sickness from which they suffered had left them incapable of doing anything to help themselves) (180/245–46), that is, they were as good as dead anyway. Joinville continues, in a still more gripping passage:

> Il me fist amener mes mariniers devant moy, et me dist que il estoient tuit renoié; et je li dis que il n'eust jà fiance en aus; car aussi tost comme il nous avoient lessiez, aussi tost les lairoient-il, se il véoient ne lour point ne lour lieu. Et li amiraus me fist response tel, que il s'acordoit à moy; que Salehadins disoit que on ne vit onques de mauvais crestien bon sarrazin, ne de mauvais sarrazin bon crestien. (180)
>
> (He subsequently had all my crew brought before me, and told me that every one of them had renounced their faith. I warned him not to put any trust in them, for just as lightly as they had left our side so they would leave his, if they saw either time or opportunity to do so. The admiral replied that he agreed with me, for as Saladin used to say, one never saw a bad Christian become a good Saracen, nor a bad Saracen become a good Christian.) (246)

There is much to be said about this rich exchange. Having been presented with the case of his crew's total conversion (under circumstances not described in the text), Joinville again replies levelheadedly, with an argument of analogy and similarity of plight: just as they have done to us, so too they'll do to you (*aussi tost . . . aussi tost*). The admiral then answers Joinville's mirroring analogy by offering a second citation of the sayings of Salahadin, partaking in a veritable contest in the sayings of a mutually revered figure from the not-so-distant crusading past. And in a dialogue of verbal forms, the admiral has duplicated and answered Joinville's mirror with one of his own. The proverb he cites yokes *bon Sarrazin* and *bon Chretien* together in likeness and value, setting them off against the less than faithful of their respective faiths—very close indeed to valuing the faithful of either faith as equally good (because equally faith-ful) as the faithful of the other, an ecumenical outlook anticipating that found in another text of the Mediterranean contact zone over which Salahadin presides, *Decameron* 1.3. Indeed, regarding as it does Muslims and Christians in much the same way and from the same perspective ("on ne vit . . . "), Salahadin's proverb is appropriable by either side of a Christian-Muslim debate. In the exchange between the admiral and Joinville, the voice of Salahadin reemerges to fill a space that is, uncannily, neither that of the other nor of the self, but one constituted precisely in their relation, in their hybridizing zone of contact. Just who is casting the other's glance and who that of the self is, finally, here impossible to say. The dialogue amid crusade resolves into a single image of agreement and identity, Muslim and Christian perspectives mirroring and mirrored in each other in a way wholly unanticipated and unscripted by crusading ideology. Through such instances, Joinville's text does not merely cite heteroglossia but becomes heteroglossic, other to itself, allowing the reader to take, if momentarily, a sideways glance on the official, prescribed agendas of the text: those of narrating a crusade waged by a saintly king from a Christian perspective and of reporting on the religious or ethnic differences of the Levant from a European one. In this late medieval crusade chronicle cum ethnography, the self-ascribed agenda of describing the differences of the other gives way to something new: an ethnography composed in light of another's word that dramatically stages the heteroglossic embodiment of the other's worldview and the heterodox citation of his teachings, thus doubling and subverting the monologues and monovision of official crusading ideology. In the context of crusader ethnography, perhaps there is no more subversive an image than seeing the other reflecting back oneself in the mirror.

And yet, as we know, the history of the Crusades, the emblematic history of militant, ideological, and religious confrontation, echoes with the instances of leaders revered by their enemies. Of these, Salahadin, Europe's "Saladin," surely stands apart, the subject of numerous legends and romances in medieval Europe, in which he is appropriated and imagined as being, in addition to a paragon of chivalry, the son of a Christian mother, the paramour of Eleanor of Aquitaine, the conqueror of England, a deathbed convert to Christianity, and a wise, ecumenical ruler over the three faiths.[58] Muslims, for their part, found in Frederick II the friendly image of a Mozarabic figure, a mirror of their own princely virtues. Such mirroring was aided, no doubt, as much by existing resonances between the cultures of medieval Christianity and Islam[59] as by a certain cultural portability, even doubleness, to the figures of Salahadin and Frederick respectively. And what of the saint-king? To what extent did his image and reputation lend itself to appropriation by admiring Muslims?

In Europe, the leader of the Seventh Crusade and "martyr" of the Eighth Crusade was and still is regarded as a paragon of Christian virtues—"*christianissimus*," or "the most Christian king"[60]—evidenced, in the *Vie* alone, through Louis's almsgiving, his patronage of the mendicant orders, his extolling the moral virtue of dealing with lepers, and his personal hand in burying war dead. Louis's orthodoxy also accounts for a degree of inflexibility in his treatment of non-Christians, observable in the *Vie* in his favoring of lay violence over disputation with Jews at Cluny, and in his categorical refusal to speak to the Provencal convert to Islam, interviewed by Joinville.[61] As we know, Louis likewise refused to negotiate with al-Salih at the opening of the Seventh Crusade, turning down his offer of the holy city in exchange for the recently captured Damietta. On the other hand, Louis's initial inflexibility toward negotiating with Muslims gave way to ample, multipronged diplomacy between the Mamluks and Syrians when these became necessary, and his diplomacy seems to have earned him a local reputation for honesty.[62] Louis's life, moreover, shows some mirroring of Islamic practice. While in captivity in Egypt, Louis learned of a great library of a Muslim prince and decided to start his own book collection, culminating in his great library at Sainte Chapelle.[63] And of course, readers of the *Vie* can hardly forget the tantalizing image of Louis as the sultan of Egypt, dressed, as he was upon entering Acre in the aftermath of the crusade, in Oriental clothing.

The idea of a King Louis thus Islamicized contends, of course, with the reality that the king continued his crusade against Islam literally to his dying day. And yet, "the word in language is half some else's . . . As a living, socio-ideological concrete thing, as heteroglot opinion, language, for the individual consciousness, lies on the border between oneself and the other. . . . It becomes 'one's own' only when the speaker populates it with his own intention, his own accent, when he appropriates the word."[64] The life of Saint Louis does not end with his death in 1270 from illness while crusading upon North Africa's shores. Its ending, or one of them, is told by Tunisians in the French colonial period. Nineteenth-century visitors to Tunisian coastal cities returned with stories of a village named after Saint Louis, a Sufi saint who converted to Islam while on the Eighth Crusade. The legend has various versions, but the general picture in them is the same: while in Tunisia, King Louis takes a solitary walk and meets a marabout, or Muslim saint, telling him the crusade is going poorly and that he does not wish to return to domestic problems facing him in France. The marabout tells him of a local man of high birth who resembles him uncannily and with whom, he suggests, the king could exchange places: "The king of France pondered it. His faith was too pure to attach much importance to a change of religion. What bothered him was Queen Isabelle; even while feigning death, he had scruples. At that moment a pretty infidel passed whose copper arms were holding a jar. She headed for the village, shockingly white above the waves. 'What is that place?' Saint Louis asked the marabout. 'Sidi Bou Said.'"[65] Sidi Bou Said, Louis's alter ego, dies that night, and after some language and Qur'anic instruction, King Louis becomes a Muslim, namely the saint Sidi Bou Said. The historical Sidi Bou Said Khalaf bin Yahiya at-Tamini al-Begi (1156–1231) died forty years before Louis's death in 1270 in Gabal al-manar, the previous name of the village. A Sufi, Sidi Bou Said had a shrine named after him in the eponymous village, which bore a particular reputation for holiness.[66]

In the context of colonial Tunisia, the appropriation of Saint Louis's legend is fascinating enough. The legend effectively constitutes what Malek Alloula calls a "colonial postcard" sent back to its sender,[67] for as Afrodesia McCannon notes, "The Tunisians revised history to counter the story of the great crusading Christian saint who died trying to teach the Arabs the error of their ways. They replaced that history with a king converted by Tunisia"[68]—a transculturation of medieval history for modern colonial times (resting on a reading of the Crusades as similarly colonialist). This is all the more so in light of the legends' knowing, writing back to that well-worn medieval European romance fantasy of the Saracen princess (cum her subjects) converted by a handsome Christian knight. Here, instead, a local Muslim beauty plays a suggestive hand in Louis's own conversion, his misgivings about deceiving his queen aside.[69] But equally interesting are the elements of the medieval Saint Louis legend that lent themselves to appropriation for a Sufi saint's legend in the first place. For it is Louis's reputation for scruples and for holiness that seem to prepare him for his annexation to a saint's life in an alternative faith. And lest we be skeptical of such a seemingly ironic turn, the legend lays bare its own assumption for us: "His faith was too pure to attach much importance to a change of religion."[70] Or as Salahadin once said, "on ne vit onques de mauvais crestien bon sarrazin, ne de mauvais sarrazin bon crestien."

CHAPTER 5

Dis-Orienting the Self

The Uncanny Travels of John Mandeville

The era of the *Travels*' composition may be characterized as one in which Europe both turned away from the East and turned inward.¹ The fall of Acre, the last Christian outpost of Outremer, to the Mamluks in 1291 meant that trading, missionary, and pilgrimage routes to the East were significantly slowed. In 1316 the khans of Persia adopted Islam, thereby constituting a Muslim block on the trade routes to India and China. By the time Mandeville wrote in the mid-1350s, calls for a new crusade on the Holy Land were hampered by the reality of absorption of resources in the domestic Hundred Years' War. In 1370, the xenophobic Ming dynasty replaced the Mongols of China, ending the dramatic medieval chapter of exploration of and missions to Asia; the mission of Mandeville's contemporary, John Marignolli, to the khan of Cathay (1339–52) constituted the last of the great medieval European missionaries to China.² This is the context out of which *Mandeville's Travels*, a text distinctly outward looking in its curiosity about the ethnic and natural diversity of the world in its time, paradoxically emerged. Even the composition of the *Travels* from a remix of already received authorities and sources, seemingly a sign of its inward turn, reflects a prodigious appetite for the knowledge of others, and indeed the *Travels* can and has been treated as an encyclopedia of Middle Eastern and Asian travel and ethnographic knowledge as it stood in the late Middle Ages.³ In addition to Mandeville's two main sources, William of Boldensele's *Liber de quibusdam ultramarinis partibus* [Book of certain overseas regions] (1336) and Friar Odoric of

Pordenone's *Relatio* (1330), a partial list of the Mandeville author's vast array of sources would include some two dozen other texts, including Vincent of Beauvais' *Speculi* (c. 1256–59), Jacques de Vitry's *Historia Orientalis* (early thirteenth century), Hayton of Armenia's *Flor des estoires de la terre d'Orient naturale* (1307), William of Tripoli's *Tractatus de statu Saracenorum* (1273), the *Littera Presbyteris Johannis* (late twelfth century), the *Roman de Alexandre* (mid-twelfth century), and John of Wurzburg's *Descriptio Terrae Sanctae* (c. 1165), as well as selective use of the encyclopedic and historical works of early medieval authorities such as Josephus, Orosius, Macrobius, and Isidore of Seville.[4]

The ethnographic status of *Mandeville's Travels* is complex and contested: while earlier critics tended to view its armchair-traveling author as a plagiarist and a purveyor of ethnographic legend and lore rather than ethnography,[5] more recent critics have viewed the text as comparable or superior in geographic and ethnographic knowledge to contemporary travel texts;[6] have found in his text evidence of the later medieval period's interest in curious personal observation,[7] a hallmark of empirical ethnography; and noted the text's enduring influence on the genres of travel and ethnography well into the sixteenth century.[8] Although the Mandeville author's reworking of existing travel sources cannot be said to represent empirical ethnography, his careful imitation of the form and genre secures the work an important place in our examination of the dialogic mode in late medieval ethnographic poetics, amply on display in the *Travels*. Indeed, *Mandeville's Travels* reflects strong continuities with the works studied in the previous chapters of this book in writing ethnography in light of another's word. Like them, it shows an openness to alternative perspectives and voices, highlights the limits of a single-point Latin Christian perspective on a diverse world, and perhaps more than works analyzed in any other chapter shows the *difficulty* in confronting unfamiliar worldviews that dialogize, relativize, and interrogate Latin Christian ones throughout its pages. These continuities are just the starting point for the *Travels*, however, whose extensive troubling of self-other boundaries runs deeper than we have previously witnessed. The *Travels* stands, then, as both an appropriate bookend and a limit for the mode of seeing and writing ethnography that we have been plotting.

THE TERRORS OF UNCANNY TRAVEL

Mandeville's Travels has justifiably received critical attention as a text preoccupied with human diversity and difference—with, in the knight John Mandeville's own words, the "many dyuerse folk and [of] dyuerse maneres and lawes and [of] dyuerse schappes of men" (prol.).[9] The main critical reading of the *Travels*' preoccupation with otherness has been a Christian pedagogical one that insists on the text's use of its diverse others as objects against which to project an "ironic" or "satiric" image of a sinful Christian self for the purposes of its redisciplining.[10] But "irony," as we know, resorts to a stable viewpoint,[11] and in what follows, I argue that the many moments in the *Travels* that have rightfully been associated with an instability of tone derive this quality less from narrative irony than from a narrative perspective that is fundamentally irreconcilable with and split off from itself. This condition, I show, is born out of the work of the uncanny on the *Travels*' narrator, with decidedly unnerving results for the *Travels*' narrations of otherness: the production of representations that blur the boundaries between Christians and their supposed others, be they monsters, Saracens, or pagans, placing them in a relation of near indistinguishability from each other. In the final section of the chapter, I explore the special role of the narrator's gaze in the boundary-blurring moments of the uncanny, as well as the way the text's attention to his gaze follows the visual poetics of the medieval ethnographic gaze generally, highlighting its limits, contingency, and subjectivity in a diverse world.[12] Throughout, I argue that the *Travels*' collapsing of self and other may best be understood as part of the phenomenological crisis particular to aesthetics of the uncanny. It is the threat of the Latin Christian self's precarious slip into otherness, dissolution, or fracture that lends the *Travels* its famous instability of tone and, I argue, a quality of terror rooted in the uncanny. While the narrator boasts the pleasures of a text about difference—"for many men han gret likying to here speke of straunge thinges of dyuerse contreyes" (iv)—as indeed have many of the *Travels*' readers,[13] below its textual surface, the *Travels*' treatment of otherness brings its readers into unwitting contact with emotions that are far from pleasurable.

I locate the source for the copious play of the uncanny in the *Travels*, with its loosening of the boundaries between Christian and non-Christian, within a specific intellectual and social context: the late fourteenth century's precarious faith in the exclusivity of Christian salvation and increasing openness to the possibility of non-Christian salvation. Scholars have acknowledged the importance of the theme of non-Christian salvation in the vernacular literature of fourteenth-century writers from Dante to William Langland,[14] but the full import of the virtuous pagan theme to *Mandeville's Travels* has yet to be appreciated.[15] Such an appreciation is not possible without consideration of the rich fourteenth-century theological and literary background against which the *Travels'* investment in non-Christian salvation comes into focus and finds its meaning. Nor is it possible without acknowledgment of the way in which non-Christian salvation acts as much more than a thematic preoccupation in the *Travels*, but rather triggers its very representational crises, giving shape to its essential formal features.

IN LIGHT OF ANOTHER'S WORD: INHABITING THE OTHER'S PERSPECTIVE IN THE *TRAVELS*

The narrator John Mandeville loses no time in alerting us to some rather unusual techniques of ethnographic observation that he will deploy in his narrative. In the third chapter, "Of the Cytee of Constantynoble and of the Feith of Grekes," for instance, he notes that "thei [Greeks] suffre not the Latynes to syngen at here awteres, and yif thei don be ony aventure, anon thei wasschen the awteer with holy water" (iii). This striking remark has the Greeks washing the pollution of Latins from their communal realm in the incidence of their unwelcome presence at the church altar—not a view of the self the Latin Christian reader may have expected to discover in *Mandeville's Travels*. The paragraph continues to delineate the differences between Greek and Latin Christian belief and practice for its remainder, but solely from the perspective of Greeks, introducing this perspective into each of its sentences with the phrase, "And thei seye . . ." Already in an opening chapter within the "pilgrimage" section of his book, Mandeville would have his readers see how they are seen from without.

This foregrounding of the outside perspective on Western Christian practice soon resurfaces in another telling context. In "Ebron," the narrator notes that the Saracens keep the sepulchres of Old Testament figures such as Abraham and Isaac "full curyously and han the place in reuerence for the holy fadres the patriarkes that lygn there" (ix). Mandeville follows this observation with another, made on behalf of Saracens, which is typical of what is taken by critics to manifest his "ironic" tone in the *Travels*: "And thei suffre no Cristene man entre into that place but yif it be of specyalle grace of the Soudan, for thei holden Cristene men and Iewes as dogges and thei seyn that thei scholde not entre into so holy place." Not only are Christians and Jews failing to maintain the central sites of their faith, they are barred from them as potential polluting agents, dogs amid holy things. A reading of verbal irony here would presumably be premised on the notion that our narrator has gone too far in representing the outside perspective: a Christian writing about how Christians are dogs in the eyes of Saracens cannot mean merely to convey this viewpoint, but must also be condemning it.

The trouble with such a condemnatory reading of the Saracen perspective, with diffusing it into an ironic Christian one, is that soon enough Mandeville reveals information that suggests he himself knows better. In chapter 15, "Of the Customes of Sarasines and of Hire Lawe," Mandeville notes the Qur'an's agreement with a number of Christological points, including Jesus's prophethood and sinlessness, the virginity of Mary and the Incarnation, and the truth of the Gospels.[16] But, he continues, in spite of these shared beliefs, "the Sarazines seyn that the Iewes ben cursed for thei han defouled the lawe that God sente hem be Moyses. And the Cristene ben cursed also, as thei seyn, for thei kepen not the commandementes and the preceptes of the gospelle that Ihesu Crist taughte hem" (xv). This information, in which Mandeville offers his readers a fundamental Muslim belief, casts new light on the question of the narrator's would-be irony when he asserts the Saracen desire to guard the tomb of the patriarchs from Jewish or Christian impurity. For as Mandeville himself seems to know fully, Muslims believed Jews and Christians to be the recipients of the same message of God attested to by Islam, passed down through their respective prophets Moses and Jesus but then corrupted by them, making Muhammad its rightful inheritor and final bearer.[17] Mandeville, then, is very close indeed to voicing the perspective of a Muslim in representing Saracens as the reverential and careful (Middle English: *curious*) keepers of the patriarchs' sepulchres—the more so as Muslims consider Abraham the first Muslim and the original prophet of their faith, also known to them as the religion of Abraham (*millat Ibrahim*).[18] Once again, our narrator has chosen to see from the perspective of an "other" of Latin Christendom, here Islam.

From these early examples, we can see the perspective of the *Travels*' narrator is complex and that this complexity derives not from irony but from the narrator's occasional tendency to slip, unannounced, into a position hard to align with that of a Christian self. At the same time, as we will see, what the narrator says and does at these very moments frequently serves to render Christian and non-Christian less distinguishable. Many moments that have been read as doing ironic work in the *Travels* derive their destabilizing and edgy quality not from irony but from a fundamental instability of perspective in the moment of their telling. Whether the instability is a product of the play of narrative perspective as above, or, as we will frequently find, of the violation of the corporeal integrity of depicted Christians and their supposed others—be they monsters, Saracens, or pagans—at their moments of representation, the aesthetic effect and import of these representations are the same: the unnerving, disorienting, even frightening production of an indistinguishability between Christians and their others. In the following sections I examine the many instances of representational and phenomenological uncertainty within the pages of *Mandeville's Travels*.

FRACTURED VIEWERS, FRACTURED VIEWS

One striking narrative mode in the *Travels* is the deployment of a special sort of ventriloquism, whereby the voices of the "self"—received European authorities and debates—occupy bodies of the other and vice versa with resulting blurring between European selves and Eastern others. The narrator's "Nota of a Merueyle," whereby a creature that is half man and half goat asks an Egyptian hermit to pray for the salvation of all men, provides an early and important example. What is striking here is not that the hermit should come upon a speaking half man, half goat, or even that he should ask that hermit to pray for his soul, although these would suffice as marvelous in another author's hands. Rather, what is notable is that when it speaks, this monster-other cites a large and lively medieval Christian debate as to both the existence of monsters and the salvation of non-Christians, topics that affect its own existence and status directly. The other, then, is challenging the Christian self to recognize its existence by speaking in the language of the self. For the reader informed about such a debate, the moment is a strange and unnerving one: in recognizing the other, the European reader recognizes a European discourse about that other's existence, catching him- or herself in the mirror. For the narrator, who plays the curious and open-minded cosmopolitan traveler, this is one of the strange and yet familiar events that go without commentary during his travels eastward. Even the Christian "self" is not simply disposed of in this boundary-crossing self-other encounter: our Egyptian hermit is a reminder of the diversity of Christianities in the Eastern landscape, many of which, as our narrator constantly reminds us, differ in crucial articles of faith from "official" Latin Christendom, itself precariously split into two papal centers for much of the fourteenth century (1309–77), including, of course, the period of the *Travels*' composition circa 1357.[19]

The narrator's interview with the sultan of Egypt provides perhaps the paradigmatic example of boundary-crossing ventriloquism in the text. After being invited into the sultan's private chamber "voyden" out of his lords and council, Mandeville is also made privy to the sultan's private thoughts on his coreligionists: "And there he asked me how the Cristene men gouerned hem in oure contree, and I seyde him, 'Right wel, thonked be God.' And he seyde me: 'Treulych nay.'" So begins the sultan's long diatribe against the current state of Christendom, where he criticizes its gluttony, deceit, fractiousness, decadence, licentiousness, and impiety, among other sins. The sultan ends by attributing the Christian loss of "alle this lond that wee holden" to their "foul" and "unclene lyvynge" (xv). It is easy to see how this interview can be read as part of the text's strategic use of its others as disciplining counterexamples designed to reorient Christian readers away from sin. According to such a reading, the efficacy of the other's making such a rebuke to Christendom would presumably depend on the greater sting of a critique from without to Christian pride, made as it is by those understood by narrator and readers (modern and contemporary) to be morally ill equipped for such judgments. Indeed Mandeville says as much: "Allas, that it is great sclaundre to oure feith and to oure lawe, whan folk that ben withouten lawe schulle repreuen vs and vndernemen vs of oure synnes" (xv).

But the narrator follows this statement with another that undermines our sense of the stability of his perspective in these pages. He concludes the episode with the sultan with the following assessment of Muslims and their faith: "And treuly thei sey soth. For the Sarazines ben gode and feythfulle, for thei kepen entierly the commandement of the holy book Alkoran that God sente hem be His messenger Machomet, to the whiche, as thei seyn, seynt Gabreille the aungel often tyme tolde the wille of God" (xv). This passage posits Muslims' following of their law in juxtaposition to Christians, who have earlier been described as failing to uphold their own. It also identifies Muhammad as the messenger of God, a rare position indeed in the "lives of Muhammad" genre,[20] as well as noting Islam's shared belief with Christianity in the angel Gabriel. The chapter has thus far been filled with the tag "as thei seyn," signaling Mandeville's citation of the Saracen perspective. In each instance, the tag carries an ambivalent edginess, potentially undermining or affirming the truth value of what follows. But here, in the last instance of its use in the chapter, Mandeville chooses to affirm explicitly the truthfulness of the perspective at issue: "And treuly thei sey soth. For the Sarazines ben gode and feythfulle." Muslims and their faith, then, by passage's end have been depicted as at once good and true, and not all that different from Christians and their faith; indeed the latter is the basis on which Mandeville has just asserted that the Saracens "ben lightly conuerted to Cristene lawe" (xv). These statements in effect overturn the sting of the rebuke of the sultan, based as it is on the notion of a less moral outsider delivering it. Muslims are depicted in the closing lines of the interview episode as neither entirely outside the community of Christian beliefs nor less morally upright and true for their beliefs. Instead of didactic rebuke, we are left with a sense of uncertainty as to the narrator's point about the relationship between Islam and Christianity, the two great faiths put into dialogue in this chapter.

The boundary confusion on display in this episode is rarely acknowledged by critics who wish to limit its aim to didacticism alone. Like the uncanny scene between the hermit and the monster, what is strange and unnerving about the sultan is less that he should be critical of Christendom, his adversary in over two centuries of crusade, than his deployment of utterly Christian arguments in the launching of his critique—here too is an other who speaks in the voice of the Christian self. And rather than separating the voice of Christian self-rebuke from the body of a sultan as critics are wont to do in seeking to explain the passage's "message," we might, as readers of fiction, challenge ourselves to recognize the specific aesthetics here—the simultaneity of self and other inhabiting one body as such. In the figure of the sultan, Mandeville stages a frightful event: out of the depths of the body of the other springs the self. This "springing" recalls one of the most palpable and memorable definitions of the uncanny, provided by Freud: "'Heimlich'? . . . What do you understand by 'heimlich'?"

"Well, . . . they are like a buried spring or a dried-up pond. One cannot walk over it without always having the feeling that water might come up there again." The uncanny, Freud concludes, is in fact the anxiety of repression and the return of repressed content: "'Unheimlich' is the name for everything that ought to have remained . . . secret and hidden but has come to light."[21] In his influential critique and elaboration of Freud's essay, Samuel Weber links the uncanny and its signature aesthetic components rather to the castration complex. In this reading, fear of castration marks a crisis in perception and phenomenality, the first fissure between perception and ontology in the life of the infant: the absence of the maternal phallus forces the infant to recognize its own body as alienated from the mother's with which it had been heretofore wholly integral.[22] Caught in the rift between identification with the (m)other and its "not-quite-nothing" difference from the same, the subject is in "a mortal danger . . . the 'integrity' of its body and thus . . . its very identity" threatened, instantiating feelings of dread and panic. The uncanny is thus marked by both feelings of terror and "a certain indecidability" at the level of representation, features at the core of *Mandeville's Travels*.[23] Critics who reduce the scene of a sultan speaking in Christian tongue to one of the author's knowing and even amusing satire flatten and strip the scene of its deeper power, which lies in its ability to call up the fear of the indistinguishability between ourselves and our supposed others, the terror of our confrontation with the unstable limits of our selves in the world.

It is fitting that this chapter, located as it is on the seam between the pilgrimage and Eastern travel sections of Mandeville's book, should stage the uncanny collapse of self and other via the sultan's voice. Nor is this the sole medium for the collapse of boundaries between Christian selves and Muslim others presented to us in the chapter. The narrator has also twice noted, however casually, the ease of the conversion of Muslims to Christianity given the proximity of their beliefs. He concludes the chapter by alluding to the threat of conversion in the opposite direction as well: "Also it befalleth sumtyme that Cristene men becomen Sarazines outher for pouertee or for sympleness or elles for here owne wykkednesse" (xv). Though our narrator calls such would-be converts to Islam "wicked," he follows this statement, stunningly, by reciting the *shahada*, the Muslim profession of faith, the recitation of which is one of the five duties of Muslims. He recites it in both Arabic and English—appropriating, in such recitation, a quintessentially Muslim voice. We ought not be surprised by our narrator's familiarity with Islamic teaching: he has already declared that "I haue often tyme seen and radd" the "Alkaron." But the reader now recalls his close brush with conversion by seduction in an earlier chapter in a somewhat different light. In chapter 6, Mandeville boasted sufficient intimacy with the sultan to have had him offer his "gret princes doughter yif I wolde han forsaken my lawe and my beleue, but I thanke God I had no wille to don it for no thing that he behighte me" (vi). The anecdote is shaped to reveal a narrator impermeable to the seductions of both princess (in a pastiche of countless romances bearing an "enamoured Muslim princess" theme)[24] and faith. But the incident, now coupled with his intimacy with practices of Islam and his uncanny recitation of the shahada in chapter 15, suggests something other than the safe distance of the narrator from the dangers of Muslim conversion.

The chapter offers more instances of slippage between the increasingly porous categories of Christians and Muslims. Muslim spies dressed as merchants, the sultan informs us at the interview's end, have been penetrating and surveying "euery contree amonges Cristene men" and reporting such information back to the sultan for years: "And than he leet clepe in alle the lordes that he made voyden first out of his chambre, and there he schewed me iiii. that weren great lordes in the contree, that tolden me of my contree and of manye other Cristene contrees als wel as thei had ben of the same contree, and thei spak Frensch right wel and the Sowdan also; whereof I had gret meruaylle" (xv). This scene imagines a fitting response to the ethnographic approach of John Plano de Carpini, one of Mandeville's sources via Vincent of Beauvais's encyclopedic collection *Speculum Historiale*, among the Mongols. Carpini had written of how much Europeans could learn from Mongol war strategies even as he described them for European audiences, making the link between reported cultural information and war making explicit. The Mandeville author here subversively suggests that the other has its own ethnographic reconnaissance work in mind, reversing the gaze so that it works on unsuspecting Christians in their own lands.[25] In doing so, he knowingly targets specific skills—ability in foreign languages and in the merchant trade—that break down cultural borders and permit the free mixing of non-Christians in Christian lands. But the force of the scene resides, I believe, in the way in which it is staged as a return. For we have seen this language before. Having opened the interview with the sultan by describing how the latter "leet voyden out of his chambre alle manner of men, lordes and othere," our narrator closes it by noting that he "leet clepe in alle the lordes that he made voyden first out of his chambre." Such repetition calls attention unmistakably to the return at work, and more particularly, to the way it is staged with a difference. The Muslim counselors return self-like, or more precisely, as ready to disclose their masquerading capabilities as Christians, complete with a cultural and linguistic fluency so equal to Mandeville's own that he marvels at it—"whereof I had gret meruaylle." Marveling and wondering, as Caroline Bynum has recently written, may be characterized as responses ranging from terror to disgust to delight at "credible though deeply unusual events" that defy human understanding. Moreover, the "marveling and astonishment as reactions seem to be triggered most frequently and violently by what Bernard of Clairvaux called *admirabiles mixturae*: events or phenomena in which ontological and moral boundaries are crossed, confused, or erased"[26]—linking them here inextricably to the workings of the uncanny.[27]

The permeability of Christian selves and Muslim others extends, as we might expect, beyond chapter 15 and its particular interests. In other chapters, we are confronted with other ways of thematizing uncanny slippage between Christians and Muslims, and again our narrator plays a pivotal role in the slippage. In chapter 6, for instance, he tells us that he fought "as a soudyour" in the sultan of Egypt's "werres a gret while ayen the Bedoynes." Likewise at the court of the great khan, he discloses: "And ye schulle vndirstonde that my felawes and I with oure yomen, we serueden this emperour and weren his soudyoures xv. monethes ayenst the kyng of Mancy that held werre ayenst him" (xxiii). In indicating his experiences as a mercenary soldier in the East, the narrator slyly places himself within an important and destabilizing shift in the military organization of Europe in the fourteenth century, which saw the increasing rise of mercenary armies or "companies" for hire in place of the service of feudal tenant-knights and communal militias.[28] Lacking in feudal or national loyalties, better organized and stronger than available local or state armies in a period of weak centralized authority and papal direction on the continent, the companies threatened widespread social destruction when turned on local populations.[29] The *routiers,* as they were called, also caused significant social confusion and fragmentation, blurring national lines and threatening the integrity of Christian community. It is no surprise, then, to find them likened to pagans and deemed "worse than Saracens" by chroniclers of the period, such as the Metz chronicler, as well as by Pope Urban V, who was not the only fourteenth-century pope to try, and fail, to entice the "heathenish tormentors" to redirect their destructive energies toward an eastern theater on crusade. In fighting for hire in the East, Mandeville positions himself within a notable subgroup of this larger maligned and destabilizing phenomenon: Christians working in the service of Arab rulers, in particular in North Africa but also in Asia Minor,[30] not far from the two sites, Egypt and Central Asia, where the narrator himself claims to have done service.

As we head farther east on Mandeville's itinerary, away from the sites of Christian pilgrimage, the boundary confusion between European selves and Eastern others steadily heightens, though the others in question shift from Muslims to the various pagan groups of Asia. This Eastern travel section features many descriptions in which the Christian reader is forced to see himself in a form both recognizably self-like and slightly altered, to peer, in short, into a "not-quite-nothing" difference. Again the critical tendency has been to diffuse unsettling uncanny moments into Christian self-rebuke posing as satire. Donald Howard, for example, reads the closeness between depictions of pagans and Christian practices and beliefs in the latter half of Mandeville's journey as a "parody" of Christianity, an effort that "make[s] the customs of the East a distorted reflection of the West, forcing a comparison between the two."[31] While an East-West comparison may characterize the reader's most basic response, it does not suffice to describe the far more complicated aesthetic and emotional effect of the reader's confrontation with these passages. Many moments within the narrator's depictions of the pagan practices are surprising, unsettling, and unnerving because we cannot fathom the perspective from which he is viewing them, or we know them to be irreconcilable to a single, unified picture.

For example, in the "yles abouten Ynde" in the city of Polombe, Mandeville calls our attention to men who "worschipen the ox of his sympleness and his mekeness and for the profite that cometh of him." He follows this safely pagan and thus "other" description with one much closer to home: "And thei seyn that he is the holyest best in erthe, for hem semeth that whosoeuere be meke and pacyent he is holy and profitable, for thenne they seyn he haath alle vertues in him" (xviii). With this statement, Christian readers observe the comfortable distance between themselves and pagan ox worshippers dissolve.

Presented with an underlying and invisible similarity between themselves and ox worshippers—the common assumption that the meek are holy—as well as a quite visible difference, the ox versus the body of Christ, Christian readers are forced to weigh material differences against spiritual similarities—forced to engage, that is, in uncomfortable phenomenological questions.

Only pages later, we are confronted with another challenge to our readerly perceptions. At first, Mandeville describes the pilgrimage rites of idol worshippers. Making a number of overt comparisons between pagans and Christians, Mandeville here supports a reading of the *Travels*' use of the East in the service of Christian self-rebuke. His opening words are exemplary in this regard: "And to that ydole gon men on pilgrimage als comounly and with als great deuocoun as Cristene men gon to Seynt Iames or other holy pilgrimages" (xix). As are his closing words: "And, schortly to seye you, thei suffren so grete peynes and so harde martyrdomes for loue of here ydole that a Cristene man, I trowe, durst not taken vpon him the tenthe part the peyne for loue of oure lord Ihesu Crist" (xix). In between, however, readers will need their sensibilities to make sense of what is being presented to them. These idol worshippers, we are told, practice bodily mutilation and praise devotion to the point of martyrdom: "And alleweyes as thei gon thei smyten hemself in here armes and in here legges and in here thyes with many hidouse woundes, and so thei scheden here blood for loue of that ydole. And thei seyn that he is blessed and holy that dyeth so for loue of his god." Likewise, during the procession of the "thronynge of the ydole, . . . [s]umme of hem fallen doun vnder the wheles of the chare and lat the chare gon ouer hem so that thei ben ded anon. And summe han here armes or here lymes alle tobroken, and somme the sydes. And alle this don thei for loue of hire god in gret deuocoun. And hem thinketh that the more peyne and the more tribulacoun that thei suffren for loue of here god, the more ioye thei schulle haue in another world" (xix). In such descriptions, it is not a system of overt comparisons or analogies that is called up—just as we, so they—but rather a description of the other that implicitly calls on the self to recognize itself therein. This is a very different rhetorical strategy, with different effects: not indoctrinating, as Christianizing readings would have it, but undoctrinating, calling on the self to question its distance from its so-called others. The same effect is achieved farther east, in the "dyuerse yles that ben abouten in the lordschipe of Prestre Iohn." Here, the narrator describes one place:

> After that is another yle where that wommen maken gret sorwe when hire children ben yborn. And whan thei dyen, thei maken gret feste and gret ioye and reuelle, and thanne thei casten hem into a gret fuyr brennynge. And tho that louen wel hire husbondes, yif hire husbondes ben dede, thei casten hem also into the fuyr with hire children and brennen hem. And thei seyn that the fuyr schalle clensen hem of alle filthes and of alle vices, and thei schulle gon pured and clene into another world to hire husbondes, and thei schulle leden hire children with hem. And the cause whi that thei wepen whan hire children ben born is this: for whan thei comen into this world, thei comen to labour, sorwe, and heuyness. And whi thei maken ioye and gladnesse at hire dyenge is because that, as thei seyn, thanne thei gon to Paradys, where the ryueres rennen mylk and hony, where that men seen hem in ioye and in habundance of godes withouten sorwe and labour. (xxxi)

Christian readers can find in a description such as this one the contours of their own image as well as lines that do not conform to it, a "not-quite" resemblance, or put differently, the violation of the bodily integrity of represented objects by a mixing of Christian and non-Christian elements. The harsh denial of worldliness and faith in an afterlife where one's joy is inversely proportional to one's sufferings on earth—these are exaggerations of, as Donald Howard has put it, "the pessimistic, the death-loving side of Christianity, with its emphasis on self-abnegation, 'mortification,' and martyrdom."[32] But the emphasis on purity via cremation, or the ritual sacrifice of self and child to purifying fires—these are not within a Christian belief system and distort readerly self-reflection. What one is left with is a picture of both familiar and foreign, domestic and exotic elements, which allows for neither identification nor its renunciation, catching the subject-reader in between contrary impulses and leaving him or her with a faint feeling of unease.

If Christian *contemptus mundi* constitutes one theme of uncanny Christian-pagan mixing in the *Travels*, the Christian Mass certainly constitutes another. In an isle called "Milke" off Java, for instance, Mandeville describes a rite whereby a "full cursed peple," who "delyten in nothing more than for to fighten and to sle men, . . . drynken gladlyest mannes blood, the whiche thei clepen *dieu*" (xxi). Had Mandeville not bothered to call this man's blood "dieu" the reverberations between this practice and the holy blood of Christ in the Christian Mass might have been avoidable; the inclusion seems to be designed to call forth a moment of unwitting identification on behalf of Christian readers with bloodthirsty cannibals.[33] The isles "costynge to

Prestre Iohnes lond," at the eastern end of Mandeville's itinerary, provide a further uncanny mirroring of the Christian Mass in the pious cannibalism of the people of Ryboth. Here, the son of a dead man "bryngeth hoom with him alle his kyn a his frendes and alle the othere to his hows and maketh hem a gret feste. . . . And whan thei ben at mete, the sone let brynge forth the hede of his fader and thereof he yeueth of the flesch to his most spcyalle frendes instede of entremess or a sukkarke. And of the brayne panne he leteth make a cuppe, and thereof drynketh he and his other frendes also with gret deuocoun in remembrance of the holy man that the aungeles of God han eten. And that cuppe the sone schalle kepe to drynken fo alle his liftyme in remembrance of his fadir" (xxxiv). The Christian reader here cannot but see the outline of the Mass and the symbolic flesh of Christ consumed according to it. At the same time, the unfamiliar is undeniably ever present: the context of a familial cannibal ritual in private home, of a skull cup to be kept and used in living memory of the father for the son's lifetime. It is this mixture of alien and grotesque with the familiar and the holy—for in Ryboth too the flesh eating is done "with gret deuocoun in remembrance of the holy man"—which makes reading this passage so uncomfortable: are Christian readers to see themselves therein or to deny the similarity and turn away in horror? Are they to uphold Christian ritual as fundamentally holy in contradistinction to this, a sacrilegious one? The latter is difficult to support, for in this passage we find no explicitly condemnatory language—Mandeville has not called these people "cursed" or "wicked" as he does so many others. Mandeville leaves Christian readers with an uncomfortable, uncanny remainder—their own reflection alienated from them, in a gruesome cannibal rite.

It is apparent from the above examples that pagans are often placed in uncanny proximity to Christians in this text. But there is a second and very different approach to pagans in the *Travels*, which, while intimately bound with the production of the uncanny, is also wholly distinct from and must be clearly differentiated from it. This second tendency may be described as the favorable representation of pagan religions as naturally "virtuous" and stemming from human reason. Mandeville begins his praise of virtuous pagans from within Christianity's own traditions, with Job: "Iob was a payneem, and he was Are of Gosra is sone, and held that lond as prynce of that contree. And he was so riche that he knew not the hundred part of his godes. And alle though he were a payneem, natheless he serued wel God after his lawe, and oure lord toke his seruice to His plesance. . . . [A]nd in that lond of Iob there nys no defaute of nothing that is nedefulle to mannes body" (xvii). In stating that God recognized Job's service "after his lawe" despite his being a pagan, Mandeville cites from a long and complex debate on the question of the salvation of pagans, to which I will turn shortly. Notably, following a tradition linking the geography of the East with the plenitude of the Earthly Paradise,[34] Mandeville here describes the lands of virtuous pagans as ones in which "there nys no defaute of nothing that is nedefulle to mannes body."

In the lands "abouten Ynde" in Chana, we find Mandeville's favorable treatment of pagans further elaborated. The idol worshippers here are assimilated into Christian monotheism by virtue of their natural beliefs: "For thei seyn wel that thei [their idols] be not goddes, for thei knowen wel that there is a god of kynde that made alle thinges, the which is in Heuene. But thei knowen wel that this may not do the meruayles that he made but yif it had ben the specyalle gifte of God" (xviii). The efficacy of pagan marvels depends on the "specyalle gifte of God," the god of nature and the maker of all things. Shortly thereafter, Mandeville follows a description of certain superstitions and auguries among the pagans with the statement "in theise thinges and in such othere ther ben many folk that beleeven because it happeneth so often tyme to fallen after here fantasyes. . . . And sith that Cristene men han such beleeve, that ben enformed and taught alle day be holy doctryne whereinne thei scholde beleeve, it is no meruaylle thanne that the paynemes that han no gode doctryne but only of here nature beleeven more largely for here symples" (xviii). Here, Mandeville calls on his readers to excuse pagan superstition by noting that pagans have only their natural beliefs to rely on whereas Christians have "holy doctryne" and yet still carry residual superstitions among them. Again and again, Mandeville praises pagan proximity to reason and nature in ways unmistakable—remarkable indeed amid the *Travels*' so many quicksand-like pages. Of the Pygmies, one of the "monstrous races" believed to occupy the East, Mandeville asserts, "And alle be it that the pygmeyes ben lytylle, yit thei ben fulle resonable after here age and conen bothen wytt and gode and malice ynow" (xxii). No note of ambiguity or problems of narrative perspective, susceptible to readings of parody or satire, is discernible here.

This is not to say that plays with perspective are not evident in Mandeville's descriptions of "virtuous pagans" as they are elsewhere in the text. The following depiction of the people of the Isle of Lamary

Dis-Orienting the Self

indicates just how playful and complicated the Mandeville author's representations of virtuous pagans can be: "And the custom there is such that men and wommen gon alle naked, and thei scornen whan thei seen ony strange folk goynge clothed. And thei seyn that God made Adam and Eue alle naked, and that no man scholde schame him to schewen him such as God made him, for nothing is foul that is of kyndely nature. And thei seyn that thei that ben clothed ben folk of another world or thei ben folk that trowen not in God. And thei seyn that thei beleeuen in God that formed the world and that made Adam and Eue and alle other thinges" (xx). It is easy to recognize the signs of the virtuous pagan tradition here: folks who believe in God that "formed the world and that made Adam and Eue," the people of Lamary live according to Adamic laws and shun clothing "for nothing is foul that is of kyndely nature." But Mandeville characteristically goes much further. Christian readers are soon turned into the object of pagan ethnographic depiction: those who clothe themselves are "strange" and "folk of another world or thei ben folk that trowen not in God." We find here the familiar repeated refrain "thei seyn" from Mandeville's depiction of the faith of Orthodox Greeks—here, too, he is preoccupied with another outside perspective on Western Christianity. But still we have not grasped the full rhetorical art of the passage, for these "thei seyns" place in the mouth of pagan others what late medieval Christians believe about them—their greater proximity to nature and the world before sin and the Fall—not, of course, what "they" say at all about themselves or about Christians. This is the language of the self coming forth from the other, another device to which we have become acclimated in the *Travels*. It takes a second or third reading to feel this last, uncanny effect, which competes with a few others for dominance within the passage's many manipulations of perspective. What is not contested, however, is the virtue of the pagans at each level of the passage's representations.

The *Travels*' favorable depictions of virtuous pagans culminates in chapter 32, devoted to the "folk of the yle of Bragman," also known as the "lond of feyth" according to Mandeville. "And alle be it that thei ben not cristned ne haue no perfyt lawe, yit natheles of kyndely lawe thei ben fulle of alle vertue," he tells us. The Brahmans obey the Ten Commandments out of their natural knowledge of good and evil; they have no thieves, beggars, or murderers among them; they fast "alle dayes"; they experience no hunger, pestilence, or tempest; they eschew worldly riches and power; they do not ordain their bodies but go as God made them; they know that naked they will reenter the earth from which they were created, "wherefore it semeth wel that God loueth hem and is plesed with hire creance for hire gode dedes." Mandeville reiterates this last point a number of times in this chapter, and it seems to be its focus.

> And alle be it that theyse folk han not the articles of ourre feyth as wee han, natheles for hire gode feyth naturelle and for hire gode entent I trowe fully that God loueth hem and that god take hire seruyse to gree, right as He did of Iob that was a paynem and held him for His trewe seruant. And therefore alle be it that there ben many dyuerse lawes in the world, yit I trowe that God loueth alweys hem that louen Him and seruen Him mekely in trouthe, and namely hem that dispysen the veyn glorie of this world, as this folk don and as Iob did also.
>
> And therefore seyde oure lord be the mouth of Ozee the prophete, *Ponam eis multiplices leges meas*, and also in another place, *Qui totum orbem subdit suis legibus*. And also oure lord seyth in the gospelle, *Alias oues habeo que non sunt ex hoc ouili*; that is to seyne that He hadde othere seruauntes than tho that ben vnder Cristene lawe. (xxxii)

The effect of these two passages is powerful and unambiguous: it is possible for pagans and those of otherwise "dyuerse lawes" to serve the Lord and be loved by him "for hire gode feyth naturelle and for hire gode entent." Using again the example of Job, the passage stresses the reciprocity of God's love: "yit I trowe that God loueth alweys hem that louen Him." Mandeville follows up this highly inclusive and tolerant perspective on the diversity of faiths with three biblical sayings. The first two emphasize the presence of God's law, by his design, in a diversity of guises throughout the whole world; the third, the only one Mandeville chooses to translate, is slightly more pointed: it affirms not just the possibility but the historical fact of non-Christian servants of the Lord.

Another paragraph later, Mandeville pronounces the words that I believe bring together the *Travels*' two discourses of pagans—uncanny self-like pagans and "virtuous" pagans: "for wee knowe not whom God loueth ne whom God hateth." In the mystery of God's love alone resides the answer to the members of his law and community, not in such markers as "Christian," "pagan," or even "Saracen." The distinction, crucial to medieval communities, is also declared unknowable to them—"for wee knowe not." This problem of differentiating those within from those outside the community of God's love and salvation is of interest to medieval theologians from a very early period. But as we shall see, it takes a turn at once more skeptical and decentering for the Christian community in the century in which Mandeville writes, the aesthetic effects of which we have been viewing.

A LATE MEDIEVAL CRISIS OF PHENOMENALITY: THE SALVATION OF NON-CHRISTIANS

Samuel Weber closes his remarks on the uncanny by addressing the important and often overlooked "question of the historical status of the Unheimliche," its relation, that is, "to socially determined objective structures which themselves involve something like that crisis of perception and representation active in the uncanny."[35] In so doing, Weber gives voice to a concern often raised by historicist medievalists in the face of the application of theoretical paradigms from the modern era to medieval materials. Here I wish to address the historical specificity and the "socially determined objective structures" of the uncanny to show that the themes and concerns of latter fourteenth-century medieval thought resonate powerfully with the structures of the uncanny.

The fourteenth century features an unusual development, one that R. W. Southern characterized as an "ambiguity about the exclusive claim of Christianity to confer the gift of eternal blessedness" and a concomitant, abiding interest in the salvation of non-Christians. While this fourteenth-century tendency "appeals to every human instinct . . . it also marks, for better or worse, a loosening of the cohesion of the Western world, an obscuring of its sense of separateness, and a blurring of the clear-cut line between the West and its neighbors."[36] The late medieval preoccupation with non-Christian salvation was a fundamentally ambivalent phenomenon, then, presenting Latin Christians at once with the opportunity to engage anew with the world's diversity of faiths and customs, and with the uneasy possibility of the diminution of their own corporate identity. As we saw in Chapter 1, the question of non-Christian salvation and of "virtuous pagans" had concerned the church from its beginnings. But in the fourteenth century, it sharpened and increasingly manifested itself inextricably in theological and philosophical discussions marked by epistemological crisis.

The fourteenth century marks certain decisive breaks with the past in Christian theology and epistemology. Perhaps the hallmark of fourteenth-century thought is the separation it evinces between the realms of theology and philosophy, faith and reason, divine and human. This separation is usually linked to the great Condemnation of 1277, a group of 219 propositions condemned by Bishop Etienne Tempier of Paris because they conflicted with Christian teachings and overly restricted divine power by a reliance on "a naturalistic determinism rooted in Aristotle's physical and metaphysical principles."[37] As Etienne Gilson points out, the condemnations were themselves "a symptom of an already existing reaction against the excessive philosophical independence of some masters in philosophy and theology."[38] They are therefore best understood as part of a larger defensive moment within Christian theology, one characterized by "a critique of human knowledge and of its foundations of evidence such as would be sufficient to show that the doctrines of theology could be neither refuted nor established by philosophy as such."[39] As a result, theology of the fourteenth century earned itself a secure detachment and independence from philosophical inquiry, and God's absolute power (*potentia Dei absoluta*) and the contingency and nonnecessity of the created world asserted themselves with renewed vigor and consequence.[40] Philosophy, for its part, pulled away from theological and metaphysical conclusions, for which it had been deemed incompetent, and turned increasingly and irrevocably toward empiricism and the sciences.[41]

Representative theologians of the age such as John Duns Scotus and William of Ockham participated in effecting this separation of faith and reason, complete with its deeply limiting effects on human knowledge. Duns Scotus, for instance, added to the number of truths that required faith without possibility of proof.[42] Ockham, perhaps the most empirical thinker of his age, held that nothing metaphysical—"in the sense of a science of suprasensory realms of being or of a priori factual truths"—could be inferred from the experiential world, even the existence of God.[43] According to his theory of intuitive cognition, knowledge of the phenomenal world could be intuited cognitively and immediately, whereas knowledge of God could not. Ockham can thus be said to have located the split between divine and human in the senses, endowing the senses with enhanced utility in the apprehension of nature on the one hand, and a futility in the apprehension of the divine on the other.[44] While Augustine, Aquinas, and Bonaventure had assumed the leap of reasoning "from the existence of things seen to the existence of things unseen," based on the notion of a "hierarchy of being," fourteenth-century thinkers like Duns Scotus and Ockham now discarded it.[45]

Nor did the knowability of the phenomenal world of nature entirely escape unscathed, as it too was conditioned, at least hypothetically, on God's absolute free will, allowing for the possibility of man's immediate, yet faulty apprehension of nonexistents if God so willed. The theory of "the intuitive cognition of non-existents," carefully restricted to cases of God's exercise of his *potentia absoluta* by Ockham, was expanded by other fourteenth-century philosophers to include the possibility of faulty apprehension as a matter of nature's course.[46] "Sensory error and . . . the possibility of divine deception" became, for instance, the most basic constructive elements of Peter Aureol's epistemology.[47] Nicholas of Autrecourt similarly held, against Ockam and others, that "if we admit that an effect . . . can be supernaturally produced without its natural cause, then we have no right to posit natural causes for any effects whatever"; in short, strictly speaking, the possibility of intuiting nonexistents as a result of divine intervention made human apprehension of all things in nature subject to error.[48] Nicholas's methods led him toward a radical skepticism in which certitude about the natural world retreated, leaving only probability in its stead, such that "the most probable hypothesis we can make is that everything that appears exists and that everything that appears to be true is true."[49] Finally, Peter of Limoges, author of the highly popular preaching manual *Liber de oculo morali* (c. 1260–1306),[50] must be counted in this company of fourteenth-century visual skeptics. Without recourse to the self-correction of an interior "eye of consideration" and "house of conscience," argues Peter, sin dooms human vision to certain error and fault. In ways that resonate deeply with the Mandeville author's own sensibilities, Peter extends visual skepticism to the realm of moral judgment of other men: whereas the body's eyes can only see others and not the self, he argues, the mind's eyes can never see others properly, and equip one only to judge the self.[51]

The preoccupation of fourteenth-century *moderni*—Ockham, Robert Holcott, Thomas Buckingham, Adam Woodham—with God's *potentia absoluta* was linked to a related preoccupation with issues of agency and free will, both God and man's, explored particularly in the context of Christian morality and the requirements of salvation.[52] Ockham and Holcott, for instance, believed in man's free will and his ability to perform virtue and earn reward of his own accord, which, they held, God could then accept according to his own absolute agency. Buckingham and Woodham, on the other hand, thought God's interpretation of man's actions, whatever their nature, alone significant for his salvation, thereby rendering traditional morality and man's natural reason inconsequential in the question of salvation.[53] All four thinkers shared the label of "Pelagian" for their belief in man's ability to achieve *merit de congruo*, virtue emerging from his own acts and of his own free will. Thomas Bradwardine, the chief anti-Pelagian, argued instead that man could do no good without God's grace; following his free will would lead to certain sin. Nor could man ever be assured of his moral status, according to Bradwardine ("Nescit homo utrum amore, an odio dignus sit").[54] Even greater confusion of traditional morality is evidenced in other discussions: Duns Scotus, for instance, argued that God's potentia absoluta could work, paradoxically enough, to free man from needing divine grace for salvation; Woodham argued that as God's potentia absoluta had no limits, sin and grace could coexist if God so willed, overturning all previous assumptions for the judgment of good and evil.[55]

While this debate assumes a Christian audience and appears to be at best only theoretically invested in non-Christian salvation, we should not thereby conclude that the salvation of non-Christians was not a specific and concrete concern for these and other fourteenth-century thinkers, who rather display the full range of dispositions on the issue. Conservative thinkers such as Bradwardine, Gregory of Remini, and Richard FitzRalph insisted on the necessity of grace, baptism, and conversion for salvation, holding infidels incapable of virtue: "ubi fides non erat, bonum opus non erat."[56] A majority of fourteenth-century thinkers, however, left the way open to non-Christian salvation, following a liberal line of thought descending from thirteenth-century thinkers like Aquinas and Alexander of Hales, each of whom had argued that a child reared outside Christianity could attain salvation "si facit quod in se est."[57] Duns Scotus held that while conversion was preferred, God's absolute power could bring about non-Christian salvation.[58] Holcott adopted the "facere quod in se est" formula, arguing that God would reveal himself to those who naturally did their best and that knowledge of God and science was available to all men.[59] Ockham too followed this formula, holding that membership in the church was not necessary for salvation, which was open to anyone who "facit quod in se est." Ockham gives the example of a pagan who grows up in Christian surroundings and has access to Christian teachings, but who does not convert and is nevertheless saved out of his love of God *ex puris naturalibus* and without the help of grace. Pagans, argues Ockham, though outside the Judeo-Christian covenant, are nevertheless subject to the divine will in the *ordinata*, or created world, by virtue of their living according to the natural laws of reason.[60] And Uthred of Boldon, a Benedictine monk, from the most conservative of orders, strikingly maintained at Oxford in the 1360s that all men, whether Jews, Saracens, pagans, or Christians, enjoyed a "claro visio" at the moment of death, when their soul either rejected or accepted God.[61] Neither grace nor natural law was necessary for salvation, Uthred held, but some sort of religious institution was—religions, like diverse manners of living, were like "many branches from one root."[62] This radically tolerant and open doctrine was soon condemned and withdrawn, but resurfaced in the writings of other thinkers, among them John Wycliff, who adopts Uthred's notion of "claro visio" and its attendant opening of salvation to any and all: "Man can be saved from any sect, even from among the Saracens" says the man who otherwise held Islam to be a heretical sect of Christianity.[63]

From the above survey, a number of fourteenth-century intellectual trends are apparent. First, we can see both how widespread is the concern for the salvation of non-Christians, and how the possibility of non-Christian salvation permeated fourteenth-century theological thinking. Also evident is the optimism of the notion of a God who revealed himself to all his children, no matter the particular circumstances of their birth, and of the agency of all men to reach out to God by "facere quod in se est." But the period shows signs of the anxiety of such self-critical, open-ended tolerance as well: God's potentia absoluta stressed the radical indeterminacy of salvation, the possible irrelevance of membership in the Christian Church, and the openness of salvation even to outright sinners. Fourteenth-century Christian thinkers were not spared the possibility that with regard to their most passionate concern, the salvation of their own souls, it neither mattered who they were nor what they did; they, in any event, were not equipped to know or distinguish who would be saved.

These countering effects of openness and skepticism are visited and visible on the *Travels'* notoriously elusive narrator, whose at-once openness and tentativeness, credulity and worldliness have struck many of his readers. In his treatment of Saracens, we observed a Mandeville unable to decide, having it both ways: converts to

Islam are "wicked" but Islam itself is not very distant from Christianity and Saracens "ben gode and feythfulle." In his depictions of pagan custom, the narrator shows a reluctance to judge cultural beliefs that contradict Christian teaching: "And sith that Cristene men han such beleeve, that ben enformed and taught alle day be holy doctryne whereinne thei scholde beleeve, it is no meruaylle thanne that the paynemes that han no gode doctryne but only of here nature beleeven more largely for here symples" (xviii), he says of Indian superstitions. The narrator's indeterminacy and uncertainty, his unwillingness to cast judgments on others on the basis of a single subject position, his unnerving tendency to say "maybe" to everything, speak an unquestionable openness and at the same time an underlying anxiety, which surely comes into sharper relief if we take the *Travels*' social and intellectual milieu into account. *Mandeville's Travels* was composed on the heels of the controversies above, and based on the diversity of its sources and the depth of learning those imply, its author could not have been positioned far from such debates. In M. C. Seymour's estimation, "such a collection of learned works" as constitute the author's sources "could have been found at this time (1351–57) only in a large ecclesiastical library, possibly Dominican or Franciscan or even papal."[64] Rather than expressing a knowing and savvy didacticism, the Mandeville narrator evinces the uncertainty peculiar to his age with regard to what set Christians apart in the eyes of God. This is not to say that the author must have "doubted that the Church of Rome was the true church and its dogmas the true faith," anymore than did the century's most prominent thinkers, but that his narrator reflects the spirit of open questioning with respect to the exclusivity of Christian blessedness unique to his times.[65]

Given the relative legitimacy accorded to non-Christian faith and practice in such social and intellectual circumstances, the others of this text, pagan or Muslim, can hardly be said to be taking part in the Western Orientalist or colonialist fantasy in which some critics have placed them.[66] If the other is made to take part in a European fantasy in the *Travels*, it is a peculiar horror fantasy of selves without borders, of the self's imminent collapse into otherness, of the unknowability of distinctions between self and other—in short, an unnerving and uncanny "crisis of phenomenality" provoked and sustained by the period's thorny preoccupation with non-Christian salvation. Very much at the expense of the self rather than the other, the self-other encounter of the *Travels* diverges significantly from Orientalist and colonialist practices. This is confirmed in a number of fascinating visually mediated encounters between self and world in the text of *Mandeville's Travels*, to which I turn in conclusion.

EYES ON THE WORLD: GLOBAL PERSPECTIVE AND RELATIVIZED GAZES IN *MANDEVILLE'S TRAVELS*

Visual experience is fundamental to the narration of the *Travels*. This assertion finds no better support than the countless claims made by its narrator as to the veracity of his report based on his own presence and eyewitnessing. This is the case whether the matter to which Mandeville is bearing witness is natural, ethnographic, or marvelous. Mandeville's statement punctuating his narration of the annual homage paid to a pious Eastern king by the various fish off the coast of his island may be taken as typical in this regard: "this, me semeth, is the moste merueylle that euere I saugh." While such assertions underscore the importance of eyewitnessing to narration in the *Travels*, Mandeville draws an even closer connection between his book and his eyes, going so far as to stake his narrative's right of existence on such eyewitnessing moments. For instance, when he reaches his description of the Paradys Terrestre, he carefully points out first that "of Paradys ne can I not speken properly, for I was not there" (xxxiii). He then relates what it looks like according to what "wise men seyn," by which he may mean ancients or sages with special knowledge, for "no man that is mortelle ne may not approchen to that Paradys." Having described the mortal effects that fall on those who endeavor to reach the Earthly Paradise, Mandeville then apologizes for his relation of the entire subject matter: "So that no mortelle man may approche to that place withouten specyalle grace of God, so that of that place I can sey you no more. And therefore I schalle holde me stille and retornen to that that I haue seen" (xxxiii). Just as men may not approach this paradise, so Mandeville suggests, can he not speak of it. He shall instead "holde . . . stille" his discourse and confine it to what he has seen, making his visual field and his discursive field the same. This means of concluding his discourse at the limits of his vision is revisited in his final pages, which are rich with visual language. Here he claims that he has had the pope read over both the things he has not seen and the things he has seen for himself: "And so my boke, alle be it that many men ne list not to yeue credence to nothing but to that that thei seen with hire eye, ne be the auctour ne the persone neuer so trewe, is affirmed and preued by oure holy fader in maner and forme as I have seyd" (xxxiv). In short, the pope's surveillance and inspection of Mandeville's eyewitnessed and reported material acts as insurance against the charge that his text is limited by blind spots, or that it is discourse unsupported by vision.

In claiming the eye as the source of its veracity, the *Travels* cites and builds on a cultural movement that had been gaining momentum since at least the twelfth century, which saw the rise of descriptive writing in the natural and human sciences founded on eyewitnessing. Scholars like Ernest Moody and Heiko Oberman have noted the empirical "shape of late medieval thought" with its increasing insistence on the test of experience, arguing importantly for the fourteenth century's continuities with modernity in having "provided the setting for modern science, replacing the authority-based deductive method with the empirical method."[67] The essentially visual nature of the fourteenth century's empiricism, moreover, has been remarked: "Ockhamist epistemology is not simply empirical; it is based on visual experience, and it takes the eye as the primary sense organ around which to build a theory of knowledge."[68] But even as the *Travels* displays and announces a modern visual empiricism, at moments it displays its breakdown and a profound visual skepticism that resonates with the thinking of contemporary theorists of visual error I noted earlier, including Peter Aureol and Nicholas of Autrecourt, who emphasized, respectively, the normativity of perceptual error and lack of visual certitude in their accounts of the workings of vision. *Mandeville's Travels* is chock-full of episodes that display visual skepticism by revealing the limits of the narrator's ethnographic gaze upon diverse others, and by extension, the limits and contingencies of the European gaze upon the world.

Mandeville's anecdote of the "three eyes" of civilizations, taken from Hayton of Armenia's *Fleurs des Histors d'Orient* (1307) and placed in his description of the palace of the great khan of Cathay, offers a particularly rich example of the text's meditations on the limits and powers of the Latin Christian gaze upon the world. Of the Chinese, Mandeville makes an assessment of their unsurpassed skills, saying "thei ben the moste sotyle men in all sciences and in alle craftes that ben in the world." He adds: "And therfore thei seyn hemself that thei seen with ii. eyen, and the Cristene men see but with on, because that thei ben more sotylle than thei. For alle other nacouns thei seyn ben but blynde in conynge and worchinge in comparisoun to them" (xxiii). The narrator's technique of delivery, his taking on the external perspective of Cathayans, marked with the repeated tags "they say that," is by now familiar. Mandeville here not only takes the Chinese perspective but delivers an authentically Eastern anecdote, attested in a range of European travel sources, in which the blind people of "other nations" are usually identified specifically as Muslims; the anecdote is, as such, suggestive of increasing tensions between Islamicized central Asian Mongols and "the settled civilizations they had conquered, from China to the fringes of Europe."[69] In presenting a hierarchy of vision based on a corresponding scale of arts and knowledge—markers of civility—the anecdote shows, first, the socially constructed nature of vision. In taking the Chinese at their word, and asserting that what and how you see depends on nationality, religion, or geography, the anecdote affirms the relational and contingent aspects of gazing. And in qualifying the Christian perspective, our narrator's own, as secondary to a more perfect Chinese one, the narrator reaffirms the relative limits of the Latin Christian perspective in a diverse world. Each of these aspects of the gaze according to the Eastern anecdote—its social construction, its contingency, and its limits from a global perspective—which are consistent with the visual poetics of the gaze in the medieval ethnographic texts we have been viewing, are recast in further episodes in the *Travels*.

Three such episodes occur within a single chapter, appropriately, the one devoted to the description of the globe itself—or the "forme and schapp" of the "erthe and the see." In a chapter that features a deluge of visual language as well as Mandeville's frequent assurances of personal eyewitnessing, one of the proofs the narrator puts his eyewitnessed evidence toward is the circularity and full inhabitability of the globe: "Be the whiche I seye you certeynly that men may envirowne alle the erthe of alle the world as wel vnder as abouen and turnen ayen to his contre, that hadde companye and schippynge and conduyt, and alleweys he scholde fynde men, londes, and yles als wel as in this contree" (xx). To further make this point, Mandeville tells a story that he claims to have heard "whan I was yong" but that, he simultaneously insists, represents not an isolated event and "hath . . . befallen may tymes." The story is of a "worthi" man who departs from "oure contrees for to go serche the world," who, like our narrator himself, passes India and the isles "beyonde Ynde." Mandeville continues:

> And so longe he went be see and lond and so enviround the world be many seisons, that he fond an yle where he herde speke his owne langage, callynge on oxen in the plowgh suche wordes as men speken to bestes in his owne contree; whereof he hadde gret meruayle, for he knew not how it myghte be. But I seye that he had gon so longe be londe and be see that he had envyround alle the erthe, that he was comen ayen envirounynge (that is to seye, goynge aboute) vnto his owne marches. And yif he wolde haue passed forth, he had founden his contree and his owne knouleche. But he turned ayen from thens fro whens he was come fro, and so he loste moche peynefulle labour, as himself seyde a gret while after that he was comen hom.

Eventually, a tempest drives the man home, whereupon he "knew wel that it was the yle where he had herd speke his owne langage before." "And that," concludes Mandeville, "was a possible thinge" (xx).

The story is, of course, about much more than the circumnavigability of the round globe or its everywhere inhabitability. What Mandeville shows as "possible" here, what is worthy of "meruayle," is the estrangement lying at the heart of "home." Such estrangement allows the traveler to find home when in "serche of the world," an uncanny substitution, and then to miss it altogether, to misapprehend it for further strange-worldliness. What is marvelous here is the changeability of the self in the face of otherness: the traveler is sufficiently othered, "worlded" or dialogized by his travels around the globe, as to misapprehend himself—a misrecognition or failure of visual apprehension attending and announcing the self's uncanny slippage into otherness. But of course this is only half of the story: the world, we are told, can also become self-like in an uncanny return, for the world, like the structure of the uncanny, is circular, and it is a matter of time before it will reappear as the "known of old and long familiar."

The "return"—of Mandeville's traveler, of any traveler—is not complete, however. For the self never returns to itself the same—as the law of castration has it, "no thing is ever the same but only the repetition of another"[70]—so that it cannot *but* misrecognize itself, cannot but return to itself as another. And it is here that we come upon another circle, and the full import of Mandeville's little story, which has all along felt unnervingly more significant than we can explain. Now Mandeville's story reveals itself as a provocative miniature of the *Travels* itself. For if the tale of the confused traveler announces the disorienting work of the world on the European self, this is something our narrator knows only too well himself. Why else, at his tale's end, upon his own "return" home to the center of Western Christianity, does he consciously and voluntarily submit himself to unworlding? As Mandeville tells us, "And yee schulle vndirstonde yif it lyke you that at myn hom comynge I cam to Rome and schewed my lif to oure holy fadir the Pope and was assoylled of alle that lay in my conscience of many a dyuerse greuous poynt, as men mosten nedes that ben in company dwellyng among so many a dyuerse folk of dyuerse secte and of beleeue as I haue ben" (xxxiv). Here he submits not just his text but his "lif" for the pope's inspection and correction, crucial after so much disorienting exposure to so much worldly diversity.

Chapter 20 presents us with further unsettling scenes of self-misrecognition. Mandeville ends the chapter seemingly innocently enough, with the following observation: "And yee schulle vundirstonde that, after the opynyoun of olde wise philosophres and astronomeres, oure contree ne Irelond ne Wales ne Scotlond ne Norweye ne the other yles costynge to hem ne ben not in the superficyalte cownted abouen the erthe, as it scheweth be alle the bokes of astronomye. For the superficialtee of the erthe is departed in vii. parties for the vii planetes, and tho parties ben clept clymates. And oure parties be not of the vii clymates, for thei ben descendyinge toward the west betwene high toward the roundness of the world" (xx). The passage, far from lending closure, is rather disturbing. Mandeville confesses his inability to find England and environs on a map: they are simply not there according to ancient philosophers and astronomers, who divide the surface of the earth into seven parts or "climates" without including the northern European isles in any one of them. According to the perspective of Mediterranean ancients, northern Europe is a blind spot, unworthy of mention. This may be understood as a sly commentary by Mandeville as to the accuracy of received traditions and authorities as against the empiricism and eyewitnessing he so frequently boasts throughout. But something further lingers about the passage, and this is the problem of perspective. For Mandeville has—inadvertently or consciously—raised the question of his own viewpoint. He stands and looks for the representation of his home, for an image of himself, from a position that does not exist according to the authorities he cites. In light of the other's word, the north European self does not exist, an acknowledgment that threatens the dissolution of this narrator's viewing position. We can hope for no clearer display, at once, of the terrors of uncanny self-annihilation, and of

European "provincialism," that is, the dangerously circumscribed limits of European knowledge of and perspective on the world.[71]

Finally, we come to chapter 20's richest vignette, one that deconstructs the gaze of the ethnographer-self on the object-world. Here Mandeville describes the two fixed stars, Transmontane and Antartyke, about which the firmament turns "right as doth a wheel," dividing the heavens into two equal parts. These "ii. egalle parties," which he designates as north and south, have more than equal mass in common: "In that lond ne in many othere beyonde that no man may see the sterre Transmontane (that is clept the *sterre of the see*) that is vnmevable and that is toward the north, that wee clepen the lodesterre. But men seen another sterre the contrarie to him, that is toward the south, that is clept Antartyk. And right as the schipmen taken here avys here and gouerne hem be the lodesterre, right so don schipmen beyonde tho parties be the sterre of the south, the whiche sterre appereth not to vs. And this sterre that is toward the north (that we clepen the lodesterre) ne appereth not to hem" (xx). The north star, Transmontane, or the lodestar, is invisible to southern hemispheric dwellers ("that lond"); the south star, Antartyk, is invisible to northern hemispheric dwellers: northerners and southerners each have a blind spot, which is the star around which the other's hemisphere turns. This analogous and symmetrical blind spot would be interesting enough in itself as an emblem of the incompleteness of northern and southern epistemologies. But Mandeville soon enough extends the implications of mutual blindness irrevocably further:

> For yee wyten welle that thei that ben toward the Antartyk, thei ben streght feet ayen feet of hem that dwellen vnder the Transmontane also wel as wee, and thei that dwellyn vnder vs ben feet ayenst feet. For alle the parties of see and of lond han here appositees habitables or trepassables and [yles] of this half and beyond half. . . . But how it semeth to symple men vnlerned that men ne mowe not go vnder the erthe, and also that men scholde falle toward the Heuene from vnder. But that may not be vpon less that wee mowe falle toward Hevene from the erthe where wee ben. For fro what partie of the erthe that man duelle, outher abouen or benethen, it semeth always to hem that duellen that thei gon more right than ony other folk. And right as it semeth to vs that thei ben vnder vs, right so it semeth hem that wee ben vnder them. (xx)

In this provocative passage, Mandeville first succinctly and elegantly encapsulates his supposition of the existence of antipodes, people on the "other side," under Europe, with the wonderfully visual metaphor of northerners and southerners living "feet ayenst feet." The question of the existence of antipodes—"men, that is who live on the other side of the earth, where the sun rises when it sets for us, men who plant their footsteps opposite ours"[72]—constituted a flourishing and controversial medieval debate dating back to Augustine at the core of which was the question of the "others" of Christianity: if antipodes in fact existed on the other side of the earth, how could they derive from Adam as Christianity insisted all human beings did? Augustine resolved the question by asserting that if the antipodes did indeed exist (which he believed not) and were indeed "human," by which he meant rational, rather than monstrous, they must necessarily derive from the first couple.[73] This left open at least the theoretical possibility that antipodes existed and were not human, but essentially as well as geographically "other," with which later medieval thinkers continued to grapple. It is to this question, the essential "otherness" of antipodal life, that Mandeville directly addresses himself, and directs our attention. Raising the point of "how it semeth to symple men vnlerned that men ne mowe not go vnder the erthe"—the problem of morality, the questionable Christianity in such down-under living—Mandeville sets out to quell whatever doubt might exist in his reader's minds as to the morality of southern dwelling with a simple formula: "For fro what partie of the erthe that man duelle, outher abouen or benethen, it semeth always to hem that duellen that thei gon more right than ony other folk." This formula recalls Mandeville's previous treatment of the invisibility of the north star to southerners and the south star to northerners, that is, the mutual blindspots of northern and southern empiricism and epistemology. Here, too, we are confronted with a visual problem—that of "seeming" or appearances; but here Mandeville has lifted the north-south symmetry of blindness into another order: cultural-moral, and hence religious. Just as northerners such as Mandeville's audience are tempted to judge southerners as morally troubled or troubling for their living opposite them, so, Mandeville asserts, do southerners assert that "thei gon more right than ony other folk" in living where they live. For "right as it semeth to vs that thei ben vnder vs, right so it semeth hem that wee ben vnder them." Social and moral apprehension, that is, depend literally, here, on where one happens to be standing; the "truth" of visually apprehended social knowledge is socially constructed, relational, and contingent rather than absolute or able to be apprehended from an objective position that does not implicate the viewer and the viewing process. It is deictically derived.

At this final juncture between self and world, then, the Mandeville author, like Peter of Limoges before him, suggests the utter unsuitability of humans to judge those in opposite or "other" positions on the basis of their senses. Such an assertion certainly resonates with one we have related to the problem of the uncanny in this late medieval text: the problem of distinguishing the good and saved from the bad and damned in this life. The author of the *Travels* has come down clearly in this heated fourteenth-century debate: the empiricism of human perspective is always partial and limited, and as such cannot but fail to penetrate the hidden and invisible signs of God's will. In doing so, he not only severs human knowledge from the divine, the realm of reason from that of faith, but epitomizes, in aesthetic and cultural form, one of the most vexing theological and epistemological problems of the fourteenth century.

The problems of human vision—the necessary contingencies of human perspective, its blind spots, the problem of appearances and seeming cultural truths—are essential to the author's point in these passages. The Mandeville author uses visual fallibility as a point of connection between self and other: northerners and southerners are both mutually ill equipped to judge each other, and less distinguishable for their likelihood to try to do just that—bound together in a common inability to make meaningful distinctions between themselves and their would-be others. He thus practices a deconstructive ethnography that turns "otherness" on its head, revealing it as a construct emerging out of the very mechanics of faulty human perspective rather than as born of necessity or truth. He performs this same visual trick when speaking of the Pygmies, of whom he says: "And of tho men of oure stature han thei als grete skorn and wonder as we wolde haue among vs of geauntes yif thei weren amonges vs"—Pygmies view humans with as much scorn as we view giants; we are linked by the contingencies of perspective. Far from constructing an "antithesis" to Western civilization in his depiction of antipodal "foot-to-foot" living, the Mandeville author sets out to collapse the very basis for such antithesis, exposing the faulty scaffolding of its construction—human vision. According to his fourteenth-century theorization, visual limits produce otherness; the gaze, its ethnographic others. Here in the late fourteenth century, *Mandeville's Travels* has essentially rearticulated the view of Gerald of Wales that human perspective on other humans is necessarily partial, incomplete, and ever imperfect.

Conclusion

On close examination, the premodern ethnographies of *In Light of Another's Word* reveal themselves to be highly complex cultural objects in which the voices and gazes of Europe's others reflect images of Europeans back to them, holding up an often startling mirror to the late medieval European self. In the *Description of Wales*, an ethnic Cambro-Norman hybrid cites native Welsh discourse in ways that show Anglo-Norman self-definition to be inextricably bound up with its colonial other. In the *Journey*, William of Rubruck reflects imperial Mongols viewing Latin Christians as adherents of a confounding faith, even as tamquam monstra, some kind of monsters. In Joinville's *Vie de Saint Louis*, the cited sayings of a revered Islamic crusading hero reflect a sanctioned view of the Christian faithful as substitutable with their Muslim counterparts. And in the funhouse reflections of *Mandeville's Travels*, sultans speak in Christian voice, holy and monstrous rites resolve into one image, and one is never sure where the self ends and the other begins. For these late medieval European travelers and ethnographers, dialogic engagement with the voices and perspectives of others was not only disorienting but productively so, challenging and altering long-held assumptions about both self and other. Thus at the end of his journey, William of Rubruck is forced to acknowledge Christian scripture as just "one story" with no inherent primacy over others in multifaith contexts, while Joinville reports on an Islam already worshipful of core Judeo-Christian patriarchs and saints. Much was at stake in such European reorientation, including a rethinking of the centrality of Latin Christians' place in a heterogeneous world such as Mandeville presses to its limit, and new, more realistic modes of thinking and writing about an assortment of Europe's others.

The empirical status of prescientific, premodern ethnographic works has been and continues to be challenged due to the presence within them of stories now marked as fantastic—the mythical Prester John, descriptions of the Earthly Paradise. But the dismissal of premodern ethnography as unscientific when compared to that of later eras is far from self-evident. It is instead guided by the widespread association of the Middle Ages with forces opposed to science—whether the occult, the mythical, the barbaric, or the fanciful.[1] And as historians of ethnography know, problems of empiricism haunt the ethnographic method well past the medieval period—today, much of the self-styled classic, "scientific" nineteenth-century ethnography reads instead as a record of European self-projection and fantasy falling under the sign of Orientalism. By contrast, premodern ethnography's production of social knowledge without recourse to claims of scientific objectivity but instead through the modest accumulation of divergent perspectives wears well from our own postmodern vantage point. So too does the mode of writing ethnography in light of another's word. Instead of fantastically projecting the other as a screen on which to play out the interests of the European self, the ethnographies of this study highlight and foreground the ineluctable materiality of the other and of difference, demonstrating their centrifugal power to disrupt and reorient the perspectives of the onlooking self. Unlike fantasy, and rather like the scientific method, dialogism tests rather than serves unstated cultural assumptions.

But from what conditions do dialogism and the production of culturally challenging ethnography emerge? The peripheral or precarious position of Latin Christians abroad witnessed in this study is not likely accidental: dialogism is less suited to conditions of fixed and asymmetrical power than to fluid and more uneven conditions. It may even flourish best when the writer-ethnographer is disempowered. Recall William's closing complaint in his remarkable *Journey* about not being able to speak openly as a mere missionary. This may well be, but had he had more authority in the realm, would he have *written* as he did? Scholars of early modern ethnography note that while that period's travelers lacked the sense of total cultural superiority that would be exhibited by their nineteenth-century counterparts over people in locales such as India, they already came armed with certainties—of the superiority of European firearms, of Christianity's sole authenticity— about which medieval Europeans abroad in Asia or the Holy Land could be less sure.[2] Such cultural uncertainty was, as we have seen, in fact boldly generative: in Europe's still-formative, precolonial era, it combined with a premodern affinity for perspectival representation to nurture a mode of ethnography that dared to step into alternative worlds and words, and refashion both self and other in their light.

NOTES

INTRODUCTION

1. A phrase I have adapted from the work of Mikhail Bakhtin. In describing Roman cultural bilingualism, Bakhtin writes: "From its very first steps, the Latin literary word viewed itself *in the light of the Greek word*, through the eyes of the Greek word; it was from the very beginning a word 'with a sideways glance'" (italics mine). See "From the Prehistory of Novelistic Discourse," in *The Dialogic Imagination: Four Essays*, ed. Michael Holquist, trans. Caryl Emerson and Holquist (Austin: University of Texas Press, 1982), 41–83, quotation on 61.

2. See, for instance, Karma Lochrie, "Provincializing Medieval Europe: Mandeville's Cosmopolitan Utopia," PMLA 124.2 (2009): 592–99; and María Rosa Menocal, *The Ornament of the World: How Muslims, Jews, and Christians Created a Culture of Tolerance in Medieval Spain* (New York: Little, Brown, 2002). For my reading of cosmopolitanism in late medieval ethnography and travel, see Shirin A. Khanmohamadi, "Worldly Unease in Late Medieval European Travel Reports," in *Cosmopolitanism and the Middle Ages*, ed. John Ganim and Shayne Legassie, New Middle Ages (New York: Palgrave, 2013), 105–20.

3. The concept of the "contact zone" has been deployed productively by critics of travel and encounter narratives such as Mary Louise Pratt to show how subjects newly brought together in a "spatial and temporal copresence . . . are constituted in and by their relations to each other" (7)—in a word, dialogically. Setting out to complicate diffusionist models of top-down, colonizer-to-colonized cultural influence, Pratt insists on the two-directional nature of cultural influence even in highly asymmetrical, modern colonial encounters. See *Imperial Eyes: Travel Writing and Transculturation* (New York: Routledge, 1992), 4–6.

4. The nature and sources of medieval ethnographic thinking and writing have recently been undergoing scholarly definition and elaboration. For a comprehensive introduction to medieval Europe's ethnography and its debt to classical sources, see Robert Bartlett, *Gerald of Wales, 1146–1223* (Oxford: Clarendon Press, 1982), especially 155–210, and *The Making of Europe: Conquest, Colonization and Cultural Change, 950–1350* (London: Allen Lane,

1993). Joan-Pau Rubiés has recently published a number of important studies, among them the collection *Medieval Ethnographies: European Perceptions of the World Beyond* (Aldershot, England: Ashgate, 2009) (which includes J. K. Hyde's essay "Ethnographers in Search of an Audience," 65–119), *Travel and Ethnology in the Renaissance: South India Through European Eyes, 1250–1625* (Cambridge: Cambridge University Press, 2002), and "Travel Writing and Ethnography," in *Cambridge Companion to Travel Writing*, ed. Peter Hulme and Tim Young (Cambridge: Cambridge University Press, 2002), 242–60; as well as Jas Elsner and Rubiés, introduction to *Voyages and Visions: Towards a Cultural History of Travel*, ed. Rubiés and Elsner (London: Reaktion Books, 1999), 1–56. See also Felipe Fernández-Armesto, "Medieval Ethnography," *Journal of the Anthropological Society of Oxford* 13.3 (1982): 275–86; and Jeffrey Jerome Cohen's recent *Hybridity, Identity and Monstrosity in Medieval Britain: On Difficult Middles*, New Middle Ages (New York: Palgrave, 2006), chapter 1, "Acts of Separation," 11–42. A number of scholars have responded to the ethnographic work of *Mandeville's Travels*. See Ian Higgins, *Writing East: The "Travels" of Sir John Mandeville* (Philadelphia: University of Pennsylvania Press, 1997); Suzanne Conklin Akbari, "The Diversity of Man in the *Book of John Mandeville*," in *Eastward Bound, Travel and Travellers from 1050–1550*, ed. Rosamund Allen (Manchester: Manchester University Press, 2004), 156–76; and Geraldine Heng, *Empire of Magic: Medieval Romance and the Politics of Cultural Fantasy* (New York: Columbia University Press, 2003), "Eye on the World: Mandeville's Pleasure Zones; Or, Cartography, Anthropology, and Medieval Travel Romance," 239–305.

5. Rubiés, "Travel Writing and Ethnography," 257–58.

6. Manners and customs discourse has long been recognized as residing at the heart of ethnographic writing, whether in its classical origins (Herodotus, Tacitus) or its early modern expression. See Margaret Hodgen, *Early Anthropology in the Sixteenth and Seventeenth Centuries* (Philadelphia: University of Pennsylvania Press, 1998). Roger Bacon, the preserver of William of Rubruck's *Itinerarium* in his *Opus Maius*, for instance, renamed William's *Itinerarium* "De Moribus Tartarorum" (On the customs of the Tartars [Mongols]). See *Opus Maius*, ed. John Henry Bridges, 3 vols. (Oxford: Clarendon Press, 1897–1900), 1:400–401, 2:368, 371, 376, 383. See Peter Jackson, introduction to William, *The Mission of Friar William of Rubruck* (London: Hakluyt Society, 1990), 1–55, on 53–54. Medieval Europeans, Robert Bartlett has argued, saw customs, along with language and laws, as a primary basis for differentiating and defining their own cultural identities against those of others. See *The Making of Europe*, 197. Bartlett emphasizes that racial, i.e., somatic, differences were relatively unimportant in making those distinctions.

7. Hyde, "Ethnographers in Search of an Audience," 167–68.

8. Bartlett, *Gerald of Wales*, 181.

9. See Hyde on Carpini's original contribution, "Ethnographers in Search of an Audience."

10. See Jackson, introduction, *The Mission of Friar William of Rubruck*, 47–51.

11. Rubiés, *Travel and Ethnology in the Renaissance*, 83.

12. The Crusades may have been thus far overlooked as a source of ethnographic production because encounters with Muslims, Jews, and oriental Christians, as opposed to pagans, often generated more polemic than curiosity in Latin Christian accounts. But this was of course not always the case, and the crusading theater did contribute to ethnographic production, particularly in the later Middle Ages during its era of contraction as opposed to its early years of expansion. In 1307, for instance, the Armenian prince Hayton (Hetoum) included in his call for a Latin-Mongol crusade against Muslims to restore the Kingdom of Cicilia an account of Eastern peoples from Syria to Cathay and histories of Muslim and Mongol dynasties. See Rubiés to this effect in his introduction to *Medieval Ethnographies*, xiii–xxxviii, on xxi, xxiii.

13. Multiplicity of perspective in medieval painting has been treated by Samuel Edgerton, *The Renaissance Rediscovery of Linear Perspective* (New York: Basic Books, 1975); Miriam Bunim, *Space in Medieval Painting and the Forerunners of Perspective* (New York: AMS Press, 1970); and more recently A. C. Spearing, *Textual Subjectivity: The Encoding of Subjectivity in Medieval Narratives and Lyrics* (Oxford: Oxford University Press, 2005). For the treatment of multifocality in chronicle writing, see Gabrielle Spiegel, *Romancing the Past: The Rise of Vernacular Prose Historiography in Thirteenth-Century France* (Berkeley: University of California Press, 1993), and "Genealogy: Form and Function in Medieval Historical Narrative," *History and Theory* 22.1 (1983): 43–53.

14. See Bakhtin's reading of Roman self-consciousness in relation to a more hegemonic Greek metropolitan culture in *The Dialogic Imagination*, 61.

15. See Sharon Kinoshita, *Medieval Boundaries: Rethinking Difference in Old French Literature* (Philadelphia: University of Pennsylvania Press, 2006); Cohen, *Hybridity, Identity, and Monstrosity*; Richard Bulliet, *The Case for Islamo-Christian Civilization* (New York: Columbia University Press, 2004); and María Rosa Menocal's earlier classic, *The Arabic Role in Medieval Literary History: A Forgotten Heritage* (Philadelphia: University of Pennsylvania Press, 1987).

16. See Rubiés, introduction to *Medieval Ethnographies*, especially xiv.

17. See James Clifford, "On Ethnographic Authority," in *The Predicament of Culture* (Cambridge, MA: Harvard University Press, 1998), 21–54, and "Partial Truths," in *Writing Culture: The Poetics and Politics of Ethnography*, ed. James Clifford and George Marcus (Berkeley: University of California Press, 1986), 1–26, quotation on 13.

18. Mary Louise Pratt, "Fieldwork in Common Places," in Clifford and Marcus, *Writing Culture*, 27–50, quotation on 32.

19. Augmenting the critiques of Clifford and Pratt, Timothy Mitchell similarly notes of the gaze of European travelers to colonial Egypt: "to establish the objectness of the Orient, as something set apart from the European presence, required that the[ir] presence itself, ideally, become invisible." See *Colonising Egypt* (Cambridge: Cambridge University Press, 1988), 26.

20. Martin Jay, *Downcast Eyes: The Denigration of Vision in Twentieth-Century French Thought* (Berkeley: University of California Press, 1993), "Sartre, Merleau-Ponty, and the Search for a New Ontology of Sight," 263–328, on 287–88.

21. See Edgerton, *Renaissance Rediscovery of Linear Perspective*; and William M. Ivins, *On the Rationalization of Sight*: Metropolitan Museum of Art Papers no. 8, 1938, New York (repr. Cambridge, MA: Da Capo Press, 1973).

22. For a description of "deictic" poetics in painting, see art historian Norman Bryson, *Vision and Painting: The Logic of the Gaze* (New Haven, CT: Yale University Press, 1983), 88–89.

23. See Janet Abu-Lughod, *Before European Hegemony: The World System, a.d. 1250–1350* (Oxford: Oxford University Press, 1991). Writing of the disjunction between early modern and nineteenth-century travel and ethnographic gazes upon others in travel and ethnographic writings, Rubiés has argued that "the blatantly imperialistic assumptions of many nineteenth-century travel writers stand in contrast with the nuanced portrayal of native courts often displayed by early modern ambassadors." See "Travel writing and ethnography," 250–51.

24. In this way, my book aligns itself with that branch of postcolonial medievalism that questions the ready application of influential postcolonial theoretical models like Orientalism to the medieval period. For a recent articulation of this critique, see Kinoshita, *Medieval Boundaries*. While Kinoshita restricts her critique of "the conventional orientalizing tropes deployed by an unreflective strain of late twentieth-century postcolonial medievalism" to pre-fourteenth-century, and non-English, literary criticism, texts like *Mandeville's Travels,* as I show, argue for the unsuitability of Orientalizing tropes well into the fourteenth century and in England.

25. Johannes Fabian's critique of anthropology's objectification of natives, for instance, rests on his critique of the objectification of knowledge via its spatialization: he believes it is specifically the ability to render knowledge as *visible* objects in space, a maneuver that distances subjects-knowers from the subject-known, that paves the way for human objectification in the human sciences. See *Time and the Other: How Anthropology Makes Its Object* (New York: Columbia University Press, 1983). Fabian's analysis is consistent with that of Edward Said, who in his groundbreaking study *Orientalism* argues that a static system of "synchronic essentialism" underpins Orientalist practice: "The Orientalist *surveys the Orient from above*, with the aim of getting hold of the whole sprawling panorama before him—culture, religion, mind, history, society. To do this he must *see every detail* through the device of a set of reductive categories (the Semites, the Muslim mind, the Orient, and so forth). . . . *A vision therefore is static,* just as the scientific categories informing late nineteenth century Orientalism are static: there is no recourse beyond 'the Semites' or 'the Oriental mind'; these are final terminals holding every variety of Oriental behavior within *a general view of the whole field*" (my italics). Edward Said, *Orientalism* (New York: Vintage, 1979), 239.

26. See Suzannah Biernoff, *Sight and Embodiment in the Middle Ages: Ocular Desires* (New York: Palgrave Macmillan, 2002).

27. See Jay, *Downcast Eyes*, 30, 45.

28. See Sarah Stanbury, "The Lover's Gaze in *Troilus and Criseyde*," in ed. *Chaucer's Troilus and Criseyde: Subgit to All Poesye*, ed. R. A. Shoaf (Binghamton, NY: Medieval and Renaissance Text Studies, 1992), 224–38, on 231. For another important study of lovers' gazes in medieval literature, see Ruth Cline, "Hearts and Eyes," *Romance Philology* 25 (1971–72): 263–97. For further analysis of the difference of the premodern "scopic regime" from the modern, see Stanbury, "Regimes of the Visual in Premodern England: Gaze, Body and Chaucer's *Clerk's Tale*," *New Literary History* 28.2 (1997): 261–89.

CHAPTER 1

1. Joan-Pau Rubiés similarly distinguishes ethnography from ethnology thus: "If we define ethnography as the description of peoples in their variety, a practice often ruled by implicit assumptions rather than explicit theories, we may distinguish ethnology as a theoretical discourse on humanity, unity and diversity (racial and cultural) which makes use of ethnography and is a subject of debate within a scientific (but not necessarily academic) discourse." See "Travel Writing and Ethnography," in *Travellers and Cosmographers: Studies in the History of Early Modern Travel and Ethnology*, ed. Rubiés (Aldershot, England: Ashgate Variorum, 2007), essay 4, 1–39, quote on 3.

2. Joan-Pau Rubiés has usefully defined the language of civility as "operat[ing] through the categories of savagery, or barbarism, and rationality," on the one hand, and the language of Christianity as "divid[ing] . . . Christians and heathens, and interpret[ing] historical agency in terms of Providence and sin," on the other. See "New World and Renaissance Ethnology," *History and Anthropology* 6.2 (1993): 157–97, quotation on 171.

3. See Robert Bartlett's classic study, *Gerald of Wales, 1146–1223* (Oxford: Clarendon Press, 1982).

4. "If these races are included in the definition of 'human,' that is, if they are rational and mortal animals, it must be admitted that they trace their lineage from that same one man, the first father of all mankind. This assumes, of course, the truth of the stories about the divergent features of those races, and their great difference from one another and from us." Augustine, *City of God*, 16.8, trans. Henry Bettenson (New York: Penguin, 1984). In chapter 9 of the same book, Augustine asserts there is not "rational ground" for belief in antipodal life.

5. John Bagnell Bury, *Idea of Progress* (London: Macmillan, 1920), 16.

6. See John Gillingham, "The Beginnings of English Imperialism," *Journal of Historical Sociology* 5.4 (1992): 392–409; and Rodney M. Thomson, *William of Malmesbury* (Woodbridge, England: Boydell Press, 1987), especially chapter 3, "William's Reading," 40–75.

7. W. R. Jones, "The Image of the Barbarian in Medieval Europe," *Comparative Studies in Society and History* 13.4 (1971): 376–407, quotation on

397. Jones notes the impact of Ciceronian ideas on late medieval intellectuals from the poet Peter of Poitiers to scholastics such as Albertus Magnus, St. Thomas Aquinas, and Roger Bacon, whom I discuss as arbiters of the discourse of Christianity below.

8. See Edward E. Best, "Classical Latin Prose Writers Quoted by Giraldus Cambrensis" (Ph.D. diss., University of North Carolina, Chapel Hill, 1957).

9. Thomson, *William of Malmesbury*, 11.

10. Julius Caesar, *The Gallic War*, trans. H. J. Edwards (Cambridge, MA: Harvard Loeb Classics, 1979).

11. Sallust, *Bellum Iugurthinum*, 17.1–19.8, 170–73, ed. J. C. Rolfe, rev. ed. (London: Loeb Classical Library, 1931).

12. Arthur O. Lovejoy and George Boas, *Primitivism and Related Ideas in Antiquity* (1935; repr., New York: Octagon, 1965); see chapters 8 and 9 on Lucretius and Cicero, respectively.

13. For a complete account of Lucretian progressivist anthropology, see Lovejoy and Boas, *Primitivism and Related Ideas*, chapter 8, "Lucretius: Primitivism and the Idea of Progress," 222–42. See also Thomas Cole, *Democritus and the Sources of Greek Anthropology*, Philological Monographs no. 25, (Chapel Hill, NC: American Philological Association, 1967), 3. Cole adds the following reservation: "The estimate is certainly one which makes too little allowance for the possibility that Lucretius' narrative represents a specifically Epicurean treatment of the subject. But the text is so detailed and comprehensive that it must occupy a prominent, if not necessarily central, place in one's researches."

14. Lucretius, *De rerum natura* V.1011–1027, cited in Lovejoy and Boas, *Primitivism and Related Ideas*, 228–29, quotation on 229.

15. Lucretius, *De rerum natura* V.1143–1160, cited in Lovejoy and Boas, *Primitivism and Related Ideas*, 234.

16. Lucretius, *De rerum natura* V.1448–57, cited in Lovejoy and Boas, *Primitivism and Related Ideas*, 236–37.

17. Robert Nisbet, *History of the Idea of Progress* (New York: Basic Books, 1980), 42.

18. Cicero, *De Officiis* 2.4.15, cited in Lovejoy and Boas, *Primitivism and Related Ideas*, 251.

19. Lovejoy and Boas, *Primitivism and Related Ideas*, 243.

20. For contemporary uses of the term, see R. R. Davies, *The First English Empire: Power and Identities in the British Isles, 1093–1343* (New York: Oxford University Press, 2000), 128n63.

21. Cicero, *Pro Sestio* 42.91–92, cited in Lovejoy and Boas, *Primitivism and Related Ideas*, 243–44.

22. "Si . . . stabilique magis pugnae quam agilitati dimicando confisi fuerint." Gerald of Wales [Giraldi Cambrensis], *Descriptio Kambriae* 2.10, in *Opera*, 6 vols, ed. James F. Dimock (London: Longman, 1861–91).

23. English text from Gerald of Wales, *The History and Topography of Ireland*, trans. John O'Meara (New York: Penguin, 1982), 101–2; Latin from Gerald, *Topographia Hibernica* 3.10, *Opera*, vol. 5 (1867).

24. William of Malmesbury, *Gesta Regum Anglorum*, ed. and trans. R. A. B. Mynors, vol. 1, chapter 409 (Oxford: Clarendon Press, 1998), 738–40.

25. Bury, *Idea of Progress*, 21.

26. Matthew Paris, *Matthew Paris' English History from the Year 1235 to 1273*, vol. 1, trans. J. A. Giles (New York: AMS Press, 1968), 312–13.

27. Pliny, *Natural History in Ten Volumes*, ed. H. Rackham, vol. 2 (books 3–7) (Cambridge, MA: Harvard University Press, 1949), bk. 7.2.

28. John Block Friedman, *The Monstrous Races in Medieval Art and Thought* (Cambridge, MA: Harvard University Press, 1981), 26.

29. It is in India where we find the gymnosophists, Cynocephales, races exhibiting various anomalous childbirth practices, and those with no tongues or no speech. In Africa, especially Ethiopia, we find Garamants sharing their women, Nomads, more Dogheads, cannibal Anthropophages, and Libya is home of cave-dwelling Troglodites, devil-worshipping Augyles, trade-abstaining Gamphasants, and headless Blemmyes. See Solinus [C. Iulii Solini], *Collectanea Rerum Memorabilium*, ed. Theodor Mommsen (Berlin: Weidmannsche, 1958), 183–203, on 129–37.

30. Solinus, *Collectanea* 152, 182, 184–85, 198–99.

31. Ibid., 88.

32. Isidore [Isidori Hispalensis Episcopi], *Etymologiarum sive Originum Libri XX*, ed. W. M. Lindsay (Oxford: Clarendon Press, 1985), vol. 2, bk. 11.3. Isidore provides further relevant ethnographic models elsewhere in the *Etymologies*; in bk. 9, devoted to languages and social groups, he notes the eruption of new customs or mores into the Roman Empire upon the Germanic invasions, and parses Germanic culture according to the diversity of its arms, *habitus* or aspect, and languages (dissonant and impure ones as compared to the purity of Latin). See *Etymologies*, ed. Marc Reydellet (Paris: Societe d'Editions, 1984), 37, 96.

33. See Richard Bernheimer, *Wild Men in the Middle Ages: A Study in Art, Sentiment, and Demonology* (Cambridge, MA: Harvard University Press, 1952), chapter 4, "The Learned Aspect," 85–120.

34. This, Roger Bartra's phrase, reveals the shared contours of discourses of the human, ethnography, and discourses of the wild man. See Bartra, *Wild Men in the Looking Glass*, trans. Carl T. Berrisford (Ann Arbor: University of Michigan Press, 1994).

35. Albeit they were doing so just after the great missions of Carpini and Rubruck, and so their classifications were unavailable to these seminal thirteenth-century ethnographic writers.

36. H. W. Janson, *Apes and Ape Lore in the Middle Ages and the Renaissance* (London: Warburg and Courtauld Studies, 1952), 83.

37. Ibid., 85.

38. Albertus Magnus, *On Animals: A Medieval Summa Zoologica*, trans. Kenneth F. Kitchell Jr. and Irven Michael Resnick, 2 vols. (London: Johns Hopkins University Press, 1999), vol. 2, 1416n23. Albertus had never seen a Pygmy but had accumulated data about it on the basis of reports. See Janson, *Apes and Ape Lore*, 88.

39. Albertus, *On Animals*, 1417–18.

40. In Janson's estimation, Albertus Magnus's work represents "as close an approximation to genuinely scientific anthropology as the intellectual

horizon of the Middle Ages would permit," raising questions "not to be raised again until four centuries later." Janson, *Apes and Ape Lore*, 93.

41. Albertus Magnus, *Ethicorum*, bk. 7, tract 1, ch. 1, in *Opera Omnia*, ed. Augustus Borgnet, (Paris: Vivès, 1891), quoted in Anthony Pagden, *The Fall of Natural Man: The American Indian and the Origins of Comparative Ethnology* (Cambridge: Cambridge University Press, 1982), 21.

42. Scythians, like Tartars after them, had been identified by antique writers as the "enclosed nations" of Alexander's Gate, and in this way may be seen as the forerunners of the Tartars in the European imaginary. See Jones, "Image of the Barbarians," 399.

43. Thomas Aquinas, *Commentary on the Politics*, trans. Ernest L. Fortin and Peter D. O'Neill, in *Medieval Political Philosophy*, ed. Ralph Lerner (New York: Free Press, 1963), 305–6.

44. Quoted in Benjamin Kedar, *Crusade and Mission: European Approaches Towards the Muslims* (Princeton, NJ: Princeton University Press, 1984), 183, 218.

45. William Rockhill, "Introductory Notice," in *The Journey of William of Rubruck to the Eastern Parts of the World*, ed. Rockhill (1990; repr., London: Hakluyt Society, 1998), xiii–xliv, xxii.

46. James Muldoon, *Popes, Lawyers, and Infidels: The Church and the Non-Christian World, 1250–1500* (Philadelphia: University of Pennsylvania Press, 1979), 42.

47. Ibid., 6–7.

48. Ibid., 9–11.

49. Ibid., 48.

50. Ibid., 19–21.

51. In doing so, they reveal the popularity of the argument of "sin," for Innocent had made the preclusion of missionaries a ground for "just war" without recourse to calling such preclusion a sin.

52. Hemmerlin's *De Nobilitate ac Rusticitate* is quoted in Felipe Fernández-Armesto, *Before Columbus: Exploration and Colonisation from the Mediterranean to the Atlantic, 1229–1492* (London: Macmillan, 1987), 235.

53. Muldoon, *Popes, Lawyers, and Infidels*, 158.

54. Ibid., 19–20.

55. Ibid., 121.

56. Friedman, *The Monstrous Races*, 206. Elsewhere, the natives' immodest dress was also seen as a sign of their imperfect humanity. See ibid., 203.

57. This point is made eloquently by Fernández-Armesto, *Before Columbus*.

58. Muldoon, *Popes, Lawyers, and Infidels*, 156–58.

59. Ibid., 124.

60. See Friedman, *Monstrous Races*, 199.

61. The genre included such twelfth-century texts as the *Vita Mahumeti*, Walter of Compiègne's *Otia de Machomete*, and Guibert of Nogent's *Gesta Dei per Francos*, 1.3, and the thirteenth-century *Roman de Mahomet*. See R. W. Southern's discussion of the group in *Western Views of Islam in the Middle Ages* (Cambridge, MA: Harvard University Press, 1972), 29–33. See

also Norman Daniel, *Islam and the West: The Making of an Image* (Edinburgh: Edinburgh University Press, 1959), 67.

62. Dorothee Metlitzki, *The Matter of Araby in Medieval England* (New Haven, CT: Yale University Press, 1977), 204; and Samuel C. Chew, *The Crescent and the Rose: Islam and England During the Renaissance* (Oxford: Oxford University Press, 1937), 413.

63. Bernard Hamilton, "Knowing the Enemy: Western Understanding of Islam at the Time of the Crusades," *Journal of the Royal Asiatic Society of Great Britain and Ireland* ser. 3, 7 (1997): 373–87, on 374–75.

64. Ibid., 376–78.

65. Ibid., 378.

66. Jean-Pau Rubiés, introduction to *Medieval Ethnographies: European Perceptions of the World Beyond*, ed. Rubiés (Aldershot, England: Ashgate, 2009), xiii–xxxviii, xxi.

67. J. K. Hyde, "Ethnographers in Search of an Audience," in Rubiés, *Medieval Ethnographies*, 65–119, on 73.

68. Hamilton, "Knowing the Enemy," 379.

69. Ibid., 380.

70. See John V. Tolan, "Mirror of Chivalry: Salah al-Din in the Medieval European Imagination," in *Images of the Other: Europe and the Muslim World Before 1700*, ed. David Blanks, Cairo Papers in Social Science, vol. 19, monograph 2 (Cairo: American University in Cairo Press, 1996), 7–38. See, too, Saladin's representation in Boccaccio, *Decameron* 1.3.

71. As Bernard Hamilton has aptly remarked, owing to "the greater degree of contact with Muslims and their civilization which the crusades produced . . . an attempt was made to accommodate good Muslims in the thought-world of western Christendom as honorary knights in this world or as honorary antique pagans in the next." See Hamilton, "Knowing the Enemy," 387.

72. See George Boas, *Primitivism and Related Ideas in the Middle Ages* (Baltimore: Johns Hopkins University Press, 1948), "The Noble Savage," 137–51.

73. Ibid., "Earthly Paradises," 154–74.

74. See Hyde, "Ethnographers in Search of an Audience," 102–3. See also David Wallace's discussion in *Premodern Places: Calais to Surinam, Chaucer to Aphra Behn* (Oxford: Blackwell, 2004), "Canaries (The Fortunate Islands)," 203–38.

75. Cited in Boas, *Primitivism*, 174.

76. Cindy Vitto, *The Virtuous Pagan in Middle English Literature* (Philadelphia: American Philosophical Society, 1989), 14–15.

77. Ibid., 23.

78. Ibid., 17–22.

79. Ibid., 23–25.

80. Ibid., 25–28. The relevant statements are found in Aquinas's *De Veritate*:

Non sequitur inconveniens posito quod quilibet teneatur aliquid explicite credere, si in silvis vel inter bruta animalia nutriatur: hoc enim ad divinam providentiam pertinet ut cuilibet provideat de necessariis ad salutem, dummodo ex parte eius non impediatur. Si enim aliquis taliter nutritus, ductum naturalis rationis sequeretur in appetitu boni et fuga mali, *certissime est tenendum, quod ei Deus vel per internam inspirationem revelaret ea quae sunt ad credendum necessaria, vel aliquem fidei praedicatorem ad eum dirigeret*, sicut misit Petrum ad Cornelium. (my italics)

Quamvis non sit in potestate nostra cognoscere ea quae sunt fidei, ex nobis ipsis; tamen, si nos fecerimus quod in nobis est, ut scilicet, ductum naturalis rationis sequamur, Deus non deficiet nobis ab eo quod nobis est necessarium.

Quoted in T. P. Dunning, "Langland and the Salvation of the Heathen," *Medium Aevum* 12 (1943): 45–54, on 49–50.

81. Dunning, "Langland and the Salvation of the Heathen," 50.

CHAPTER 2

1. See his "First Preface" to the *Descriptio Kambriae* in *The Journey Through Wales and the Description of Wales*, trans. Lewis Thorpe (New York: Penguin, 1978), 211–13.

2. *Mos/mores* shares its meaning with a number of Latin synonyms such as *consuetudo*, *ritus*, and *cultus*, the latter term having particularly fertile meanings, from dress or appearance alone to agricultural cultivation, to the cultivation of high manners and morals. *Natura* usually designates more innate or permanent characteristics, in the work of Gerald especially. For this observation and others, see Robert Bartlett's groundbreaking work on Gerald of Wales, in *Gerald of Wales, 1146–1223* (Oxford: Clarendon Press, 1982).

3. Ibid., 180–81, 193; and John Howland Rowe, "The Renaissance Foundations of Anthropology," in *Readings in the History of Anthropology*, ed. Regna Darnell (New York: Harper and Row, 1974), 61–77.

4. Antonia Gransden, "Realistic Observation in Twelfth-Century England," *Speculum* 47 (1972): 29–51.

5. Along with Walter Map and William Fitz Stephen; see ibid., 42. See also Urban T. Holmes, "Gerald the Naturalist," *Speculum* 11 (1936): 110–21.

6. As Bartlett notes, Sallust's *Bellum Iugurthinum*, which was available to Gerald, could have provided him the model of digressive, ethnographic excurses lodged in the middle of historical narratives, a balance of history writing and ethnography better approximated in the *Topographia Hibernica*. See Bartlett, *Gerald of Wales*, "Gerald's Ethnographic Achievement," 178–210.

7. For an argument for Marie de France's comparable cultural "salvage work" of Breton-Briton materials in the *Lais*, see my article "Salvage Anthropology and Displaced Mourning in Marie de France's *Lais*," *Arthuriana* 21.3 (Fall 2011): 49–69, where I consider the many biographical, historical, and thematic ties between Marie and Gerald.

8. For a description of the role of "salvage anthropology" in Western anthropology, see Jacob W. Gruber, "Ethnographic Salvage and the Shaping of Anthropology," *American Anthropologist* 72 (1970): 1289–99.

9. Mary Louise Pratt, *Imperial Eyes: Travel Writing and Transculturation* (New York: Routledge, 1992), 7.

10. Mary Louise Pratt, "Transculturation and Autoethnography: Peru, 1615/1980," in *Colonial Discourse/ Postcolonial Theory*, ed. Francis Barker, Peter Hulme, and Margaret Iversen (Manchester: Manchester University Press, 1994), 24–46, quotation on 28.

11. All Latin citations are from Gerald of Wales [Giraldi Cambrensis], *Opera*, vol. 6, ed. James F. Dimock (London: Longman, 1868); all English translations from Gerald of Wales, *The Journey Through Wales and the Description of Wales*, trans. Lewis Thorpe (New York: Penguin, 1978).

12. Notably, Scotland was afforded exemption from much of the negative stereotyping that characterizes Anglo-Norman descriptions of the Irish and Welsh because of the proximity of its political structures and assumptions to those of Anglo-Norman England. See R. R. Davies, *The First English Empire: Power and Identities in the British Isles, 1093–1343* (New York: Oxford University Press, 2000), especially 112.

13. See Robert Bartlett, *The Making of Europe: Conquest, Colonization and Cultural Change, 950–1350* (London: Allen Lane, 1993).

14. So, for instance, the anonymous *Gesta Stephani* describes Wales as "a land of wood and pasture . . . rich in deer and fish, in milk and herds," and Scotland likewise as "a region of fertile woods." Bartlett, *Gerald of Wales*, 160.

15. See Davies's discussion, "Political Heartlands and Political Backwaters," in *The First English Empire*, 89–112.

16. See R. R. Davies, "The Survival of the Blood Feud in Medieval Wales," *History* 54 (1969): 338–57.

17. Bartlett, *Gerald of Wales*, 164.

18. Gerald's knowledge of the native Welsh tongue was probably insufficient to write in that language and the *Descriptio* remained untranslated into Welsh until the twentieth century. Brynley F. Roberts, "Gerald of Wales and the Welsh Tradition," in *The Formation of Culture in Medieval Britain: Celtic, Latin, and Norman Influences*, ed. Francoise Le Saux (Lewiston, NY: Mellen Press, 1995), 129–47, on 133. For the view that Gerald wrote primarily for English audiences, see also Michael Richter, *Giraldus Cambrensis: The Growth of the Welsh Nation* (Aberystwyth: National Library of Wales, 1972), 69.

19. See Jeffrey Jerome Cohen, *Hybridity, Identity and Monstrosity in Medieval Britain: On Difficult Middles*, New Middle Ages (New York: Palgrave, 2006), especially "In the Borderlands," 77–108.

20. This is a return to the site of what Cohen has analyzed as the grass-eating Welshman Guidan's colonial mimicry in the *Journey Through Wales*. See Ibid., 90–95.

21. R. R. Davies, *Conquest, Coexistence, and Change: Wales, 1063–1415* (Oxford: Clarendon Press, 1987), 79.

22. Davies, *The First English Empire*, 143.

23. Ibid., 147–48, 155–56.

24. Davies, *Conquest, Coexistence, and Change*, 160, 164.

25. Davies, *The First English Empire*, 167.
26. Ibid., 156.
27. Davies, *Conquest, Coexistence, and Change*, 104–5.
28. Elsewhere, in the *Expugnatio Hibernica* 2.37, Gerald refers to the Normanni, the Angli, and "*nostri*," by which latter he means the marchers and to whom he is surely more closely identified than the natives of Wales. See Gerald of Wales, *Expugnatio Hibernica*, ed. and trans. A. B. Scott and F. X. Martin (Dublin: Royal Irish Academy, 1978).
29. Pratt, "Transculturation and Autoethnography," 44.
30. Ibid., 38.
31. Ibid., 28, 27.
32. Patricia Ingham shows the uses of the Celtic for claims of British sovereignty in a later phase of English history in *Sovereign Fantasies: Arthurian Romance and the Making of Britain* (Philadelphia: University of Pennsylvania Press, 2001).
33. John Gillingham, "The Context and Purposes of Geoffrey of Monmouth's History of the Kings of Britain," collected with other of his essays in *The English in the Twelfth Century* (Rochester, NY: Boydell Press, 2000), 19–40, on 37, first published in *Anglo-Norman Studies* 13 (1991): 99–118. Notably, Gerald of Wales himself wrote two accounts of Arthur's exhumation at Glastonbury, which he claims to have witnessed, one in the *Liber de Principis instructione* c. 1193, and another in the *Speculum Ecclesiae*, c. 1216.
34. *The Gesta Regis Ricardi*, ed. William Stubbs, Rolls Series (London: 1867), 2.159; cited in Gillingham, "Context and Purposes," 23.
35. See Rhonda Knight, "Stealing Stonehenge: Translation, Appropriation, and Cultural Identity in Robert Mannyng of Brunne's *Chronicle*," *Journal of Medieval and Early Modern Studies* 32.1 (2000): 41–58, on 52. The political expropriation of Arthur by the English and the vogue in Welsh story may well be linked with what seems to be a much wider set of appropriative procedures on the part of Anglo-Normans in the twelfth century. Davies notes, for instance, that Normans harnessed Welsh traditions to their own ends in order to prop up their religious and secular institutions, by commissioning biographies of local Welsh saints and collecting folktales and anecdotes for aristocratic court consumption as did Walter Map in the De Nugis Curialium. See *Conquest, Coexistence, and Change*, 104–7. And Ceri Lewis similarly notes:

> Disdainful at first of the native culture and hagiographical traditions of the population which they had subjugated, the Anglo-Norman conquerors eventually came to realize that . . . an investigation of the origin and development of the native traditions which they encountered could be a profitable as well as an intellectually fascinating exercise. So they began gradually to explore the traditions surrounding the native saints whose names were borne by the Welsh *clas* churches and to whose festivals the Welsh people were deeply devoted. A combination of interests of this kind eventually impelled a group of Anglo-Norman monks to

compile what is generally regarded as the best extant text of the *Vitae Sanctorum Wallensium*. . . . This manuscript contributed to the preservation of traditions of the Celtic Church in the west . . . [and] provide[s] us with another instructive example of that historical or pseudo-historical research into the traditions of the early Celtic Church which was one characteristic feature of the literary activity of the Anglo-Norman regime.

See Ceri Lewis, "The Court Poets: Their Function, Status and Craft," in *A Guide to Welsh Literature*, ed. A. O. H. Jarman and Gwilym Rees Hughes, vol. 1 (Swansea: Christopher Davies, 1976), 118–56, quotation on 133.

36. So joined, the dialogue of Anglo-Norman and Welsh discourses in the twelfth century may be understood in the way Aron Gurevich proposes that we understand the dialogue between official and unofficial cultures in the Middle Ages: "as the presence of one culture in the thought and world of the other, and vice versa." See *Medieval Popular Culture: Problems of Belief and Perception*, trans. J. M. Bak and P. A. Hollingsworth (Cambridge: Cambridge University Press, 1988), 180.

37. See Homi Bhabha's celebrated account of the twinning of desire and derision in the colonizer for the colonized, "The Other Question: Stereotype, Discrimination and the Discourse of Colonialism," in *The Location of Culture* (London: Routledge, 1994), 94–120, on 96.

38. Pratt, *Imperial Eyes*, 6.

39. See Jeffrey Cohen's persuasive reading of Gerald's deployment of sly civility against the colonialist stereotype of "the grass-eating Welshman" in the *Journey Through Wales* in "Hybrids, Monsters, Borderlands: The Bodies of Gerald of Wales," in *The Postcolonial Middle Ages*, ed. Cohen, New Middle Ages (New York: Palgrave, 2000), 85–104, on 86–89.

40. Gerald of Wales, *The History and Topography of Ireland*, trans. John O'Meara (New York: Penguin, 1982), 101.

41. Johannes Fabian, *Time and the Other: How Anthropology Makes Its Object* (New York: Columbia University Press, 1983), 80.

42. Bartlett, *Gerald of Wales*, 38.

43. In the 1960s, Jacques Maquet suggested that anthropologists' attraction to "traditional" forms of culture and to their preservation, as against the progressive, modernizing elements of culture, aligned them with the conservative forces of the colonial regime, for which the rise of modernizing movements within the ranks of the colonized were a distinct threat. See "Objectivity in Anthropology," *Current Anthropology* 5 (1964): 47–55, on 49–50.

44. Records show that some chose to settle near churches, towns, and Norman-style castles such as those possessed by Rhys ap Gruffudd in both Cardigan and Llandovery. See Huw Pryce, "In Search of a Medieval Society: Deheubarth in the Writings of Gerald of Wales," *Welsh History Review* 13.3 (1986–87): 265–81, on 269.

45. In fact, the use of stone for houses was not unusual, and Gerald's generalizations apply best to the upland summer houses. Davies, *Conquest, Coexistence, and Change*, 151.

46. Ibid., 153.

47. Pryce, "In Search of a Medieval Society," 272.

48. Gerald, *Descriptio Kambriae*, in *Journey Through Wales*, 255.

49. Gabrielle Spiegel, "Genealogy: Form and Function in Medieval Historical Narrative," *History and Theory* 22.1 (1983): 43–53, on 44–46.

50. Gabrielle Spiegel, *Romancing the Past: The Rise of Vernacular Prose Historiography in Thirteenth-Century France* (Berkeley: University of California Press, 1993), 221.

51. Spiegel, "Genealogy," 46.

52. Miriam Bunim, *Space in Medieval Painting and the Forerunners of Perspective* (New York: AMS Press, 1970), 60.

53. Samuel Edgerton, *The Renaissance Rediscovery of Linear Perspective* (New York: Basic Books, 1975), 8–10. Edgarton's negative valuation of medieval painting, which he has likened to the immersed and naive outlook of a child, has been rightly critiqued, but the aptness of his description stands. Suzannah Biernoff places him within a general critical tendency to pathologize medieval vision. See *Sight and Embodiment in the Middle Ages: Ocular Desires* (New York: Palgrave Macmillan, 2002), 10. But Edgerton's account of the essentially subjective aims of medieval painting—its attempt to convey subjective experience—align with Biernoff's own thesis that medieval vision inextricably connected truth apprehension to the body of the viewer, subjects to their objects. See *Sight and Embodiment*.

CHAPTER 3

1. All citations are from Anastasius Van den Wyngaert's edition of the *Itinerarium* in *Sinica Franciscana*, vol. 1, *Itinera et relationes fratrumminorum saeculi XIII et XIV* (Florence: Quaracchi-Firenze, 1929), 164–332; all translations are from *The Mission of Friar William of Rubruck*, ed. Peter Jackson (London: Hakluyt Society, 1990), except where I have adapted the translation, as indicated. An earlier version of this chapter appeared as "The Look of Medieval Ethnography: William of Rubruck's Mission to Mongolia," *New Medieval Literatures* 10 (2008): 87–114. I thank *New Medieval Literatures* and the Brepols Press for permission to reprint.

2. At the time of William's mission, the vast Asian empire was effectively divided into two realms of rule, one being the Golden Horde and the other eastern Asia as far as Cathay; later, in 1258, Persia would be added to the Mongol realm, and a third distinct dynasty of Mongolian rulers, the Il-Khans, formed.

3. This fact further suggests Bacon's instrumental hand in its preservation. See Peter Jackson, introduction to *The Mission of Friar William of Rubruck*, 1–55, on 52–53.

4. See William Rockhill, "Introductory Notice," in *The Journey of William of Rubruck to the Eastern Parts of the World*, ed. Rockhill (1990; repr. London: Hakluyt Society, 1998), xiii–xliv, on xl–xliv.

5. See Christopher Dawson, ed., *The Mongol Mission: Narratives and Letters of the Franciscan Missionaries in Mongolia and China in the*

Thirteenth and Fourteenth Centuries (New York: Sheed and Ward, 1955), xxi–xxiii; and more recently, Jackson, introduction to *The Mission of Friar William of Rubruck*, especially 47–51.

6. Compare the dual authorship and voice of Marco Polo and his collaborator, Rustichello of Pisa, in Marco Polo's *Travels*, or the author of *Mandeville's Travels*, whom Stephen Greenblatt has called "the fictive body made up of fragments of other bodies" and "a violation of the presumption of a unitary material body that has produced the text ... with a travel narrative or an eyewitness history, this presumption is particularly irresistible." See Greenblatt, *Marvelous Possessions: The Wonder of the New World* (Chicago: University of Chicago Press, 1992), 35, 34.

7. Mary Campbell, *The Witness and the Other World: Exotic European Travel Writing, 400–1600* (Ithaca, NY: Cornell University Press, 1988), 114. The relative lack of attention to the *Journey*'s literariness comes into particular relief when compared with the treatment of fellow texts of medieval travel writing like *Mandeville's Travels*, whose complexities of form, variants, and ethnographic representation attract ever more criticism. Recent examples of an empirical approach to the *Journey* include Stéphane Mund, "Travel Accounts as Early Sources of Knowledge About Russia in Medieval Western Europe from the Mid-Thirteenth to the Early Fifteenth Century," *Medieval History Journal* 5.1 (2002): 103–20; Walter Pohl, "The *regia* and the *hring*: Barbarian Places of Power," in *Topographies of Power in the Early Middle Ages*, ed. Frans Theuws, Carine van Rhijn and Mayke de Jong (Leiden: Brill, 2001); and Gregory Guzman, "European Clerical Envoys to the Mongols: Reports of Western Merchants in Eastern Europe and Central Asia, 1231–1255," *Journal of Medieval History*, 22.1 (1996): 53–67. Notable exceptions include Campbell, *Witness*, 112–21, which discusses the subjectivity and precocious modernity of William's account; Caroline Walker Bynum, *Metamorphosis and Identity* (New York: Zone Books, 2001), which treats the *Journey*'s perspectivalism as part of the discourse of wonder; and Michèle Gueret-Laferté, "Les gestes de l'autre," in *Le Geste et les gestes au Moyen Age*, Conference Proceedings of Centre Universitaire d'Etudes et de Recherches Médiévale d'Aix (Aix-en-Provence: CUERMA / Sénéfiance 41, 1998), which highlights the *Journey*'s reliance on gestural communication.

8. Linda Lomperis has theorized the fluidity of medieval cultural and religious boundaries in "Medieval Travel Writing and the Question of Race," *Journal of Medieval and Early Modern Studies* 31.1 (2001): 149–64, in which she argues with respect to "Christianity" and "Non-Christian otherness" in *Mandeville's Travels* that "neither of these identity categories in the *Travels* is stable or entirely separate one from the other" (156). For a recent argument for the interpenetration of Old French literature and literary meaning with cultural and geographic spaces external to Europe, in particular the Arab world, see Sharon Kinoshita, *Medieval Boundaries: Rethinking Difference in Old French Literature* (Philadelphia: University of Pennsylvania Press, 2006). See also Maria Rosa Menocal's classic study of the syncretism of Andalusian, Provencal, and Italian literature with Arabic culture, with repercussions for all Europe, *The Arabic Role in Medieval*

Literary History: A Forgotten Heritage (Philadelphia: University of Pennsylvania Press, 1987). Kinoshita and Menocal each insist on the exceptionalism and difference of medieval relations with the Arab world from modern Orientalist modes.

9. Postquam ergo recessimus de Soldaia, tertia die invenimus Tartaros, inter quos cum intravi, visum fuit michi recte quod ingrederer quoddam aliud seculum, quorum vitam et morem vobis describo prout possum (1.14).

10. "A detestable nation of Satan, to wit, the countless army of the Tartars, broke loose from its mountain-environed home and piercing the solid rocks [of the Caucasus], poured forth like devils from the Tartarus, so that they are rightly called Tartari or Tartarians." Mathew Paris, *Matthew Paris' English History from the Year 1235 to 1273*, vol. 1, trans. J. A. Giles, (New York: AMS Press Press, 1968), 312.

11. W. R. Jones, "The Image of the Barbarian in Medieval Europe," *Comparative Studies in Society and History* 13.4 (1971): 376–407, on 400.

12. Matthew Paris, *Matthew Paris' English History*, 312–13.

13. John Block Friedman, *The Monstrous Races in Medieval Art and Thought* (Cambridge, MA: Harvard University Press, 1981).

14. Richard Bernheimer, *Wild Men in the Middle Ages: A Study in Art, Sentiment, and Demonology* (Cambridge, MA: Harvard University Press, 1952); and Roger Bartra, *Wild Men in the Looking Glass*, trans. Carl Berrisford (Ann Arbor: University of Michigan Press, 1994), 124–25.

15. Anthony Pagden, *The Fall of Natural Man: The American Indian and the Origins of Comparative Ethnology* (Cambridge: Cambridge University Press, 1982, 21. Aquinas's definition of barbarism, also influential, is distinctive for its emphasis on the presence of written language in particular: "Hence barbarism is appropriately manifested by this sign, that men either do not live under laws or live under irrational ones, and likewise that among certain peoples there is no training in writing." Thomas Aquinas, *Commentary on the Politics*, trans. Ernest L. Fortin and Peter D. O'Neill, in *Medieval Political Philosophy*, ed. Ralph Lerner (New York: Free Press, 1963), 305–6.

16. Apart from Isidore and Solinus, compilers of Pliny's monstrous races, William's ethnographic ideas cannot be grounded in any specific textual tradition. Textual traces in the *Journey* itself only assure us of his knowledge of the scriptures and the Franciscan Rule, Peter Lombard's *Sentences*, Isidore and Solinus, and the *Aeneid*. Although William mentions the important mission of John of Plano Carpini once in his text (19.5), his misspelling of the name as "John of Policarpo" together with a lack of evidence that he ever met Carpini in Paris after his mission (as he did Bacon and King Louis) have suggested to some editors that William of Rubruck did not in fact know of either Carpini or his earlier text. See Jackson, introduction to *The Mission of Friar William of Rubruck*, 40n4. Van den Wyngaert lists Carpini and his companion Benedict the Pole as sources for William of Rubruck. See *Itinerarium*, 213.

17. Roger Bacon, *The Opus Maius of Roger Bacon*, 3 vols., ed. John Henry Bridges (Oxford: Clarendon Press, 1897–1900), 1:400–401, 2:368,

371, 376, 383. See also Jackson, introduction to *The Mission of Friar William of Rubruck*, 53–54.

18. For instance, Peter Kolb's 1719 account "of the several Nations of the Hottentots" includes in its description of their "manners and customs": "Their Religion, Government, Laws, Customs, Ceremonies, and Opinions; Their Art of War, Professions, Language, Genius." See Mary Louise Pratt, *Imperial Eyes: Travel Writing and Transculturation* (London: Routledge, 1992), 41.

19. William's categories closely match those of Carpini's earlier missionary tract. For a treatment of the originality and importance of Carpini's contribution to medieval ethnography, see J. K. Hyde, "Ethnographers in Search of an Audience," in *Medieval Ethnographies European Perceptions of the World Beyond*, ed. Joan-Pau Rubiés (Aldershot, England: Ashgate, 2009), 65–119.

20. R. W. Southern, *Western Views of Islam in the Middle Ages* (Cambridge, MA: Harvard University Press, 1962), 47–51. Southern credited "the dialectical superiority of the Latins" with William's rhetorical success at this debate, but as dialectic and logical argument assume *reasoning* opponents, the debate may be seen as equally demonstrative of Latins' assumptions of non-Christian rationality. William's disappointment regarding the lack of converts in spite of his demonstrated superiority in arguments of faith is therefore all the greater—a blow to the tools and assumptions of scholasticism as much as a lost opportunity to save souls.

21. Roger Bacon, *The Opus Maius of Roger Bacon*, 2 vols., trans. Robert Belle Burke (Philadelphia: University of Pennsylvania Press, 1928), 1:321; Bacon, *Opus Maius*, ed. Bridges, 1:301–2.

22. In particular, their ignorance of the Syriac in which they chant the office and the holy scriptures renders them totally corrupt: "totaliter sunt corrupti," he declares in 26.12.

23. On this, see Felipe Fernández-Armesto, *Before Columbus: Exploration and Colonisation from the Mediterranean to the Atlantic, 1229–1492* (London: Macmillan, 1987).

24. Johannes Fabian, *Time and the Other: How Anthropology Makes Its Object* (New York: Columbia University Press, 1983), 26.

25. Vision is indeed overdetermined in William's text: it is at once a source of his authorial legitimacy, the privileged sense of his empiricism, a communicative substitute for many failures of language plotted by the text, a means of supplementary illustration, a form of religious tutorial and invocation to God, a dangerous inducement to sin, and perhaps most interestingly, a painful source of self-scrutiny from the viewpoint of the other.

26. Bacon. *Opus Maius*, trans. Burke, 2:419–20.

27. William M. Ivins, *On the Rationalization of Sight*, Metropolitan Museum of Art Papers no. 8, 1938, New York (repr. Cambridge, MA: Da Capo Press, 1973), 13.

28. Bacon, *Opus Maius*, trans. Burke, 2:420.

29. As on route from Baatu's court to Mangu's, where the letter takes on a troubling new meaning: Louis's request for Mongol military aid against the Saracen enemy (27.11).

30. See Jackson, appendix 1 to *The Mission of Friar William of Rubruck*, 279.

31. See also Gueret-Laferté, "Les gestes de l'autre," 244–47, to this effect. Gueret-Laferté suggestively analyzes the ambiguity and flexibility of gestures as opposed to words in a number of provocative kneeling scenes before the Mongol emperors.

32. There is an extensive literature on the relative efficacy of images over language in preaching the Christian faith. See Margaret Caviness, "Biblical Stories in Windows: Were They Bibles for the Poor?" in *The Bible in the Middle Ages: Its Influence on Literature and Art*, ed. B. S. Levy (Binghamton, NY: Medieval and Renaissance Texts and Studies, 1992), 103–47; Hans Belting, *The Image and Its Public in the Middle Ages*, trans. M. Bartusis and R. Meyer (New Rochelle, NY: Caratzas, 1990); and Herbert Kessler, "Pictorial Narrative and Church Mission in Sixth-century Gaul," *Studies in the History of Art* 16 (1985): 75–91, and "Pictures as Scripture in Fifth-Century Churches," *Studia Artium Orientalis et Occidentalis* 2.1 (1985): 75–91. Notably, William of Rubruck's patron, Louis IX, seems to have been particularly sensitive to the persuasive power of images. As his famous biographer Jean de Joinville reports, having been visited by envoys from Mongolia in Cyprus just before the launch of the Seventh Crusade: "By these men his Majesty sent the King of the Tartars a tent arranged for use as a Chapel—a very costly gift indeed, for it was made throughout of fine scarlet cloth. Moreover, in the hope of making our religion appear attractive to the Tartars, the king had ordered for this chapel a series of little figures carved in stone, representing the Annunciation of our Lady, and all other subjects relating to the Christian faith." See Joinville and [Geoffrey de] Villehardouin, *Chronicles of the Crusade*, trans. M. R. B. Shaw (New York: Penguin, 1963),198. On the subject of Louis IX and images, see Daniel Weiss, *Art and Crusade in the Age of Saint Louis* (Cambridge: Cambridge University Press, 1998).

33. Timothy Mitchell, *Colonising Egypt*, (Cambridge: Cambridge UP, 1988), 24–26.

34. Pratt, *Imperial Eyes*, 60.

35. For as James Clifford has written, while "the ethnographer's personal experiences, especially those of participation and empathy, are recognized as central to the research process . . . they are firmly restrained by the impersonal standards of observation and 'objective' distance. . . . The subjectivity of the author is separated from the objective referent of the text." See Clifford, "Partial Truths," in *Writing Culture: The Poetics and Politics of Ethnography*, ed. Clifford and George Marcus (Berkeley: University of California Press, 1986), 1–26, quotation on 13.

36. Fabian, *Time and the Other*.

37. Norman Bryson, *Vision and Painting: The Logic of the Gaze* (New Haven, CT: Yale University Press, 1983), 88–89. According to art historians such as Bryson, modern Western painting, much like modern travel and ethnographic writing, "is predicated on the disavowal of deictic reference, on the disappearance of the body as the site of the image" whereas, by contrast,

traditional non-Western painting technique, what he calls the "painting of the glance," "does not seek to bracket out the process of viewing, nor . . . the traces of the body of labour."

38. Pratt, *Imperial Eyes*, 52.

39. See Clifford, "Partial Truths," 13.

40. Bynum aptly locates this scene in the wider perspectivalist tendencies of medieval travel and wonder literature, which sometimes turns a "gently ironic comment" on Latin Christianity itself, here Franciscan ascetic practice. See *Metamorphosis and Identity*, 55–56. But ironic commentary, as I argue in the final chapter of this book, requires a stable viewpoint, something that William, unlike his readers, does not enjoy the luxury of during his disorienting missionary travels among the Mongols.

41. Dallas George Denery II, *Seeing and Being Seen in the Later Medieval World: Optics, Theology and Religious Life* (Cambridge: Cambridge University Press, 2005), 79.

42. See his anthropologically influenced study, Aron Gurevich, *Medieval Popular Culture: Problems of Belief and Perception*, trans. J. M. Bak and P. A. Hollingsworth (Cambridge: Cambridge University Press, 1988), especially 2–3.

43. Michael Baxandall, *Painting and Experience in Fifteenth Century Italy: A Primer in the Social History of Pictorial Style* (Oxford: Clarendon Press, 1972), 61–71.

44. Humbert of Romans, *Liber de eruditione praedicatorum* IV.18, 421–22: "non una eademque cunctis exhortatio congruit, quia nec cunctos par morum qualitas astringit. Saepe namque aliis officiunt quae aliis prosunt." Quoted in Denery, *Seeing and Being Seen*, 24.

45. Thomas Aquinas, *Summa Contra Gentiles*, bk. 1, *God*, trans. and ed. Anton C. Pegis (1955; Notre Dame: University of Notre Dame Press, 1975), 62.

46. Humbert, *Liber*, VII.35, 455–56: "Item, praedicatorum interest procurare salutem aliorum modis quibus possunt. Quandoque vero melius procuratur per bonam conversationem quam per verbum." Quoted in Denery, *Seeing and Being Seen*, 27.

47. "Numquam ita securus sis et absconsus, quin ita disciplinate et caste te habeas in visu, gestu, tactu, et in onmibus aliis, ac si ab aliquo videreris." David of Augsburg, *De institutione novitiorum*, I.16, in Bonaventure, *Opera Omnia*, vol. 12 (Paris: Vives, 1868): 292–312, on 298. Quoted in Denery, *Seeing and Being Seen*, 7–98.

48. Denery, *Seeing and Being Seen*, 16, 27–29.

49. Ibid., 16.

50. But see Aron Gurevich's insistence on the central role of "dialogue-conflict" at the interface of official Christianity with popular belief throughout the medieval period, as evidenced in ecclesiastical literature including preaching manuals. See *Medieval Popular Culture*, especially 5, 6–7, 12.

51. This is the same conclusion reached by Gurevich in his study of the official ecclesiastical literature's ambivalent but necessary engagement with the pre-Christian popular worldview: "As a matter of fact, the efficacy of

this type of literature depended on the degree to which the authors were able to enter into the thought-structure of their audience. . . . Here is an ecclesiastical literature which, because it is directed to the illiterate mass of simple people, and therefore oriented towards their minds, is in turn strongly influenced by them. Intentionally or not, these texts are 'infected' by folklore." Gurevich, *Medieval Popular Culture*, 5.

52. Again, Gurevich's readings of medieval popular Christianity are instructive: "the paradox of medieval culture . . . lies in the fact, documented in the intersection of popular culture and the culture of educated people, that Latin writings of scholars and teachers contain substantial elements of non-literate folklore tradition *almost against their author's will*" (my italics). Gurevich goes on to ask probing questions we might well put to William of Rubruck as he preached in Mongolia: "How can these levels combine and penetrate each other within a single mind? What transformations do they suffer in this confluence?" See Gurevich, *Medieval Popular Culture*, xvii. As Gurevich later reasserts, authorial intention is frequently thwarted in dialogic engagements with unofficial views, which "break through" anyway and express what the author "could not have consciously disclosed" (7).

53. Denery, *Seeing and Being Seen*, 38.

54. David L. Clark, "Optics for Preachers: The *De oculo morali* by Peter of Limoges," *Michigan Academician* 9 (1977): 329–43.

55. Denery, *Seeing and Being Seen*, 38.

56. Dawson, *The Mongol Mission*, 73–76, quotation on 76.

57. Ibid., 85–86.

58. The Armenian monk who so vexes William shows a willingness to acquiesce to Mongol expectations such as Guyuk's when he considers brokering the submission of all the Latins, including the pope, to Mangu Khan in exchange for the Mongols' conversion to Christianity (27.8).

59. Such stringent requirement no doubt left a wide gulf between practice and theory, indicated in William's own occasional, frustrated calls for crusade upon the Mongols.

60. Sartre quoted in Martin Jay, *Downcast Eyes: The Denigration of Vision in Twentieth-Century French Thought* (Berkeley: University of California Press, 1993), 87–88. Jay himself, notably, explores medieval intersubjectivity as an implication of the optical theory of extramission, a potentially participatory view of subject-object relations prevalent in the ancient and medieval world that intertwined viewer and viewed in the visual process. See *Downcast Eyes*, 30, 45. In medieval literary criticism, Sarah Stanbury has argued for an intersubjective blurring of subject-object boundaries at work in amatory discourse: "One can argue, rightly I think, that the use in Book 1 [of *Troilus and Criseyde*] of ocular iconography affords Chaucer a flexible tool for depicting intersubjectivity, the experience, central to the ethics of the Western love tradition, of loss of boundaries." Sarah Stanbury, "The Lover's Gaze in *Troilus and Criseyde*," in *Chaucer's Troilus and Criseyde: Subgit to All Poesye*, ed. R. A. Shoaf (Binghamton, NY: Medieval and Renaissance Texts Studies, 1992), 224–38, quotation on 231. Blurring of self-other boundaries is, of course, less startling and bears different implications in a

discourse about merger, such as amatory discourse, than in one about religious, racial or ethnographic difference, such as ethnography.

61. Denery, *Seeing and Being Seen*, 94–95.
62. Ibid., 89.
63. Ibid., 92.

CHAPTER 4

1. See Benjamin Kedar, *Crusade and Mission: European Approaches Toward the Muslims* (Princeton, NJ: Princeton University Press, 1984).
2. Frederick II's "Bloodless" Crusade, the sixth, managed to regain Jerusalem for a ten-year period through negotation, but it was not officially sanctioned by the church.
3. I will be citing the original Old French from Jean de Joinville, *L'Histoire de Saint Louis*, ed. Natalis de Wailly (Paris: Firmin Didot, 1874), followed by the English translation, from Joinville and [Geoffrey de] Villehardouin, *Chronicles of the Crusade*, trans. M. R. B. Shaw (New York: Penguin, 1963), except where I have adapted the translation, as indicated. The double citation at the end of quotations gives page numbers from the original and translation, respectively. An earlier version of this chapter appeared as "Casting a 'Sideways Glance' at the Crusades: The Voice of the Other in Joinville's *Vie de Saint Louis*," *Exemplaria: A Journal of Theory in Medieval and Renaissance Studies* 22.3 (2010): 177–99. I thank *Exemplaria* for the permission to reprint.
4. Christopher Tyerman, *God's War: A New History of the Crusades* (Cambridge, MA: Belknap-Harvard University Press, 2006), 784–802.
5. See, as one sample, the essays in Jean Dufournet and Laurence Harf, eds., *Le Prince et son historien* (Paris: Champion, 1997); and Danielle Quéruel, ed., *Jean de Joinville: De la Champagne aux royaumes d'outremer* (Langres: Gueniot, 1998).
6. Queen Jeanne de Navarre was the wife of Philippe IV le Bel, grandson of Louis IX.
7. But see Caroline Smith, *Crusading in the Age of Joinville* (Aldershot, England: Ashgate, 2006), 48–58, for a summary of the two-stage theory of the text's composition, first set forth by Gaston Paris, according to which the crusade section well predates the hagiographical opening and closing. See also Cecilia M. Gaposchkin, *The Making of Saint Louis: Kingship, Sanctity, and Crusade in the Later Middle Ages* (Ithaca, NY: Cornell University Press, 2008), 181–96, on the dual chronicle and hagiographical functions of the text.
8. Christine Ferlimpin-Archer, "Joinville, de l'hagiographe à l'autobiographe: Approche de *La Vie de saint Louis*," in Quéruel, *Jean de Joinville*, 73–91, on 80; and Elisabeth Gaucher, "Joinville et l'écriture biographique," in Dufournet and Harf, *Le Prince et son historien*, 101–22.
9. Michèle Perret, "À la fin de sa vie ne fuz je mie," *Revue de sciences humaines* 183 (1981): 16–37.
10. Ferlimpin-Archer, "Joinville, de l'hagiographe à l'autobiographe," 85.

11. See Yvette Guilcher-Pellat, "Joinville et Paennime, l'autre l'ailleurs," in Quéruel, *Jean de Joinville*, , 193–206; Henriette Benveniste, "Joinville et les 'autres': Les procédés de représentation dans *l'Histoire de saint Louis*," *Le Moyen Âge: Revue d'Histoire et de Philologie* 102 (1996): 27–55; and Huguette Legros, "Images et représentations de l'Orient dan la *Vie de Saint Louis* de Joinville: De l'Orient peint dans l'historiographie à l'Orient évoqué dans les chanson de geste," in Gabriel Bianciotto and Claudio Galderisi, eds., *L'épopée romane: Actes du XVe Congrès international Roncesvals, Poitiers, 21–27 août 2000*, 2 vols (Poitiers: Centre d'Études Supérieures de Civilisation Médiévale, 2002), 2:705–13.

12. In 1894, Henri-Francois Delaborde called the *Vie* "rather the transcription of a conversation than a neatly composed book"; quoted in Smith, *Crusading in the Age of Joinville*, 58. Likewise, Gaston Paris, citing Joinville's final words that "j'ai fait escrire en cest livre" (412), commented that "non seulement Joinville écrit comme il parle, mais en réalité son livre n'est pas écrit, il est parlé" (not only does Joinville write like he talks, but in reality his book was not written but dictated) (translation mine); quoted in Ferlampin-Acher, "Joinville, de l'hagiographe à l'autobiographe," 85.

13. Bakhtin, *The Dialogic Imagination*, 61. On current approaches, see Legros, "Images et représentations"; and Benveniste, "Joinville et les 'autres.'"

14. For recent examples, see Sharon Kinoshita, *Medieval Boundaries: Rethinking Difference in Old French Literature* (Philadelphia: University of Pennsylvania Press, 2006); and Jeffrey Jerome Cohen, *Hybridity, Identity and Monstrosity in Medieval Britain: On Difficult Middles*, New Middle Ages (New York: Palgrave, 2006). See also Maria Rosa Menocal's classic study, *The Arabic Role in Medieval Literary History: A Forgotten Heritage* (Philadelphia: University of Pennsylvania Press, 1987).

15. See Tyerman, *God's War*, 213. For a survey of voices from the First Crusade, see Edward Peters, ed., *The First Crusade: The Chronicle of Fulcher of Chartres and Other Source Materials* (Philadelphia: University of Pennsylvania Press, 1971); and August C. Krey, ed., *The First Crusade: The Accounts of Eye-witnesses and Participants* (Gloucester, MA: Peter Smith, 1958). The official propaganda of the First Crusade is well manifested in the various accounts of Pope Urban II's address at the Council of Clermont in 1095. See Peters, *First Crusade: Chronicle*, 1–16; and Krey, *First Crusade: Accounts*, 22–43.

16. Ronnie Ellenblum, *Frankish Rural Settlement in the Latin Kingdom of Jerusalem, 1174–1277* (Cambridge: Cambridge University Press, 1998), 280.

17. Urban T. Holmes, "Life Among Europeans in Palestine and Syria in the Twelfth and Thirteenth Centuries," in *A History of the Crusades*, ed. Kenneth M. Setton, 4 vols. (Madison: University of Wisconsin Press, 1969–89), 4: 3–35, on 22.

18. Ellenblum, *Frankish Rural Settlement*, 281.

19. R. C. Smail, *Crusading Warfare, 1097–1193* (Cambridge: Cambridge University Press, 1957), 40–46; and Ellenblum, *Frankish Rural Settlement*, 3–11. See also Holmes, "Life Among Europeans."

20. See Joshua Prawer, *The Latin Kingdom of Jerusalem: European Colonialism in the Middle Ages* (London: Weidenfeld and Nicolson, 1972); and Smail, *Crusading Warfare*.

21. Jonathan Phillips, "The Latin East, 1098–1291" in *The Oxford Illustrated History of the Crusades*, ed. Jonathan Riley-Smith (Oxford: Oxford University Press, 1995), 112–40.

22. Ibid., 119.

23. Tyerman, *God's War*, 238; and Hans Mayer, *The Crusades*, 1965, trans. John Gillingham (Oxford: Oxford University Press, 1972), 175–76.

24. Adrian Boas, "Archaeological Sources for the History of Palestine: The Frankish Period: A Unique Medieval Society Emerges," *Near Eastern Archaeology* 61.3 (1998): 138–73, on 163.

25. Ellenblum, *Frankish Rural Settlement*, 286, 19; and Carole Hillenbrand, *The Crusades: Islamic Perspectives* (Chicago: Fitzroy Dearborn, 1999), 81–83, 246–51.

26. Ibn Jubayr, *The Travels of Ibn Jubayr*, trans. Roland Broadhurst (1952; New Delhi: Goodward, 2004), 300–301.

27. Jonathan Riley-Smith attributes the particular tolerance of the Outremer church as much to the reality of spontaneous popular accommodation and syncretism on the ground as to the pragmatism required of a minority church. See *The Crusades, a History*, 2nd ed. (New Haven, CT: Yale University Press, 2005), 72.

28. Usamah Ibn-Munqidh, *An Arab-Syrian Gentleman and Warrior in the Period of the Crusades: Memoirs of Usamah Ibn-Munqidh*, trans. Philip K. Hitti (1929; Princeton, NJ: Princeton University Press, 1987), 163–64.

29. Ibn Jubayr, *Travels*, 318.

30. Jonathan Riley-Smith, "Government and the Indigenous in the Latin Kingdom of Jerusalem," in *Medieval Frontiers: Concepts and Practices*, ed. David Abulafia and Nora Berend (Aldershot, England: Ashgate, 2002), 121–31, on 124.

31. Benjamin Kedar, "Convergences of Oriental Christian, Muslim and Frankish Worshippers: The Case of Saydnaya and the Knights Templar," in *The Crusades and the Military Orders: Expanding the Frontiers of Medieval Latin Christianity*, ed. Zsolt Hunyadi and Jozsef Laszlovszky (Budapest: Society for the Study of the Crusades and the Latin East, 2001), 89–100, on 91. In still more forms of improvised religious convergence, Oriental Christians, Muslims, and Franks are known to have engaged in a common Islamo-Christian Marian cult at a church in Saydnaya, near Damascus (Kedar, "Convergences," 96), and the Jewish traveler Jacob ben Nathaniel describes a likely syncretic, Jewish-Christian cult at the tomb of Rav Kahana near Tiberias (Riley-Smith, "Government and the Indigenous," 125). We know, too, of Oriental Christians adopting the Latin rite, and even founding a Latin church. See Benjamin Kedar, "Latins and Oriental Christians in the Frankish Levant, 1099–1291," in *Sharing the Sacred: Religious Contacts and Conflicts in the Holy Land*, ed. Arieh Kofsky and Guy G. Stroumsa (Jerusalem: Yad Izhak Ben Zvi, 1998), 209–22, on 220.

32. Crusader art itself has been defined by the syncretism of local styles, "in which the Western tradition, whatever it is, has already been synthesized

with the Byzantine and the local Levantine components." Jaroslav Folda, *Crusader Art in the Holy Land: From the Third Crusade to the Fall of Acre* (Cambridge: Cambridge University Press, 2005), 309.

33. While the earliest study of this hybrid Islamic art assumed it was aimed at Frankish consumption (Ranee Katzenstein and Glenn Lowry, "Christian Themes in Thirteenth Century Islamic Metalwork," *Muqarnas* 1 [1983]: 53–68), scholars now believe that local Oriental Christians and elite Muslims themselves were as likely an audience for such hybrid art as elite crusaders and European visitors. See Eva Baer, *Ayyubid Metalwork with Christian Images* (Leiden: Brill, 1989).

34. Maria Georgopoulou, "Orientalism and Crusader Art," *Medieval Encounters* 5.3 (1999): 289–321, quotation on 292.

35. Baer, *Ayyubid Metalwork with Christian Images.*

36. Georgopoulou, "Orientalism and Crusader Art," 295–96, 291. Barbara Zeitler similarly sees in the depiction of Muslims within a Crusader manuscript evidence of "the material culture of the Levant that Westerners shared with the Muslims, the result of a substantial process of accommodation between Crusaders and Muslims, in the Latin East, regardless of the antagonistic relations between them." See "'Sinful Sons, Falsifiers of the Christian Faith': The Depiction of Muslims in a 'Crusader' Manuscript," *Mediterranean Historical Review* 12 (1997): 25–50, quotation on 43.

37. The epic view of crusading was dealt a particular blow by the confusing events of the Fourth Crusade, as narrated by Joinville's contemporaries Geoffrey de Villehardouin and Robert de Clari, in which Christian forces putatively en route to the East sacked Constantinople instead. See Kinoshita's reading of the disruptions to Frankish identity resulting from this chaotic crusade, the chapter "Brave New Worlds: Robert de Clari's *La Conquête de Constantinople*," in *Medieval Boundaries*, 139–75.

38. The transfer was also without papal sanction—Frederick had been excommunicated a year earlier by Gregory IX for postponing a promised crusade due to illness. See Tyerman, *God's War*, 739.

39. Ibid., 749.

40. See Ibid., 746.

41. Bernard Hamilton, "Knowing the Enemy: Western Understanding of Islam at the Time of the Crusades," *Journal of the Royal Asiatic Society of Great Britain and Ireland* ser. 3, 7 (1997): 373–87, on 385, 382–33.

42. See Folda, *Crusader Art in the Holy Land*, 254. Frankish alliance making with Mongols, then the victorious Mamluks, continued into the final days of the Latin Kingdom. See P. M. Holt, *Early Mamluk Diplomacy, 1260–1290: Treaties of Baybars and Qalawun with Christian Rulers* (Leiden: Brill, 1995).

43. See Anthony Cutler, "Everywhere and Nowhere: The Invisible Muslim and Christian Self-Fashioning in the Culture of the Outremer," in *France and the Holy Land: Frankish Culture at the End of the Crusades*, ed. Daniel H. Weiss and Lisa Mahoney (Baltimore: Johns Hopkins University Press, 2004), 253–81.

44. The envoys were Nestorians David and Mark, sent by Aljigiday, envoy to the great khan, who wanted friendly relations with Louis against their

common Ayyubid enemy in the Near East. Christopher Dawson, *The Mongol Mission*, repr. ed., *Mission to Asia* (Cambridge, MA: Medieval Academy Press, 1980), xix.

45. Mary Louise Pratt, *Imperial Eyes: Travel Writing and Transculturation* (New York: Routledge, 1992), 7.

46. Steven Runciman, *A History of the Crusades*, vol.3, *The Kingdom of Acre and the Later Crusades* (Cambridge: Cambridge University Press, 1954), 273.

47. Joinville "impose sa proper vision des faits, souvent partielle, et nous livre le point de vue d'un combattant engagé dans une stratégie complexe, qu'il ne peut saisir dans sa totalité surtout la croisade se résume à une série de micro-récits où l'éclairage se déplace d'un détail à l'autre, sans perspective générale." Gaucher, "Joinville et l'écriture biographique," 118, 114. Translations mine.

48. For a greater elaboration on the debt of Gerald of Wales and of the book's ethnographers in general to medieval representational disciplines like historiography, see my discussion in Chapter 2, in the section "Gerald's Partial Gazes."

49. Mikhail Bakhtin, *The Dialogic Imagination: Four Essays*, ed. Michael Holquist, trans. Caryl Emerson and Holquist (Austin: University of Texas Press, 1981, 345–46. Note the convergence of vocabulary between theorists of linguistic and cultural contact around the notion of "contact zones." Mary Louise Pratt borrows "contact zone" from linguistics; see her introduction to *Imperial Eyes* (6–7), as well as her essay "Linguistic Utopias," in *The Linguistics of Writing: Arguments Between Language and Literature*, ed. Nigel Fabb et al. (New York: Methuen, 1987), 48–66.

50. Bakhtin, *Dialogic Imagination*, 45–46, 61.

51. Ibid., 342.

52. As Riley-Smith has shown, oath taking on multiple scriptures was practiced at Acre's *cours de la Fonde*, to which were brought minor commercial disputes involving all indigenous communities: "Jewish claimants could take oaths on the Torah (*la Tore de sa lei*), Samaritans on their version of the 'five books of Moses (*les cinq livres de Moyses que il tient*),' Muslims on the Koran, Jacobites and Greeks on an image of the Cross and gospel books written in their own script." See "Government and the Indigenous," 130.

53. As Hamilton has noted, "What Yves Le Breton would seem to have been reporting was a discussion of the Ismāʿīlī belief in the succession of speaking prophets each succeeded by a silent, spiritual legatee who interpreted the esoteric meaning of the prophet's revelation to the initiated. According to that tradition Simon Peter (Shamūn al-Safā) was the silent interpreter of the teaching of the prophet Jesus." See "Knowing the Enemy," 377.

54. Joinville and Villehardouin, *Chronicles*, 280.

55. For a concordant reading of the limits of the late medieval European gaze in *The Book of John Mandeville*, see Karma Lochrie, "Provincializing Medieval Europe: Mandeville's Cosmopolitan Utopia," *PMLA* 124.2 (2009): 592–99.

56. See Ibn al-Athir's account of "Prince Arnat's Treachery" in Francesco Gabrieli, *Arab Historians of the Crusades*, trans. E. J. Costello (Berkeley: University of California Press, 1984), 115–16.

57. The Near Eastern sanctity of breaking bread is mirrored in Usamah's story of having had his own life saved at a crowded market through association with an acculturated Frank, at whose house he'd formerly eaten. See Usamah, *Arab-Syrian Gentleman*, 169–70.

58. See John V. Tolan, "Mirror of Chivalry: Salah al-Din in the Medieval European Imagination," in ed., *Images of the Other: Europe and the Muslim World Before 1700*, ed. David Blanks, Cairo Papers in Social Science, vol. 19, monograph 2 (Cairo: American University in Cairo Press, 1996), 7–38.

59. See Richard Bulliet, *The Case for Islamo-Christian Civilization* (New York: Columbia University Press, 2004). Bulliet argues for the "sibling-like" parallel trajectories of Islam and Christianity from the medieval period forward.

60. This epithet was popularized after Louis IX's reign, but already in circulation during it. See William Chester Jordan, *Louis IX and the Challenge of the Crusade: A Study in Rulership* (Princeton, NJ: Princeton University Press, 1979), 182.

61. These incidents are recounted in Joinville, *L'Histoire* (Jews at Cluny, 34–36) and Joinville and Villehardouin, *Chronicles* (interviewed by Joinville, 262). See Jacques Le Goff, *Saint Louis* (Paris: Gallimard, 1996), 781–825.

62. See Claude Cahen, "Saint Louis et l'Islam." *Journal Asiatique* (1970): 3–12, on 6–7.

63. Daniel Weiss, *Art and Crusade in the Age of Saint Louis* (Cambridge: Cambridge University Press, 1998), 208–9.

64. "Prior to this moment of appropriation . . . [the word] exists in other people's mouths, in other people's contexts, serving other people's intentions." Bakhtin, The *Dialogic Imagination*, 293–94.

65. Afrodesia E. McCannon, "The King's Two Lives: The Tunisian Legend of Saint Louis," *Journal of Folklore Research* 43.1 (2006): 53–74, quotation on 55–56.

66. Ibid., 59.

67. "A reading of the sort I propose to undertake would be entirely superfluous if there existed photographic traces of the gaze of the colonized upon the colonizer. In their absence, that is, in the absence of a confrontation of opposed gazes, I attempt here, lagging far behind History, to return this immense postcard back to its sender." Alloula Malek, *The Colonial Harem*, trans. Myrna Godzich and Wlad Godzich (Minneapolis: University of Minnesota Press, 1986), 5.

68. McCannon, "The King's Two Lives," 65.

69. Louis's misgivings about deceiving his queen (here given as Isabelle rather than Margaret) seem to be in dialogue with the medieval Muslim view of Frankish respect for their women, a view memorably depicted by Usamah, but also suggested in Joinville's depiction of Louis's deference to his wife's judgment in the handling of required ransom moneys being demanded by the Egyptians during negotiations: asked if she would pay the ransom, "li roys respondi que il ne savoit se la royne le vourroit faire, pour ce que elle estoit sa dame" (the King had answered that he did not know whether or not the queen would consent, since, as his consort, she was mistress of her actions) (186/249).

70. McCannon, "The King's Two Lives," 55.

CHAPTER 5

1. See R. W. Southern, *Western Views of Islam in the Middle Ages* (Cambridge, MA: Harvard University Press, 1962), 74.
2. See Josephine Bennett, *The Rediscovery of Sir John Mandeville* (New York: Modern Language Association of America, 1954), 16–19.
3. See Christiane Deluz, *Le Livre de Jehan de Mandeville: Une "Géographie" au XIVe siècle*, Publications de l'Institut d'Etudes Médiévales: Textes, Etudes, Congrès, 8 (Louvain-la-Neuve: Université Catholique de Louvain, 1988).
4. See also Ian Higgins, *Writing East: The "Travels" of Sir John Mandeville* (Philadelphia: University of Pennsylvania Press, 1997), 9; and Bennett, *Rediscovery*, 15–25.
5. For a history of the plagiarist theory of the *Travels*, see Bennett, *Rediscovery*.
6. Josephine Bennett writes: "Mandeville's geography is, on the whole, as good as that of other travelers of his day." See *Rediscovery*, 67. Deluz sees the *Travels* not as a travelogue but an *imago mundi*, or a description of the world, drawing on a wide range of sources. See *Livre de Jehan de Mandeville*.
7. See Christian Zacher, *Curiosity and Pilgrimage: The Literature of Discovery in Fourteenth-Century England* (Baltimore: Johns Hopkins University Press, 1976). See also Jas Elsner and Joan-Pau Rubiés, introduction to *Voyages and Visions: Towards a Cultural History of Travel, ed.* Rubiés and Elsner (London: Reaktion Books, 1999).
8. Joan-Pau Rubiés, *Travel and Ethnology in the Renaissance: South India Through European Eyes, 1250–1625* (Cambridge: Cambridge University Press, 2002), 83.
9. All citations will be from *Mandeville's Travels*, ed. M. C. Seymour (Oxford: Clarendon Press, 1967), the most recent critical edition of the British Library MS Cotton Titus C.xvi. The Cotton mss, composed circa 1400, is based on the insular version of the text, itself based on a French recension of the original and available by 1390 in England. See Ian Higgins, introduction to *Writing East*, 1–27.
10. See Donald Howard, "The World of Mandeville's Travels," *Yearbook of English Studies* 1 (1971): 1–17, and *Writers and Pilgrims: Medieval Pilgrimage Narratives and Their Posterity* (Berkeley: University of California Press, 1980); and Douglas Butturff, "Satire in *Mandeville's Travels*," *Annuale Mediaevale* 13 (1972): 155–64.
11. As Wayne Booth has argued in *The Rhetoric of Irony* (Chicago: University of Chicago Press, 1974).
12. See Karma Lochrie's similar, recent reading of Mandeville's interest in showing the limits of the late medieval European gaze, "Provincializing Medieval Europe: Mandeville's Cosmopolitan Utopia," *PMLA* 124.2 (2009): 592–99. Unlike Lochrie, I do not locate the text's provincializing project as

emerging from hopeful cosmopolitan or utopian expression, but rather from the fearful play of uncanny forces rooted in a distinctive fourteenth-century crisis of indeterminacy. See also Shirin A. Khanmohamadi, "Worldly Unease in Late Medieval European Travel Reports," in *Cosmopolitanism and the Middle Ages*, ed. John Ganim and Shayne Legassie, New Middle Ages (New York: Palgrave, 2013), 105–20.

13. See, for example, Linda Lomperis, "Medieval Travel Writing and the Question of Race," *Journal of Medieval and Early Modern Studies* 31.1 (2001): 149–64. See also Geraldine Heng, *Empire of Magic: Medieval Romance and the Politics of Cultural Fantasy* (New York: Columbia University Press, 2003), "Eye on the World: Mandeville's Pleasure Zones; Or, Cartography, Anthropology, and Medieval Travel Romance," 239–306. The pleasures of peering into difference no doubt in part explain the enormous popularity of the *Travels*, which survives in nearly three hundred manuscripts and was circulating in eight European languages within fifty years of its release, probably on the Continent, in 1356/57.

14. These studies generally focus on Dante, Langland, and the *St. Erkenwald* poet, either in combination, as in Cindy Vitto, *The Virtuous Pagan in Middle English Literature* (Philadelphia: American Philosophical Society, 1989); R. W. Chambers, "Long, Will, Dante and the Righteous Heathen," *Essay and Studies by Members of the English Association* 9 (1924): 50–69; and Frank Grady, "Piers Plowman, St. Erkenwald, and the Rule of Exceptional Salvations," *Yearbook of Langland Studies* 6 (1992): 61–88; or singly, as in Gina Rizzo, "Dante and the Virtuous Pagans," in *A Dante Symposium: In Commemoration of the 700th Anniversary of the Poet's Birth*, ed. William DeSua and Gino Rizzo, University of North Carolina Studies in the Romance Languages and Literatures 58 (Chapel Hill: University of North Carolina Press, 1965), 115–40; Janet Coleman, *Piers Plowman and the Moderni* (Rome: Edizioni di Storia e Letteratura, 1981); T. P. Dunning, "Langland and the Salvation of the Heathen," *Medium Aevum* 12 (1943): 45–54; G. H. Russell, "The Salvation of the Heathen: The Exploration of a Theme in *Piers Plowman*," *Journal of the Warburg and Courtauld Institute* 29 (1966): 101–16; and Gordon Whatley, "Heathens and Saints: *St. Erkenwald* in Its Legendary Context," *Speculum* 61 (1986): 330–63, and "The Uses of Hagiography: The Legend of Pope Gregory and the Emperor Trajan in the Middle Ages," *Viator* 15 (1984): 25–63.

15. But see Frank Grady, *Representing Righteous Heathens in Late Medieval England*, New Middle Ages (New York: Palgrave, 2005); and Thomas Hahn, "God's Friends: Virtuous Heathen in Later Medieval Thought and English Literature" (Ph.D. diss., University of California, Los Angeles, 1974).

16. As well as Islam's departure from a number of articles of Christian faith, such as the Crucifixion and the Trinity.

17. Heribert Busse, *Islam, Judaism, and Christianity: Theological and Historical Affiliations*, trans. Allison Brown (Princeton, NJ: Markus Weiner, 1998), 59. See also M. T. Houtsma et al., eds., *The Encyclopædia of Islam: A Dictionary of the Geography, Ethnography and Biography of the Muhammadan Peoples*, 4 vols. and suppl. (Leiden: Brill; London: Luzac,

1913–38), s.v. "Ahl al-Kitab" and "Ibrahim." The sequence of prophets is variably cited in the Qur'an: sura 42:13/11–14 relates them as Noah, Abraham, Moses, Jesus, and Muhammad; a number of suras trace the Muslim line of inheritance through Abraham, Ishmael, Isaac, Jacob, "the Tribes" (i.e., the twelve tribes of the Children of Israel), Moses, Jesus, and the Prophets; sura 42:13/11 mentions only Abraham, Moses, and Jesus, and sura 87:19 only Abraham and Moses. See Busse, *Islam*, 32, 40. For a recent argument for the wide-ranging influence of Islamic ideas, references, and travel narrative form on *Mandeville's Travels*, see Ana Pinto, "*Mandeville's Travels*: A Rihla in Disguise," in *Travels and Travelogues in the Middle Ages*, ed. Jean-Francois Kosta-Théfaine (New York: AMS Press, 2009), 3–57.

18. Both Isaac and Abraham are mentioned in the Qur'an, the latter appearing in twenty-five suras. See Busse, *Islam*, 59–60; and Houtsma et al., *Encyclopedia of Islam*, s.v. "Ahl al-Kitab" and "Ibrahim."

19. During the Avignon papacy, which culminated in the Great Schism of 1378–1417.

20. This genre includes such twelfth-century texts as the *Vita Mahumeti*, Walter of Compiègne's *Otia de Machomete*, and Guibert of Nogent's *Gesta Dei per Francos*, 1.3, and the thirteenth-century *Roman de Mahomet*. See Southern's discussion of the group in *Western Views of Islam*, 29–33.

21. Sigmund Freud, *Writings on Art and Literature* (Palo Alto, CA: Stanford University Press, 1997), 199.

22. Samuel Weber, "The Sideshow, or: Remarks on a Canny Moment," *Modern Language Notes* 88 (1973): 1102–33, on 1119.

23. Ibid., 1131–32.

24. See F. M. Warren, "The Enamoured Moslem Princess in Orderic Vital and the French Epic," *PMLA* 29 (1914): 341–58; C. Meredith Jones, "The Conventional Saracen of the Songs of Geste," *Speculum* 17.2 (1924): 201–25; William Comfort, "The Literary Role of the Saracens in the French Epic," *PMLA* 55 (1940): 628–59; and A. Robert Harden, "The Element of Love in the *Chansons de Geste*," *Duquesne Studies: Annuale Medievale* 5 (1965): 65–80.

25. "Frensch" here stands in for the international courtly language of the Latin West. Readers of the Middle English Cotton manuscript who may themselves not have been conversant in French would find the notion of Muslim fluency in it all the more jarring. On the porousness of the boundary between Christianity and Islam posed by this moment and others in the *Travels*, see Suzanne Conklin Akbari, "The Shape of the World," in *Idols in the East: European Representations of Islam and the Orient, 1100–1450* (Ithaca, NY: Cornell University Press, 2009), 53–58.

26. Caroline Walker Bynum, *Metamorphosis and Identity* (New York: Zone Books, 2001), 53, 69.

27. Even if the marvelous and the uncanny have overlapping emotional and structural symptoms, which they seem to, they are not mutually substitutable, nor would the admirabiles mixturae account for the particular mixtures—of Christian and Saracen, Christian and pagan—at work in the *Travels*.

28. Norman Housley, "The Mercenary Companies, the Papacy, and the Crusades, 1356–1378," *Traditio* 38 (1982): 253–80.

29. Housley notes that this was particularly the case in France and Italy in the second half of the fourteenth century.

30. Norman Daniel, *The Arabs and Medieval Europe* (1975; London: Longman, 1979),.219; Terry Jones, *Chaucer's Knight: The Portrait of a Medieval Mercenary*, rev. ed. (London: Methuen, 1985), 87–88.

31. Howard, "The World of Mandeville's Travels," 13, 16.

32. Ibid. 14.

33. The basic French word for god, *dieu*, would very likely have been known through its use in Middle English by general readers of or listeners to the Cotton mss of *The Book of John Mandeville*, as is suggested by its citation at the end of the prologue to *Piers Plowman*, wherein the narrator quotes workers singing, "Dew vous saue, dame Emme" (God save you, dame Emma), a refrain from a popular song. See George Economou, trans., *Piers Plowman: The C Version* (Philadelphia: University of Pennsylvania Press, 1996), 9.

34. As Columbus notes in his records of his New World voyages, "St. Isidore, Bede, Strabo, and the Master of the Scholastic History [Peter Comestor], with St. Ambrose, and Scotus, and all the learned theologians, agree that the earthly paradise is in the east," where he expected to find it. See George Boas's discussion in "Earthly Paradises," in *Primitivism and Related Ideas in the Middle Ages* (Baltimore: Johns Hopkins University Press, 1948), 154–74, on 173.

35. Weber, "The Sideshow," 1133.

36. Southern, *Western Views of Islam*, 76–77.

37. Edward Grant, "The Condemnation of 1277, God's Absolute Power, and Physical Thought in the Late Middle Ages," *Viator* 10 (1979): 211–44, quotation on 212–13.

38. Etienne Gilson, *History of Christian Philosophy in the Middle Ages* (New York: Random House, 1955), 408.

39. Ernest Moody, "Empiricism and Metaphysics in Medieval Philosophy," *Philosophical Review* 67 (1958): 145–63, quotation on 155.

40. William J. Courtenay, "Nominalism and Late Medieval Religion," in *The Pursuit of Holiness in Late Medieval and Renaissance Religion*, ed. Charles Trinkaus and Heiko Oberman (Leiden: Brill, 1974), 26–59, on 42. God's potentia absoluta had been proclaimed by Saint Peter Damian in the eleventh century, affirmed by Peter Lombard's in the twelfth, and reaffirmed by Thomas Aquinas in the thirteenth, but it acquired a different cultural currency in the defensive theological environment with which we are concerned. See Grant, "Condemnation of 1277," 214.

41. See especially Moody, "Empiricism and Metaphysics."

42. Vitto, *The Virtuous Pagan*, 29.

43. Lawrence Eldridge, "Boethian Epistemology and Chaucer's Troilus in the Light of Fourteenth Century Thought," *Mediaevalia* 2 (1976): 49–75, quotation on 53. See also Moody, "Empiricism and Metaphysics," 157; Courtenay, "Nominalism and Late Medieval Religion," 46; and Vitto, *The Virtuous Pagan*, 29.

44. Moody, "Empiricism and Metaphysics," 158; and Eldridge, "Boethian Epistemology," 53.

45. Moody, "Empiricism and Metaphysics," 151; and Eldridge, "Boethian Epistemology," 53.

46. Courtenay, "Nominalism and Late Medieval Religion," 43; and Eldridge, "Boethian Epistemology," 52.

47. Dallas George Denery II, "The Appearance of Reality: Peter Aureol and the Experience of Perceptual Error," *Franciscan Studies* 55 (1998): 27–52, quotation on 42, and *Seeing and Being Seen in the Later Medieval World: Optics, Theology and Religious Life* (Cambridge: Cambridge University Press, 2005), 129.

48. Ernest A. Moody, "Ockam, Buridan, and Nicholas of Autrecourt: The Parisian Statutes of 1339 and 1340," *Franciscan Studies* 7 (1947): 113–46, quotation on 122.

49. See Nicholas of Autrecourt, *Exigit*, 228 (lines 5–12), quoted in Denery, *Seeing and Being Seen*, 155.

50. Over 150 manuscripts are extant today and records suggest another 100 copies were made. See David L. Clark, "Optics for Preachers: The *De oculo morali* by Peter of Limoges," *Michigan Academician* 9 (1977): 329–43.

51. Peter of Limoges, *Liber de oculo morali*, 7:8: "Octavo oculus corporalis est non sui sed alterius cognitiuus. Et in hoc differt oculus carnis ab oculo mentis. Nam oculi corporis semetipsos videre nequeunt sed alis conspiciunt econtrario oculi cordis de se non de aliis infallibiter iudicare possunt. Unde qui alios iudicunt et seipsos non, hii oculos mentales conuertunt in corporales." Quoted in Denery, *Seeing and Being Seen*, 109.

52. Coleman, *Piers Plowman and the Moderni*, 25.

53. Vitto, *The Virtuous Pagan*, 29–30.

54. Ibid., 32.

55. Ibid., 30–31.

56. Coleman, *Piers Plowman and the Moderni*, 118–20. FitzRalph did reserve the possibility of divine caprice, asserting that "no man . . . can choose his ultimate end freely." Cited in ibid., 120.

57. Ibid., 111–12.

58. Ibid., 117.

59. Ibid., 118.

60. Ibid., 117–18.

61. Southern, *Western Views of Islam*, 76; and Coleman, *Piers Plowman and the Moderni*, 121.

62. Coleman, *Piers Plowman and the Moderni*, 121–22.

63. Southern, *Western Views of Islam*, 82; and Coleman, *Piers Plowman and the Moderni*, 123.

64. *Mandeville's Travels*, ed. Seymour, commentary on select bibliography, 277.

65. Donald Howard asserts that "there is not a scrap of evidence that Mandeville entertained such doubts" in "The World of Mandeville's Travels," 9.

66. See Andrew Fleck, "Here, There, and in Between: Representing Difference in the *Travels* of Sir John Mandeville," *Studies in Philology* 97.4

(2000): 379–400. Fleck contends that in "Mandeville's attempt to colonize and incorporate non-Christian religions into his own ... Mandeville's *Travels* reveals the hegemonic impulse of pre-colonial Western Christianity" (389–90).

67. Heiko Oberman, "The Shape of Late Medieval Thought: The Birthpangs of the Modern Era," in Trinkaus and Oberman, *The Pursuit of Holiness*, 3–25, quotation on 14.

68. Courtenay, "Nominalism and Late Medieval Religion," 57. As Martin Jay has pointed out, this runs counter to the official view of the late medieval period offered to us by cultural critics and eminent historians of the late medieval and early modern periods alike. Lucien Febvre, for instance, dates the rise of visual empiricism with the seventeenth century: "it was then that *vision* was unleashed in the world of science as it was in the world of physical sensations, and the world of beauty as well" (original italics); quoted in Jay, *Downcast Eyes: The Denigration of Vision in Twentieth-Century French Thought* (Berkeley: University of California Press, 1993), 34. Robert Mandrou likewise rates seeing third in the hierarchy of the senses, "behind hearing and touch, and far after them," in the fifteenth century; quoted in Jay, *Downcast Eyes*, 34. Intellectual historians of the fourteenth century and the literature and culture of the period offer an important corrective to this generalized view.

69. Joan-Pau Rubiés, "Late Medieval Ambassadors," in *The "Booke" of Travels: Genre, Ethnology, and Pilgrimage, 1250–1700*, ed. Palmira Brummett, Studies in Medieval and Reformation Traditions: History, Culture, Religion, Ideas (Leiden: Brill, 2009), 37–112, quotation on 43.

70. Weber, "The Sideshow," 1122.

71. Lochrie, "Provincializing Medieval Europe."

72. Augustine's own definition in *City of God*, 16.9, trans. Henry Bettenson (New York: Penguin, 1984).

73. "If these races are included in the definition of 'human,' that is, if they are rational and mortal animals, it must be admitted that they trace their lineage from that same one man, the first father of all mankind. This assumes, of course, the truth of the stories about the divergent features of those races, and their great difference from one another and from us." Augustine, *City of God*, 16.8. In chapter 9 of the same book, Augustine asserts there is not "rational ground" for belief in antipodal life.

CONCLUSION

1. See Umberto Eco's enumeration of the various forms of medievalism, the "ten little Middle Ages," in "Dreaming of the Middle Ages," in *Travels in Hyperreality*, trans. William Weaver (New York: Harcourt Brace Jovanovich, 1986), 61–72.

2. See Joan-Pau Rubiés, "Travel Writing and Ethnography," in *Cambridge Companion to Travel Writing*, ed. Peter Hulme and Tim Young (Cambridge: Cambridge University Press, 2002), 242–60, on 250–51.

BIBLIOGRAPHY

Abu-Lughod, Janet. *Before European Hegemony: The World System a.d. 1250–1350*. Oxford: Oxford University Press, 1991.
Akbari, Suzanne Conklin. "The Diversity of Man in the *Book of John Mandeville*." In *Eastward Bound: Travel and Travellers from 1050–1550*, ed. Rosamund Allen, 156–76. Manchester: Manchester University Press, 2004.
———. *Idols in the East: European Representations of Islam and the Orient, 1100–1450*. Ithaca, NY: Cornell University Press, 2009.
Albertus Magnus, *On Animals: A Medieval Summa Zoologica*. Trans. Kenneth F. Kitchell Jr. and Irven Michael Resnick. 2 vols. Baltimore: Johns Hopkins University Press, 1999.
Alloula, Malek. *The Colonial Harem*. Trans. Myrna Godzich and Wlad Godzich. Minneapolis: University of Minnesota Press, 1986.
Aquinas, Thomas. *Commentary on the Politics*. Trans. Ernest L. Fortin and Peter D. O'Neill. In *Medieval Political Philosophy*, ed. Ralph Lerner. New York: Free Press, 1963.
———. *Summa Contra Gentiles*. Book 1, *God*. Trans. and ed. Anton C. Pegis. 1955. Notre Dame, IN: University of Notre Dame Press, 1975.
Augustine. *City of God*. Trans. Henry Bettenson. New York: Penguin, 1984.
Bacon, Roger. *The Opus Maius of Roger Bacon*. Ed. John Henry Bridges. 3 vols. Oxford: Clarendon Press, 1897–1900.
———. *The Opus Maius of Roger Bacon*, Trans. Robert Belle Burke. 2 vols. Philadelphia: University of Pennsylvania Press, 1928.
Baer, Eva. *Ayyubid Metalwork with Christian Images*. Leiden: Brill, 1989.
Bakhtin, Mikhail. *The Dialogic Imagination: Four Essays*. Ed. Michael Holquist. Trans. Caryl Emerson and Michael Holquist. Austin: University of Texas Press, 1981.
Bartlett, Robert. *Gerald of Wales, 1146–1223*. Oxford: Clarendon Press, 1982.

———. *The Making of Europe: Conquest, Colonization and Cultural Change, 950–1350.* London: Allen Lane, 1993.

Bartra, Roger. *Wild Men in the Looking Glass.* Trans. Carl T. Berrisford. Ann Arbor: University of Michigan Press, 1994.

Baxandall, Michael. *Painting and Experience in Fifteenth Century Italy: A Primer in the Social History of Pictorial Style.* Oxford: Clarendon Press, 1972.

Belting, Hans. *The Image and Its Public in the Middle Ages.* Trans. Mark Bartusis and Raymond Meyer. New Rochelle, NY: Caratzas, 1990.

Bennett, Josephine. *The Rediscovery of Sir John Mandeville.* New York: Modern Language Association of America, 1954.

Benveniste, Henriette. "Joinville et les 'autres': Les procédés de représentation dans *l'Histoire de saint Louis.*" *Le Moyen Age: Revue d'Histoire et de Philologie* 102 (1996): 27–55.

Bernheimer, Richard. *Wild Men in the Middle Ages: A Study in Art, Sentiment, and Demonology.* Cambridge, MA: Harvard University Press, 1952.

Best, Edward E. "Classical Latin Prose Writers Quoted by Giraldus Cambrensis," Ph.D. diss., University of North Carolina, Chapel Hill, 1957.

Bhabha, Homi. "The Other Question: Stereotype, Discrimination and the Discourse of Colonialism," *The Location of Culture*, 94–120. London: Routledge, 1994.

Biernoff, Suzannah. *Sight and Embodiment in the Middle Ages: Ocular Desires.* New York: Palgrave Macmillan, 2002.

Boas, Adrian. "Archaeological Sources for the History of Palestine: The Frankish Period: A Unique Medieval Society Emerges." *Near Eastern Archaeology* 61.3 (1998): 138–73.

Boas, George. *Primitivism and Related Ideas in the Middle Ages.* Baltimore: Johns Hopkins University Press, 1948.

Booth, Wayne. *The Rhetoric of Irony.* Chicago: University of Chicago Press, 1974.

Bryson, Norman. *Vision and Painting: The Logic of the Gaze.* New Haven, CT: Yale University Press, 1983.

Bulliet, Richard. *The Case for Islamo-Christian Civilization.* New York: Columbia University Press, 2004.

Bunim, Miriam. *Space in Medieval Painting and the Forerunners of Perspective.* New York: AMS Press, 1970.

Bury, John Bagnell. *Idea of Progress.* London: Macmillan, 1920.

Busse, Heribert. *Islam, Judaism, and Christianity: Theological and Historical Affiliations.* Trans. Allison Brown. Princeton, NJ: Markus Weiner, 1998.

Butturff, Douglas. "Satire in *Mandeville's Travels.*" *Annuale Mediaevale* 13 (1972): 155–64.
Bynum, Caroline Walker. *Metamorphosis and Identity.* New York: Zone Books, 2001.
Caesar, [Julius]. *The Gallic War.* Trans. H. J. Edwards. Cambridge, MA: Harvard Loeb Classics, 1979.
Cahen, Claude. "Saint Louis et l'Islam." *Journal Asiatique* (1970): 3–12.
Campbell, Mary. *The Witness and the Other World: Exotic European Travel Writing, 400–1600.* Ithaca, NY: Cornell University Press, 1988.
Caviness, Margaret. "Biblical Stories in Windows: Were They Bibles for the Poor?" In *The Bible in the Middle Ages: Its Influence on Literature and Art*, ed. B. S. Levy, 103–47. Binghamton, NY: Medieval and Renaissance Texts and Studies, 1992.
Chambers, R. W. "Long, Will, Dante and the Righteous Heathen." *Essay and Studies by Members of the English Association* 9 (1924): 50–69.
Chew, Samuel C. *The Crescent and the Rose: Islam and England During the Renaissance.* Oxford: Oxford University Press, 1937.
Clark, David L. "Optics for Preachers: The *De oculo morali* by Peter of Limoges." *Michigan Academician* 9 (1977): 329–43.
Clifford, James. "Partial Truths." In *Writing Culture: The Poetics and Politics of Ethnography*, ed. James Clifford and George Marcus, 1–26. Berkeley: University of California Press, 1986.
———. *The Predicament of Culture.* Cambridge, MA: Harvard University Press, 1998.
Cline, Ruth. "Hearts and Eyes." *Romance Philology* 25 (1971–72): 263–97.
Cohen, Jeffrey Jerome. *Hybridity, Identity and Monstrosity in Medieval Britain: On Difficult Middles.* New Middle Ages. New York: Palgrave, 2006.
———. "Hybrids, Monsters, Borderlands: The Bodies of Gerald of Wales." In *The Postcolonial Middle Ages*, ed. Jeffrey Jerome Cohen, New Middle Ages. 85–104. New York: Palgrave, 2000.
Cole, Thomas. *Democritus and the Sources of Greek Anthropology.* Philological Monographs no. 25. Chapel Hill, NC: American Philological Association, 1967.
Coleman, Janet. *Piers Plowman and the Moderni.* Rome: Edizioni di Storia e Letteratura, 1981.
Comfort, William. "The Literary Role of the Saracens in the French Epic." *PMLA* 55 (1940): 628–59.
Courtenay, William J. "Nominalism and Late Medieval Religion." In *The Pursuit of Holiness in Late Medieval and Renaissance Religion*, ed. Charles Trinkaus and Heiko Oberman, 26–59. Leiden: Brill, 1974.

Cutler, Anthony. "Everywhere and Nowhere: The Invisible Muslim and Christian Self-Fashioning in the Culture of the Outremer." In *France and the Holy Land: Frankish Culture at the End of the Crusades*, ed. Daniel H. Weiss and Lisa Mahoney, 253–81. Baltimore: Johns Hopkins University Press, 2004.

Daniel, Norman. *The Arabs and Medieval Europe*. 1975. London: Longman, 1979.

———. *Islam and the West: The Making of an Image*. Edinburgh: Edinburgh University Press, 1959.

Davies, R. R. *Conquest, Coexistence, and Change: Wales, 1063–1415*. Oxford: Clarendon Press, 1987.

———. *The First English Empire: Power and Identities in the British Isles, 1093–1343*. New York: Oxford University Press, 2000.

———. "The Survival of the Blood Feud in Medieval Wales." *History* 54 (1969): 338–57

Dawson, Christopher, ed. *The Mongol Mission: Narratives and Letters of the Franciscan Missionaries in Mongolia and China in the Thirteenth and Fourteenth Centuries*. New York: Sheed and Ward, 1955. Repr. as *Mission to Asia*. Cambridge, MA: Medieval Academy Press, 1980.

Deluz, Christine. *Le Livre de Jehan de Mandeville: Une "Géographie" au XIVe siècle*. Publications de l'Institut d'Etudes Médiévales: Textes, Etudes, Congrès, 8. Louvain-la-Neuve: Université Catholique de Louvain, 1988.

Denery, Dallas George, II. "The Appearance of Reality: Peter Aureol and the Experience of Perceptual Error." *Franciscan Studies* 55 (1998): 27–52.

———. *Seeing and Being Seen in the Later Medieval World: Optics, Theology and Religious Life*. Cambridge: Cambridge University Press, 2005.

Dufournet, Jean, and Laurence Harf, eds. *Le Prince et son historien*. Paris: Champion, 1997.

Dunning, T. P. "Langland and the Salvation of the Heathen." *Medium Aevum* 12 (1943): 45–54.

Eco, Umberto. "Dreaming of the Middle Ages." In *Travels in Hyperreality*. Trans. William Weaver, 61–72. New York: Hartcourt Brace Jovanovich, 1986.

Economou, George, trans. *Piers Plowman: The C Version*. Philadelphia: University of Pennsylvania Press, 1996.

Edgerton, Samuel. *The Renaissance Rediscovery of Linear Perspective*. New York: Basic Books, 1975.

Eldridge, Lawrence. "Boethian Epistemology and Chaucer's Troilus in the Light of Fourteenth Century Thought." *Mediaevalia* 2 (1976): 49–75.

Ellenblum, Ronnie. *Frankish Rural Settlement in the Latin Kingdom of Jerusalem, 1174–1277*. Cambridge: Cambridge University Press, 1998.

Fabian, Johannes. *Time and the Other: How Anthropology Makes Its Object*. New York: Columbia University Press, 1983.

Ferlimpin-Archer, Christine. "Joinville, de l'hagiographe à l'autobiographe: Approche de *La Vie de saint Louis*." In *Jean de Joinville: De la Champagne aux royaumes d'outre-mer*, ed. Danielle Quéruel, 73–91. Langres: Gueniot, 1998.

Fernández-Armesto, Felipe. *Before Columbus: Exploration and Colonisation from the Mediterranean to the Atlantic, 1229–1492*. London: Macmillan, 1987.

———. "Medieval Ethnography." *Journal of the Anthropological Society of Oxford* 13.3 (1982): 275–86.

Fleck, Andrew. "Here, There, and in Between: Representing Difference in the *Travels* of Sir John Mandeville." *Studies in Philology* 97.4 (2000): 379–400.

Folda, Jaroslav. *Crusader Art in the Holy Land: From the Third Crusade to the Fall of Acre*. Cambridge: Cambridge University Press, 2005.

Freud, Sigmund. *Writings on Art and Literature*. Palo Alto, CA: Stanford University Press, 1997.

Friedman, John Block. *The Monstrous Races in Medieval Art and Thought*. Cambridge, MA: Harvard University Press, 1981.

Gabrieli, Francesco. *Arab Historians of the Crusades*. Trans. E. J. Costello. Berkeley: University of California Press, 1984.

Gaposchkin, Cecilia M. *The Making of Saint Louis: Kingship, Sanctity, and Crusade in the Later Middle Ages*. Ithaca, NY: Cornell University Press, 2008.

Gaucher, Elisabeth. "Joinville et l'écriture biographique." In *Le Prince et son historien*, ed. Jean Dufournet and Laurence Harf, 101–22. Paris: Champion, 1997.

Georgopoulou, Maria. "Orientalism and Crusader Art." *Medieval Encounters* 5.3 (1999): 289–321.

Gerald of Wales. *Expugnatio Hibernica*. Ed. and trans. A. B. Scott and F. X. Martin. Dublin: Royal Irish Academy, 1978.

———. *The History and Topography of Ireland*. Trans. John O'Meara. New York: Penguin, 1982.

———. *The Journey Through Wales and the Description of Wales*. Trans. Lewis Thorpe. New York: Penguin, 1978.

———. [Giraldi Cambrensis]. *Opera*. Ed. James F. Dimock. 6 vols. London: Longman, 1861–91.

Gillingham, John. "The Beginnings of English Imperialism." *Journal of Historical Sociology* 5.4 (1992): 392–409.

———."The Context and Purposes of Geoffrey of Monmouth's History of the Kings of Britain." In *The English in the Twelfth Century*. Rochester, NY: Boydell Press, 2000.

Gilson, Etienne. *History of Christian Philosophy in the Middle Ages*. New York: Random House, 1955.

Grady, Frank. "Piers Plowman, St. Erkenwald, and the Rule of Exceptional Salvations." *Yearbook of Langland Studies* 6 (1992): 61–88.

———. *Representing Righteous Heathens in Late Medieval England*. New Middle Ages. New York: Palgrave, 2005.

Gransden, Antonia. "Realistic Observation in Twelfth-Century England." *Speculum* 47 (1972): 29–51.

Grant, Edward. "The Condemnation of 1277, God's Absolute Power, and Physical Thought in the Late Middle Ages." *Viator* 10 (1979): 211–44.

Greenblatt, Stephen. *Marvelous Possessions: The Wonder of the New World*. Chicago: University of Chicago Press, 1992.

Gruber, Jacob W. "Ethnographic Salvage and the Shaping of Anthropology." *American Anthropologist* 72 (1970): 1289–99.

Gueret-Laferté, Michèle. "Les gestes de l'autre." In *Le Geste et les gestes au Moyen Age*. Conference Proceedings of Centre Universitaire d'Etudes et de Recherches Médiévale d'Aix. Aix-en-Provence: CUERMA / Sénéfiance 41, 1998.

Guilcher-Pellat, Yvette. "Joinville et Paennime, l'autre l'ailleurs." In *Jean de Joinville: De la Champagne aux royaumes d'outre-mer*, ed. Danielle Quéruel, 193–206. Langres: Gueniot, 1998.

Gurevich, Aron. *Medieval Popular Culture: Problems of Belief and Perception*. Trans. János. M. Bak and Paula A. Hollingsworth. Cambridge: Cambridge University Press, 1988.

Guzman, Gregory. "European Clerical Envoys to the Mongols: Reports of Western Merchants in Eastern Europe and Central Asia, 1231–1255." *Journal of Medieval History* 22.1 (1996): 53–67.

Hahn, Thomas. "God's Friends: Virtuous Heathen in Later Medieval Thought and English Literature." Ph.D. diss., University of California, Los Angeles, 1974.

Hamilton, Bernard. "Knowing the Enemy: Western Understanding of Islam at the Time of the Crusades." *Journal of the Royal Asiatic Society of Great Britain and Ireland* ser. 3, 7 (1997): 373–87.

Harden, A. Robert. "The Element of Love in the *Chansons de Geste*." *Duquesne Studies: Annuale Medievale* 5 (1965): 65–80.

Heng, Geraldine. *Empire of Magic: Medieval Romance and the Politics of Cultural Fantasy*. New York: Columbia University Press, 2003.

Higgins, Ian. *Writing East: The "Travels" of Sir John Mandeville*. Philadelphia: University of Pennsylvania, 1997.
Hillenbrand, Carole. *The Crusades: Islamic Perspectives*. Chicago: Fitzroy Dearborn, 1999.
Hodgen, Margaret. *Early Anthropology in the Sixteenth and Seventeenth Centuries*, Philadelphia: University of Pennsylvania Press, 1998.
Holmes, Urban T. "Gerald the Naturalist." *Speculum* 11 (1936): 110–21.
———. "Life Among Europeans in Palestine and Syria in the Twelfth and Thirteenth Centuries." In *A History of the Crusades*, ed. Kenneth M. Setton, 4 vols. Madison: University of Wisconsin Press, 1969–89. 4:3–35.
Holt, P. M. *Early Mamluk Diplomacy, 1260–1290: Treaties of Baybars and Qalawun with Christian Rulers*. Leiden: Brill, 1995.
Housley, Norman. "The Mercenary Companies, the Papacy, and the Crusades, 1356–1378." *Traditio* 38 (1982): 253–80.
Houtsma, M. T., et al., eds. *The Encyclopædia of Islam: A Dictionary of the Geography, Ethnography and Biography of the Muhammadan Peoples*, 4 vols. and suppl. Leiden: Brill; London: Luzac, 1913–38.
Howard, Donald. "The World of Mandeville's Travels." *Yearbook of English Studies* 1 (1971): 1–17.
———. *Writers and Pilgrims: Medieval Pilgrimage Narratives and Their Posterity*. Berkeley: University of California Press, 1980.
Humbert of Romans. *Liber de eruditione praedicatorum*. In *De Vita Regulari*, ed. Joachim Berthier, vol. 2. Rome: Befani, 1888.
Hyde, J. K. "Ethnographers In Search of an Audience." In *Medieval Ethnographies: European Perceptions of the World Beyond*, ed. Joan-Pau Rubiés, 65–119. Aldershot, England: Ashgate, 2009.
Ibn Jubayr. *The Travels of Ibn Jubayr*. Trans. Roland Broadhurst, 1952. New Delhi: Goodward, 2004.
Ingham, Patricia Clare. *Sovereign Fantasies: Arthurian Romance and the Making of Britain*. Philadelphia: University of Pennsylvania Press, 2001.
Isidore of Seville [Isidori Hispalensis Episcopi]. *Etymologiarum sive Originum Libri XX*. Ed. W. M. Lindsay. Oxford: Clarendon, 1985.
———. *Etymologies*. Ed. Marc Reydellet. Paris: Societe d'Editions, 1984.
Ivins, William M. *On the Rationalization of Sight*. New York, Metropolitan Museum of Art Papers no. 8, 1938, Repr., Cambridge, MA: Da Capo Press, 1973.
Janson, H. W. *Apes and Ape Lore in the Middle Ages and the Renaissance*. London: Warburg and Courtauld Studies, 1952.
Jay, Martin. *Downcast Eyes: The Denigration of Vision in Twentieth-Century French Thought*. Berkeley: University of California Press, 1993.

Joinville, Jean de. *L'Histoire de Saint Louis*, Ed. Natalis de Wailly. Paris: Firmin Didot, 1874.

Joinville, [Jean de], and [Geoffrey de] Villehardouin. *Chronicles of the Crusade*. Trans. M. R. B. Shaw. New York: Penguin, 1963.

Jones, C. Meredith. "The Conventional Saracen of the Songs of Geste." *Speculum* 17.2 (1924): 201–25.

Jones, Terry. *Chaucer's Knight: The Portrait of a Medieval Mercenary*. Rev. ed. London: Methuen, 1985.

Jones, W. R. "The Image of the Barbarian in Medieval Europe." *Comparative Studies in Society and History* 13.4 (1971): 376–407.

Jordan, William Chester. *Louis IX and the Challenge of the Crusade: A Study in Rulership*. Princeton, NJ: Princeton University Press, 1979.

Katzenstein, Ranee, and Glenn Lowry. "Christian Themes in Thirteenth Century Islamic Metalwork." *Muqarnas* 1 (1983): 53–68.

Kedar, Benjamin. "Convergences of Oriental Christian, Muslim and Frankish Worshippers: The Case of Saydnaya and the Knights Templar." In *The Crusades and the Military Orders: Expanding the Frontiers of Medieval Latin Christianity*, ed. Zsolt Hunyadi and Jozsef Laszlovszky, 89–100. Budapest: Society for the Study of the Crusades and the Latin East, 2001.

———. *Crusade and Mission: European Approaches Towards the Muslims*. Princeton, NJ: Princeton University Press, 1984.

———. "Latins and Oriental Christians in the Frankish Levant, 1099–1291." In *Sharing the Sacred: Religious Contacts and Conflicts in the Holy Land*, ed. Arieh Kofsky and Guy G. Stroumsa, 209–22. Jerusalem: Yad Izhak Ben Zvi, 1998.

Kessler, Herbert. "Pictorial Narrative and Church Mission in Sixth-Century Gaul." *Studies in the History of Art* 16 (1985): 75–91.

———. "Pictures as Scripture in Fifth-Century Churches." *Studia Artium Orientalis et Occidentalis* 2.1 (1985): 17–31

Khanmohamadi, Shirin A. "Casting a 'Sideways Glance' at the Crusades: The Voice of the Other in Joinville's *Vie de Saint Louis*," *Exemplaria: A Journal of Theory in Medieval and Renaissance Studies* 22.3 (2010): 177–99.

———. "The Look of Medieval Ethnography: William of Rubruck's Mission to Mongolia," *New Medieval Literatures* 10 (2008): 87–114.

———. "Salvage Anthropology and Displaced Mourning in Marie de France's *Lais*." *Arthuriana* 21.3 (Fall 2011): 49–69.

———. "Worldly Unease in Late Medieval European Travel Reports." In *Cosmopolitanism and the Middle Ages*, ed. John Ganim and Shayne Legassie, 105–20. New Middle Ages. New York: Palgrave, 2013.

Kinoshita, Sharon. *Medieval Boundaries: Rethinking Difference in Old French Literature*. Philadelphia: University of Pennsylvania Press, 2006.

Knight, Rhonda. "Stealing Stonehenge: Translation, Appropriation, and Cultural Identity in Robert Mannyng of Brunne's *Chronicle*." *Journal of Medieval and Early Modern Studies* 32.1 (2000): 41–58.

Krey, August C., ed. *The First Crusade: The Accounts of Eye-witnesses and Participants*. Gloucester, MA: Peter Smith, 1958.

Le Goff, Jacques. *Saint Louis*. Paris: Gallimard, 1996.

Legros, Huguette. "Images et représentations de l'Orient dan la *Vie de Saint Louis* de Joinville: De l'Orient peint dans l'historiographie à l'Orient évoqué dans les chansons de geste." In *L'épopée romane: Actes du XVe Congrès international Roncesvals, Poitiers, 21–27 août 2000*, ed. Gabriel Bianciotto and Claudio Galderisi, 2 vols., 705–13. Poitiers: Centre d'Études Supérieures de Civilisation Médiévale, 2002.

Lewis, Ceri. "The Court Poets: Their Function, Status and Craft." In *A Guide to Welsh Literature* ed. A. O. H. Jarman and Gwilym Rees Hughes, 1:118–56. Swansea: Christopher Davies, 1976.

Lochrie, Karma. "Provincializing Medieval Europe: Mandeville's Cosmopolitan Utopia." *PMLA* 124.2 (2009): 592–99.

Lomperis, Linda. "Medieval Travel Writing and the Question of Race." *Journal of Medieval and Early Modern Studies* 31.1 (2001): 149–64.

Lovejoy, Arthur O., and George Boas. *Primitivism and Related Ideas in Antiquity*. 1935. New York: Octagon, 1965.

Mandeville's Travels. Ed. M. C. Seymour. Oxford: Clarendon Press, 1967.

Maquet, Jacques. "Objectivity in Anthropology." *Current Anthropology* 5 (1964): 47–55.

Matthew Paris. *Matthew Paris' English History from the Year 1235 to 1273*. Trans. J. A. Giles. Vol. 1. New York: AMS Press, 1968.

Mayer, Hans. *The Crusades*. Trans. John Gillingham. 1965. Oxford: Oxford University Press, 1972.

McCannon, Afrodesia E. "The King's Two Lives: The Tunisian Legend of Saint Louis." *Journal of Folklore Research* 43.1 (2006): 53–74.

Menocal, María Rosa. *The Arabic Role in Medieval Literary History: A Forgotten Heritage*. Philadelphia: University of Pennsylvania Press, 1987.

———. *The Ornament of the World: How Muslims, Jews, and Christians Created a Culture of Tolerance in Medieval Spain*. New York: Little, Brown, 2002.

Metlitzki, Dorothee. *The Matter of Araby in Medieval England*. New Haven, CT: Yale University Press, 1977.

Mitchell, Timothy. *Colonising Egypt*. Cambridge: Cambridge University Press, 1988.

Moody, Ernest. "Empiricism and Metaphysics in Medieval Philosophy." *Philosophical Review* 67 (1958): 145–63.

———. "Ockam, Buridan, and Nicholas of Autrecourt: The Parisian Statutes of 1339 and 1340." *Franciscan Studies* 7 (1947): 113–46.

Muldoon, James. *Popes, Lawyers, and Infidels: The Church and the Non-Christian World, 1250–1500*. Philadelphia: University of Pennsylvania Press, 1979.

Mund, Stéphane. "Travel Accounts as Early Sources of Knowledge About Russia in Medieval Western Europe from the Mid-Thirteenth to the Early Fifteenth Century." *Medieval History Journal* 5.1 (2002): 103–20.

Nisbet, Robert. *History of the Idea of Progress*. New York: Basic Books, 1980.

Oberman, Heiko. "The Shape of Late Medieval Thought: The Birthpangs of the Modern Era." In *The Pursuit of Holiness in Late Medieval and Renaissance Religion*, ed. Charles Trinkaus and Heiko Oberman, 3–25. Leiden: Brill, 1974.

Pagden, Anthony. *The Fall of Natural Man: The American Indian and the Origins of Comparative Ethnology*. Cambridge: Cambridge University Press, 1987.

Perret, Michèle. "À la fin de sa vie ne fuz je mie." *Revue de sciences humaines* 183 (1981): 16–37.

Peters, Edward, ed. *The First Crusade: The Chronicle of Fulcher of Chartres and Other Source Materials*. Philadelphia: University of Pennsylvania Press, 1971.

Phillips, Jonathan. "The Latin East." In *The Oxford Illustrated History of the Crusades*, ed. Jonathan Riley-Smith, 112–40. Oxford: Oxford University Press, 1995.

Pinto, Ana. "*Mandeville's Travels*: A Rihla in Disguise." In *Travels and Travelogues in the Middle Ages*, ed. Jean-Francois Kosta-Théfaine, 3–57. New York: AMS Press, 2009.

Pliny. *Natural History in Ten Volumes*. Ed. H. Rackham. Vol. 2 (books 3–7). Cambridge, MA: Harvard University Press, 1949.

Pohl, Walter. "The *regia* and the *hring*: Barbarian Places of Power." In *Topographies of Power in the Early Middle Ages*, ed. Frans Theuws, Carine van Rhijn, and Mayke de Jong. Leiden: Brill, 2001.

Pratt, Mary Louise. "Field Work in Common Places." In *Writing Culture: The Poetics and Politics of Ethnography*, ed. James Clifford and George Marcus, 27–50. Berkeley: University of California Press, 1986.

———. *Imperial Eyes: Travel Writing and Transculturation*. New York: Routledge, 1992.

———. "Linguistic Utopias." In *The Linguistics of Writing: Arguments Between Language and Literature*, ed. Nigel Fabb et al., 48–66. New York: Methuen, 1987.

———. "Transculturation and Autoethnography: Peru, 1615/1980." In *Colonial Discourse / Postcolonial Theory*, ed. Francis Barker, Peter Hulme, and Margaret Iversen, 24–46. Manchester: Manchester University Press, 1994.

Prawer, Joshua. *The Latin Kingdom of Jerusalem: European Colonialism in the Middle Ages*. London: Weidenfeld and Nicolson, 1972.

Pryce, Huw. "In Search of a Medieval Society: Deheubarth in the Writings of Gerald of Wales." *Welsh History Review* 13.3 (1986–87): 265–81.

Quéruel, Danielle, ed. *Jean de Joinville: De la Champagne aux royaumes d'outre-mer*. Langres: Gueniot, 1998.

Richter, Michael. *Giraldus Cambrensis: The Growth of the Welsh Nation*. Aberystwyth: National Library of Wales, 1972.

Riley-Smith, Jonathan. *The Crusades, a History*. 2nd ed. New Haven, CT: Yale University Press, 2005.

———. "Government and the Indigenous in the Latin Kingdom of Jerusalem." In *Medieval Frontiers: Concepts and Practices*, ed. David Abulafia and Nora Berend, 121–31. Aldershot, England: Ashgate, 2002.

Rizzo, Gina. "Dante and the Virtuous Pagans." In *A Dante Symposium: In Commemoration of the 700th Anniversary of the Poet's Birth*, ed. William DeSua and Gino Rizzo, 115–40. University of North Carolina Studies in the Romance Languages and Literatures 58. Chapel Hill: University of North Carolina Press, 1965.

Roberts, Brynley F. "Gerald of Wales and the Welsh Tradition." In *The Formation of Culture in Medieval Britain: Celtic, Latin, and Norman Influences*, ed. Francoise Le Saux, 129–47. Lewiston, NY: Mellen Press, 1995.

Rockhill, William. "Introductory Notice." In *The Journey of William of Rubruck to the Eastern Parts of the World*, ed. William Rockhill, xiii–xliv. 1990. London: Hakluyt Society, 1998.

Rowe, John Howland. "The Renaissance Foundations of Anthropology." In *Readings in the History of Anthropology*, ed. Regna Darnell, 61–77. New York: Harper and Row, 1974.

Rubiés, Joan-Pau. "Late Medieval Ambassadors." In *The "Booke" of Travels: Genre, Ethnology, and Pilgrimage, 1250–1700*, ed. Palmira Brummett, 37–112. Studies in Medieval and Reformation Traditions: History, Culture, Religion, Ideas. Leiden: Brill, 2009.

———, ed. *Medieval Ethnographies: European Perceptions of the World Beyond*. Aldershot, England: Ashgate, 2009.

———. "New World and Renaissance Ethnology." *History and Anthropology* 6.2 (1993): 157–97.

———. "Travel Writing and Ethnography." In *Travellers and Cosmographers: Studies in the History of Early Modern Travel and Ethnology*, ed. Joan-Pau Rubiés, essay 4, 1–39. Aldershot, England: Ashgate Variorum, 2007.

———. *Travel and Ethnology in the Renaissance: South India Through European Eyes. 1250–1625.* Cambridge: Cambridge University Press, 2002.

———. "Travel Writing and Ethnography." In *Cambridge Companion to Travel Writing*, ed. Peter Hulme and Tim Young, expanded ed., 242–60. Cambridge: Cambridge University Press, 2002.

Rubiés, Joan-Pau, and Jas Elsner, eds. *Voyages and Visions: Towards a Cultural History of Travel.* London: Reaktion Books, 1999.

Runciman, Steven. *A History of the Crusades.* Vol. 3, *The Kingdom of Acre and the Later Crusades.* Cambridge: Cambridge University Press, 1954.

Russell, G. H. "The Salvation of the Heathen: The Exploration of a Theme in *Piers Plowman*." *Journal of the Warburg and Courtauld Institute* 29 (1966): 101–16.

Said, Edward. *Orientalism.* New York: Vintage, 1979.

Sallust. *Bellum Iugurthinum.* Ed. J. C. Rolfe. Rev. ed, London: Loeb Classical Library, 1931.

Smail, R. C. *Crusading Warfare, 1097–1193.* Cambridge: Cambridge University Press, 1957.

Smith, Caroline. *Crusading in the Age of Joinville.* Aldershot, England: Ashgate, 2006.

Solinus, C. Julius [C. Iulii Solini]. *Collectanea Rerum Memorabilium.* Ed. Theodor Mommsen. Berlin: Weidmannsche, 1958.

Southern, R. W. *Western Views of Islam in the Middle Ages.* Cambridge, MA: Harvard University Press, 1972.

Spearing, A. C. *Textual Subjectivity: The Encoding of Subjectivity in Medieval Narratives and Lyrics.* Oxford: Oxford University Press, 2005.

Spiegel, Gabrielle. "Genealogy: Form and Function in Medieval Historical Narrative." *History and Theory* 22.1 (1983): 43–53.

———. *Romancing the Past: The Rise of Vernacular Prose Historiography in Thirteenth-Century France.* Berkeley: University of California Press, 1993.

Stanbury, Sarah. "The Lover's Gaze in *Troilus and Criseyde*." In *Chaucer's Troilus and Criseyde: Subgit to all Poesye*, ed. R. A. Shoaf, 224–38. Binghamton, NY: Medieval and Renaissance Text Studies, 1992.

———. "Regimes of the Visual in Premodern England: Gaze, Body and Chaucer's *Clerk's Tale*." *New Literary History* 28.2 (1997): 261–89.

Thomson, Rodney M. *William of Malmesbury.* Woodbridge, England: Boydell Press, 1987.

Tolan, John V. "Mirror of Chivalry: Salah al-Din in the Medieval

European Imagination." In *Images of the Other: Europe and the Muslim World Before 1700*, ed. David Blanks, Cairo Papers in Social Science, vol. 19, monograph 2, 7–38. Cairo: American University in Cairo Press, 1996.

———. *Saracens*. New York: Columbia University Press, 2002.

Tyerman, Christopher. *God's War: A New History of the Crusades*. Cambridge, MA: Belknap-Harvard University Press, 2006.

Usamah Ibn-Muqidh. *An Arab-Syrian Gentleman and Warrior in the Period of the Crusades: Memoirs of Usamah Ibn-Munqidh*. Trans. Philip K. Hitti. 1929. Princeton, NJ: Princeton University Press, 1987.

Vitto, Cindy. *The Virtuous Pagan in Middle English Literature*. Philadelphia: American Philosophical Society, 1989.

Wallace, David. *Premodern Places: Calais to Surinam, Chaucer to Aphra Behn*. Oxford: Blackwell, 2004.

Warren, F. M. "The Enamoured Moslem Princess in Orderic Vital and the French Epic." *PMLA* 29 (1914): 341–58.

Weber, Samuel. "The Sideshow, or: Remarks on a Canny Moment." *Modern Language Notes* 88 (1973): 1102–33.

Weiss, Daniel. *Art and Crusade in the Age of Saint Louis*. Cambridge: Cambridge University Press, 1998.

Whatley, Gordon. "Heathens and Saints: *St. Erkenwald* in Its Legendary Context." *Speculum* 61 (1986): 330–63.

———. "The Uses of Hagiography: The Legend of Pope Gregory and the Emperor Trajan in the Middle Ages." *Viator* 15 (1984): 25–63.

William of Malmesbury. *Gesta Regum Anglorum*. Ed. and trans. R. A. B. Mynors. Vol 1. Oxford: Clarendon Press, 1998.

William of Rubruck. *Itinerarium*. In *Sinica Franciscana*, vol. 1, *Itinera et relationes fratrumminorum saeculi XIII et XIV*, ed. Anastasius Van den Wyngaert. Florence: Quaracchi-Firenze, 1929.

———. *The Mission of Friar William of Rubruck*. Ed. Peter Jackson. London: Hakluyt Society, 1990.

Zacher, Christian. *Curiosity and Pilgrimage: The Literature of Discovery in Fourteenth-Century England*. Baltimore: Johns Hopkins University Press, 1976.

Zeitler, Barbara. "'Sinful Sons, Falsifiers of the Christian Faith': The Depiction of Muslims in a 'Crusader' Manuscript." *Mediterranean Historical Review* 12 (1997): 25–50.

INDEX

Adam of Bremen, 3, 37
Akbari, Suzanne Conklin, 150n4, 177n25
Albertus Magnus, 20, 23–24, 59–60; definition of civility, 23
Alexander of Hales, 134
Alloula, Malek, 111, 174n67
Andrew of Longjumeau, 26, 57, 100
anthropology: modern, 3, 11, 64; medieval, 11–36; sources of, 8; discourses of civility and Christianity, 11–12, 64–65, 153n2; evolutionary (or "developmental," "progressivist") anthropology, 11, 14–20, 98; monstrous races, 11, 60–61; wild man tradition, 12, 22–23, 60–61; Innocent IV's contribution, 14, 25–30; and knowledge of Muslims, 14, 30–33, 88–90; link to missions, 14, 64; primitivism and virtuous pagans, 14, 33–36; defining the "human," 20–25; scholastic discourse of barbarism, 23–25, 60–61; application in New World context, 28–30, 33–34, 65; medieval salvation paradigm, 29–30; link to vision, 67; distinction from ethnography, 11, 153n1. *See also* ethnography
antipodes, the, 12, 22, 118–19, 142–43, 153n4. *See also* monsters
Aquinas, Saint Thomas, 20; on barbarism, 24–25, 60; approach to virtuous pagans, 35–36, 134; advice in preaching, 78; and medieval philosophy, 132; on virtuous pagans, 157–58n80
Augustine, Saint: on antipodes, 12, 153n4; and medieval philosophy, 132

Aureol, Peter, 133, 138
Ayyubids, the, 89, 97, 99, 101

Baatu khan (ruler of Golden Horde), 58, 61, 68, 70, 74–76
Bacon, Roger, 58, 59, 61, 63–64, 66–69, 83, 86
Baer, Eva, 172n33
Bakhtin, Mikhail, 91, 103, 149n1, 173n49, 174n64. *See also* contact zone; dialogism
Bartlett, Robert, 15, 149n4, 150n6
Bartra, Roger, 60
Baxandall, Michael, 77
Bede, the Venerable, 38
Bedouins, the, 36, 98, 105, 123
Benedict the Pole, 26, 57, 164n16
Bennett, Josephine, 175n5, 175n6
Bernard of Clairvaux, 123
Bernheimer, Richard, 60
Bhabha, Homi, 49, 161n37
Biernoff, Suzannah, 7, 162n53
Boccaccio, Giovanni, 33; the *Decameron*, 109
Bonaventure, Saint, 132
Bradwardine, Thomas, 134
Brahmins, the, 14, 33, 36
Bryson, Norman, 166n37
Buckingham, Thomas, 133–34
Buddhists, 63, 69, 79–80
Bulliet, Richard, 151n15, 174n59
Bynum, Caroline Walker, 123, 163n7, 167n40

Caesar, Julius 15–16, 38,
Campbell, Mary Baine, 58, 163n7
Canary Islands, 27–30, 33
Carpini, John of Plano, 4, 57–58, 84, 122, 164n16
chansons de geste, 88

chronicle writing: influence on ethnography, 38, 54–55; mixed with ethnography 39; poetics of, 53; crusade chronicles, 88–89, 97; the Metz chronicler, 124
Church Fathers, 34–35
Cicero, 11, 15, 17–19, 24, 42, 60
clash of civilizations, 93
classical anthropology: Epicurean tradition, 11, 14; progressivism (or "developmental" or "evolutionary") anthropology, 11. *See also* Cicero; Gerald of Wales; Lucretius
Clifford, James, 6, 166n35
Cline, Ruth, 153n28
Cohen, Jeffrey Jerome, 44, 150n4, 151n15, 161n39
Constantinople, 89, 172n37
contact zone, the 2, 39, 49, 82, 91–92, 100, 104, 109, 173n49. *See also* dialogism; hybridity
cosmopolitanism, and the middle ages 2
Cota, Lady (wife of Mangu khan), 62, 69
Crusades, the: changes in, 88–89, in chronicles of, 95; the First Crusade, 88, 170n15, ideology of, 92; Third Crusade, 88, 96; Fourth Crusade, 89; Richard the Lion-hearted, 88, 97; Sixth Crusade, 96; Seventh and Eighth Crusades, 110–11; as a source of ethnography, 151n11. *See also* chronicle writing; Jean de Joinville; Outremer

Daniel, Norman, 30
Dante Alighieri, 32–33, 116, 176n14
David of Augsburg, 78
Davies, R. R., 15
Dawson, Christopher, 172–73n44
deixis, 7, 51, 55, 65–66, 72–73, 91, 103, 143. *See also* ethnographic poetics and gaze
Denery, Dallas George, 83
Descartes, René, 87
dialogism, 2, 4–10, 47–50, 54, 59, 73–87, 91, 102–12, 114, 120, 140, 145–47. *See also* ethnographic poetics and gaze; ethnography
Duns Scotus, John, 35, 132, 134

Earthly Paradise, 33,128, 137, 146, 178n34
Eco, Umberto, 180n1
Edgerton, Samuel, 53, 151n13, 162n53
Eleanor of Aquitaine, 110
Ellenblum, Ronnie, 92

ethnography: medieval European ethnography, role of discomfort and difficulty in, 1, 2, 5, 10, 44, 55, 59, 74–75, 77, 81, 86, 104–9, 114, 145–47; medieval European ethnography, European disorientation in, 1, 5, 9–10, 56, 59, 73–74, 77, 79, 81–82, 91, 104–9, 118, 139–42, 145–46; self-reflexivity and self-mirroring in, 1, 73–87, 102–9, 119, 145–46; empiricism of, 2, 89, 146–47, 180n68; links to other genres, 3; defined, 3, 11, 40; as record of affect, 5; novelty of, 5, 35, 38–39, 54, 79, 82, 102, 104, 109, 145–47; modern "scientific" ethnography, 6–7, 86, 146–47; and border writing, 14, 37; of the Celtic fringe, 15, 18–19, 41; theory versus practice of, 36, 168n59; as monograph, 38; missionary ethnography, 58–87; and cultural uncertainty, 147; early modern European ethnography, 146–47, 152n23. *See also* anthropology; ethnographic poetics and gaze; European identity; manners and customs discourse
ethnographic poetics and gaze: medieval, gazes of ethnographic others upon Europeans, 1, 5, 73–77, 102–12, 114; elements of, 2, 6–7; dialogism and intersubjectivity of, 2, 4–10, 47–50, 54, 59, 73–87, 91, 102–12, 114, 120, 140, 145–47; limits of European perspective, 2, 56, 105, 114; multifocality of, 4, 6, 52–56; modern, 6–7, 10, 50–52, 54–56, 72–73, 86–87, 138, 136–37, 146–47; subjectivity of, 6, 53, 55–56; partial and incomplete gaze, 6, 52–56, 103; deictic, 7, 51, 55, 65–66, 72–73, 91, 103, 143; seeing as other, 9, 73–87; and sideways glance, 10, 91, 101–12; openness of, 53–54; vision and contamination, 83. *See also* ethnography; medieval optics and vision; multifocality
European identity: new self-consciousness, 4, 104, 145; definition through encounter, 5, 49, 91, 104–6, 139–41, 145–47; openness and fluidity of, 6, 80–81. *See also* ethnographic poetics and gaze; ethnography

Fabian, Johannes, 7, 51, 65, 72, 152n25
Fernández-Armesto, Felipe, 150n4
FitzRalph, Richard, 134

Fleck, Andrew, 179–80n66
Folda, Jaroslav, 171–72n32
Frederick II, Holy Roman Emperor, 96, 106, 110, 169n2
Freud, Sigmund, 120–21
Friedman, John Block, 21, 60

Gaucher, Elisabeth, 103, 173n47
Geoffrey of Monmouth, 48
Georgopoulou, Maria, 95
Gerald of Wales: Celtic works, 37; ambivalence of, 43; as native informant, 43; ethnic hybridity of, 43, 55–56; *Descriptio Kambriae*: 37–56; novelty of, 3, 38, 54; as auto-ethnography, 8, 37–56; rhetorical duality of, 8, 40–45; salvage anthropology, 8, 39, 46; bifocal gaze, 9, 40, 44; evolutionary anthropology in, 18–19, 40–43; *Journey Through Wales*, 37; *Topography of Ireland*, 37, 41; and colonial ethnography, 43, 45–46, 50–52; native Welsh idiom in, 44–45; and Anglo-Norman appropriation, 48–49, 160n35; colonial derision and desire, 49; sly civility in, 49; ethnographic present in, 50–52; deixis in, 51, 55; partial and subjective gazes of, 52–56. *See also* anthropology; classical anthropology; ethnographic poetics and gaze; ethnography; salvage anthropology
Gesta Francorum, 32
Gesta Stephani, 19
Gillingham, John, 15
Glaber, Ralph, 19
Grady, Frank, 176n15
Greenblatt, Stephen, 163n6
Gregory of Remini, 134
Gurevich, Aron, 77, 161n36, 167n50, 167n51, 168n52
Guy of Lusignan (king of Jerusalem), 108
Guyuk khan, 84–85, 100

Hakluyt, Richard, 58
Hamilton, Bernard, 157n71, 173n53
Hayton of Armenia, 114, 138
Helmold of Bosau, 3
Heng, Geraldine, 150n4, 176n13
Herodotus, 3, 38
heteroglossia, 103–4, 107, 109. *See also* Bakhtin, Mikhail; Jean de Joinville
Higgins, Ian, 150n4
Hodgen, Margaret, 150n6

Holcott, Robert, 133–34
Howard, Donald, 124, 126, 179n65
Humbert of Romans, 77, 83
hybridity: in Anglo-Norman Wales, 9, 39, 44–46; in Latin Kingdom, 9, 92–102; syncretism on mission in Mongolia, 59, 82–83. *See also* Gerald of Wales; Jean de Joinville; William of Rubruck
Hyde, J. K., 150n4

Ibn Jubayr, 93–94
Innocent IV, Pope, 4, 14, anthropology of, 25–30; and sponsored missions, 25–26, 57, 64; just war in, 26; and sins contra naturam, 26–27; influence on future canonists, 27–30; letter exchange with Guyuk Khan, 84–86
interpreters, 62, 68–69, 75
Isidore of Seville, 22, 66, 114, 155n32
Iugurs, the, 63
Ivins, William, 67

Jacques de Vitry, 31, 114
James of Vitry, 92
Jay, Martin, 8, 168n60, 180n68
Jean de Valery, 97
John of Marignolli, 57, 113
John of Montecorvino, 57
John of Wurzburg, 114
Joinville, Jean de, 9, 36, 88–112; voices of Muslims in, 8–9, 102–109; as conversational text, 9, 90, 103, 170n12; sideways glances of, 10, 91, 101–12; *Vie de Saint Louis*, 88–112; generic diversity of, 89–90, 169n7; as historical source, 89; Franco-Islamic dialogue in, 90–91, 102–9; deixis in, 91, 103; dialogism in, 91, 102–12; Joinville's central role in, 91, 104–9; Outremer in, 91–95; syncretism in, 91–102; and Arab customs, 98, 101; partial gazes of, 103; Franco-Islamic mirroring in, 108–12. *See also* anthropology; Bakhtin, Mikhail; Crusades, the; ethnographic poetics and gaze; ethnography; Muslims
Jones, W. R., 153–4n7
Jordanus Catalini, 57

al-Kamil, al-Malik (Sultan), 96–97
Kedar, Benjamin, 171n31
Kinoshita, Sharon, 151n15, 163n8, 172n37

Langland, William, 116, 176n14, *Piers Plowman*, 178n33
Laurence of Portugal, 84
lives of Muhammad genre, 30, 120, 156n61, 177n20. *See also* Muslims
Lochrie, Karma, 149n2, 173n55, 175–76n12
Lomperis, Linda, 163n8, 176n13
Louis IX (king of France), 1, 25, 61, 68, 76, 88–89, 96–98, 100–101, 110–12; orthodoxy, 110, 174n60; reputation for honesty, 110–12; Tunisian legend of conversion of 111–12. *See also* Crusades; Jean de Joinville; Mongols
Lucretius, 11, 14, 16–17, 38

Macrobius, 114
Mamluks, the, 98, 100–102, 113
Mandeville's Travels, 113–44; ethnographic status, 4, 114; the uncanny, 10, 115, 120–21, 129, 131, 140–41, 144, 177n27; limits of Latin Christian perspective, 10, 138–44; and non-Christian salvation, 10, 34, 36, 115, 130–37; sources, 113–14; dialogism, 114, 120, 140; unease and terror, 114–15, 118, 121, 124, 126, 140–42; Christianizing readings, 115, 117, 119, 121, 124; partial and incomplete gazes, 115, 138, 143–44; blurring of self-other boundaries, 118–31; inhabiting outside perspective, 116; Muslims in, 116–24; eastern Christians, 116, 119; self-mirroring, 119, 125; virtuous pagans, 127–31; eyewitnessing, 137–39; visual error, 138–44; disorientation, 139–42; deixis, 143. *See also* anthropology; ethnographic poetics and gaze; ethnography; medieval optics and vision
Mangu (great khan), 1, 68–69, 74, 78, 82, 85–86
manners and customs discourse, 1, 3, 38, 61, 63, 67, 150n6, 165n18. *See also* ethnography
maps: Psalter Map, 12, 13; Ebstorf Map, 12
Matthew Paris, 20–21, 59–60, 164n10
Marco Polo, 4, 58, 60, 163n6
Marie de France, 158n7
McCannon, Afrodesia, 111
medieval optics and vision, 7; extramission theory, 7–8; amatory gaze, 8; empiricism and genres of observation, 38–39; moralizing approaches in, 83; multiplication of species, 86–87; theorists of visual skepticism and error, 132–33, 138, 144. *See also* ethnographic poetics and gaze; multifocality
Menocal, María Rosa, 149n2, 151n15, 163n8
Mitchell, Timothy, 72, 151n19
Mongols, the, 1, 3–4, 113; treatment by William of Rubruck, 9, 57–87; as barbarians, 20–21; calls for crusade upon, 25; missions to, 25–26, 57; treatment by Joinville, 36, 90; and Louis IX, 99–100; and *Mandeville's Travels*, 113, 122, 139; realms of empire of, 162n2
monsters, 1, 12, 20–23, 27, 30, 48, 60–61, 65–66, 74, 115, 118, 128, 143, 145. *See also* antipodes
Moody, Ernest, 138
Muldoon, James, 156n46
multifocality: in medieval chronicle writing, 4; in medieval painting, 4. *See also* ethnographic poetics and gaze
Muslims (Saracens), 30–33, 69, 79–81, 88–112, 116–24; as virtuous pagans, 32–33, 157n71; converted Saracen princess, trope, 112, 122

Nest (grandmother of Gerald of Wales), 39, 40
Nestorian Christians, 64, 80–81
Nicolas of Autrecourt, 132, 138

Oberman, Heiko, 138
Odoric of Pordenone, 57, 114
Old Man of the Mountain (leader of Assassins), 99, 105
Orientalism, 5; and medieval ethnography, 5, 7, 84, 136–37, 146
Orosius, 114
Outremer: connectivity with surroundings, 91–95; Franco-Syrian synthesis theory, 93; segregationist theory of, 93. *See also* hybridity; Jean de Joinville

painting and visual arts: influence on medieval ethnography, 38, 54–55; multifocality in ,53–54. *See also* multifocality
Peter of Limoges, 83, 133, 144, 179n51
Peter the Venerable, 30–31
Petrus Alfonsi, 32

Pliny the Elder, 12, 20–21, 42. *See also* monsters
postcolonial medievalism, 5, 91, 152n24
Pratt, Mary Louise, 6, 39, 47, 49, 72, 149n3, 173n49
Prawer, Joshua, 93
Prester, John (mythical eastern king), 22, 57, 66, 114, 125, 127, 146
Purchas, Samuel, 58
Pygmies, the, 12, 21–23, 128, 144. *See also* monsters

Rainald of Chatillon, 108
Renaissance rediscovery of linear perspective, 7, 67, 87. *See also* ethnographic poetics and gaze
Richard the Lion-hearted (king of England), 48, 88, 96–97. *See also* Crusades
Riley-Smith, Jonathan, 171n27,n31, 173n52
Roberts, Brynley F., 159n18
routiers, the, 123
Rubiés, Joan-Pau, 149–50n4, 152n23, 153n1, 153n2

Said, Edward, 7, 152n25
Saint Erkenwald, 176n14
Salahadin (sultan of Egypt and Syria), 32, 88, 92, 94, 97, 108–10, 112. *See also* Crusades; Outremer
Sallust, 15–16
salvage anthropology, 8, 39, 46. *See also* Gerald of Wales
salvational paradigm: 29–30; concern for virtuous pagans, 34–36: in *Journey* of William of Rubruck, 59, 63–65; incorporative, 65, 72. *See also* anthropology; William of Rubruck
Sartach (son of Baatu khan), 68, 73
Sartre, Jean-Paul, 6; 86
Scythians, the, 156n42
Seneca, 15
Seymour, M. C., 136
Smail, R. C., 93
Solinus, 22, 24, 42, 66, 155n29
Southern, R. W., 63, 131, 156n61, 165n20
Spanish Reconquest, 27–29
Spiegel, Gabrielle, 53, 151n13
Stanbury, Sarah, 153n28, 168n60

Tacitus, 3, 38
Tempier, Bishop Etienne, 132
Templars, the, 94. *See also* Outremer
Turanshah (sultan of Egypt), 101, 106
Tyerman, Christopher, 92

uncanny, the, 10, 115, 120–21. *See also Mandeville's Travels*
Urban V, Pope, 124
Usamah ibn-Munqidh, 94–95, 174n57, 174n69. *See also* Outremer
Uthred of Boldon, 135

Vincent of Beauvais, 22, 57–60, 114, 122
virtuous pagans, 14, 33–36, 127–31; Muslims as, 157n71. *See also Mandeville's Travels*

Weber, Samuel, 121, 131
William of Boldensele, 113
William of Malmesbury, 15, 19
William of Newburgh, 19
William of Ockham, 132, 132, 135, 138
William of Poitiers, 19
William of Rubruck: disorientation, 1, 59, 73–74, 77, 79, 81–82; Latin Christian alterity, 1, 73–77; self-reflexivity, 1, 73–87; primacy of vision, 4, 59, 165n25; salvational paradigm and missionary ethnography, 9, 58–59, 63–65, 72, 77, 84, 86; depiction of Mongols, 36, 59–63, 85–86; the *Journey*, 57–87; dialogism, 59, 76–77, 81–82, 86–87; anthropological influences upon, 59–60; syncretism, 59, 82; Orientalism, 59, 84; debate at Caracorum in, 63, 69, 79–81; and Nestorian Christians, 64, 80, 82; deixis, 65–73; and incorporation, 65–87; eyewitnessing, 66–68; failures of language, 68–71; efficacy of pictures, 70–71, 166n32; role of emotions, 71, 73–76, 82, 85; seeing as other, 73–87; in contemporary preaching manuals, 77–84; and Muslims, 79–81; vision and contamination, 83. *See also* anthropology; ethnographic poetics and gaze; ethnography; interpreters; medieval optics and vision; salvational paradigm
William of Tripoli, 30
William of Tyre, 31, 92
Woodham, Adam, 133–34
Wycliff, John, 135

Yule, Henry, 58
Yves Le Breton, Brother, 105

Zeitler, Barbara, 172n36

ACKNOWLEDGMENTS

I want to begin by thanking Robert Hanning, my mentor and friend, for his constant, expert intellectual guidance and boundless support for the research and writing of this book. He, Robert Stein, and Margaret Pappano provided invaluable early support and direction for the project through insightful readings and provocative questions. Paul Strohm and Joan Ferrante also shared their expert commentary on many of its chapters. I am deeply grateful for the close reading and feedback provided on the manuscript in its late stages by John Ganim, Brenda Deen Schildgen, Sharon Kinoshita, and Patricia Ingham. I want to thank San Francisco State University for funding a Presidential Fellowship in 2007–8 that allowed the book to take its current form. At SFSU, I have been blessed with the personal and intellectual support of my wonderful colleagues in the Department of Comparative and World Literature, Ellen Peel, Dane Johnson, and Chris Weinberger. A vibrant junior faculty reading group at SFSU, including Jillian Sandell, Mohammad Salama, Christopher Weinberger, Laura Garcia-Moreno, Gillian McIntosh, and Kasturi Ray, provided meaningful and detailed comments on each of the book's chapters as well as perspective on the project's potential from those trained outside medieval, European, and literary studies. Dean Paul Sherwin supported my research at every juncture, not least through his intimate knowledge of the book's stages of development and his detailed and insightful commentary on each of its chapters. I want to thank the two anonymous readers at the University of Pennsylvania Press for their deep and engaged readings of the book manuscript and for comments that greatly improved the final shape and arguments of the book. I thank Jerry Singerman, Senior Humanities editor at Penn, for his expert guidance and navigation of the project through the publication process and for his consummate professionalism throughout. I also thank Caroline Winschel, Noreen O'Connor-Abel, Melissa Marshall, Sara Davis and the entire Penn Press team, along with managing editor Tim Roberts and copyeditor Robert Milks of the Mellon Modern Language Initiative, all of whom so expertly brought the book to press. Earlier versions of Chapters 3 and 4 appeared in *New Medieval Literatures* 10 (2008): 87–114, and *Exemplaria* 22.3 (2010): 177–99, respectively, and I thank the journals for allowing me to publish them in revised form here.

I have been the beneficiary of wonderful and sustaining friendships through the years of this book's making, especially those of Mara de Gennaro, Elizabeth Weinstock Phillips, and Ruchi Chaturvedi, all of whom have provided me with intellectual, moral, and emotional support without which I would have faltered. I could not have embarked on the academic life without the unending stability and support of my parents, Mehdi and Moloud Khanmohamadi, whose practicality, work ethic, and love of vocation still serve as my abiding model. I thank my sister Azin for her constant support through the long path to this book, and my brother Ali for his intellectual camaraderie in literary study. I thank and cherish my husband, Amit, and our two jewels, Saurab and Sabina, for the daily joys that have nourished this book and made writing it worthwhile. This book is dedicated to my father, for the many gifts he gave me freely, not least his playful love of tradition and words.

www.ingramcontent.com/pod-product-compliance
Lightning Source LLC
Chambersburg PA
CBHW031436160426
43195CB00010BB/755